CONTENTIOUS KWANGJU

Asia/Pacific/Perspectives
Series Editor: Mark Selden

Identity and Resistance in Okinawa
by Matthew Allen

Woman, Man, Bangkok: Love, Sex, and Popular Culture in Thailand
by Scot Barmé

Making the Foreign Serve China: Managing Foreigners in the People's Republic
by Anne-Marie Brady

The Mongols at China's Edge: History and the Politics of National Unity
by Uradyn E. Bulag

Transforming Asian Socialism: China and Vietnam Compared
edited by Anita Chan , Benedict J. Tria Kerkvliet , and Jonathan Unger

China's Great Proletarian Cultural Revolution: Master Narratives and Post-Mao Counternarratives
edited by Woei Lien Chong

North China at War: The Social Ecology of Revolution, 1937–1945
edited by Feng Chongyi and David S. G. Goodman

Social and Political Change in Revolutionary China: The Taihang Base Area in the War of Resistance to Japan, 1937–1945
by David S. G. Goodman

Local Democracy and Development: The Kerala People's Campaign for Decentralized Planning
by T. M. Thomas Isaac with Richard W. Franke

Islands of Discontent: Okinawan Responses to Japanese and American Power
edited by Laura Hein and Mark Selden

Women in Early Imperial China
by Bret Hinsch

Postwar Vietnam: Dynamics of a Transforming Society
edited by Hy V. Luong

Wife or Worker? Asian Women and Migration
edited by Nicola Piper and Mina Roces

Biology and Revolution in Twentieth-Century China
by Laurence Schneider

CONTENTIOUS KWANGJU

The May 18 Uprising in Korea's Past and Present

Edited by
Gi-Wook Shin
and
Kyung Moon Hwang

ROWMAN & LITTLEFIELD PUBLISHERS, INC.
Lanham • Boulder • New York • Oxford

ROWMAN & LITTLEFIELD PUBLISHERS, INC.

Published in the United States of America
by Rowman & Littlefield Publishers, Inc.
A Member of the Rowman & Littlefield Publishing Group
4501 Forbes Boulevard, Suite 200, Lanham, Maryland 20706
www.rowmanlittlefield.com

PO Box 317
Oxford
OX2 9RU, UK

British Library Cataloguing in Publication Information Available

Library of Congress Cataloging-in-Publication Data

Contentious Kwangju : the May 18 Uprising in Korea's Past and Present /
edited by Gi-Wook Shin and Kyung Moon Hwang.
     p. cm.
Includes index.
  ISBN 0-7425-1961-9 (cloth : alk. paper) — ISBN 0-7425-1962-7 (pbk. :
alk. paper)
  1. Kwangju Uprising, Kwangju-si, Korea, 1980. 2. Kwangju-si
(Korea)—History. I. Title: Kwangju uprising revisited. II. Shin,
Gi-wook. III. Hwang, Kyung Moon.
  DS922.445.865 2003
  951.9504'3—dc21
                                                    2003002672

⊗™ The paper used in this publication meets the minimum requirements of American
National Standard for Information Sciences—Permanence of Paper for Printed Library
Materials, ANSI/NISO Z39.48-1992.

Contents

Tables

Acknowledgments

This book draws upon papers presented at the conference on "Kwangju after Two Decades: Historical and Comparative Perspectives," held in Los Angeles. Cohosted by the USC Korean Studies Institute and the UCLA Center for Korean Studies, and cosponsored by the 5.18 Memorial Foundation, Dongshin and Kwangju universities, the conference was designed to commemorate the twentieth anniversary of the Kwangju Uprising of 1980. We are particularly grateful to Joseph Aoun, Ken Klein, and Joy Kim of USC; Robert Buswell and Eileen Sir of UCLA; and Kim Dongwŏn, Chŏng Suman, and Hŏ Yŏnsik of the 5.18 Memorial Foundation. Keun-sik Jung and Jong-chul Ahn greatly supported our conference from the beginning. We also would like to thank Mark Selden for excellent suggestions and comments; Susan McEachern and Kärstin Painter of Rowman & Littlefield for their professional work; and James Freda, Paul Chang, Sophia Kim, and Chris Evans for their assistance. It is our sincere hope that this collection will enhance our understanding of the May 1980 event that still affects the lives of many people in Kwangju and elsewhere.

Introduction

Gi-Wook Shin

KOREA'S ROAD TO BECOMING A MODERN SOCIETY, contrary to the still popular statist view of social change, has not been a smooth evolutionary process dictated by the state. Rather, Korea has seen strong resistance to state power and foreign forces, which in turn has crucially shaped its path to modernity. The Tonghak peasant rebellion and war of 1894, various forms of peasant and labor activism during colonial rule (1910–1945), the October uprisings during the American occupation (1945–1948), the April student revolution of 1960, and the June uprising of 1987 exemplify a path wrought with societal contention. These movements exacted social and political changes in Korea from colonial and postcolonial agrarian reforms to the downfall of the Syngman Rhee government (1948–1960) to political democratization of the 1980s.[1]

The Kwangju uprising that occurred in May 1980 is another major event in this sequence of contentious politics. Beginning as a student protest in the southwestern city of Kwangju, the uprising escalated into an armed civilian struggle and was met by brutal acts of violence enacted by government troops. While the ten-day struggle ultimately ended in military suppression, its legacy and effect were of lasting significance. It was arguably the single most important event that shaped the political and social landscape of South Korea in the 1980s and 1990s.

This volume examines the uprising two decades later. Unlike recent publications that have taken the form of diaries,[2] testimonials,[3] or memoirs,[4] this book combines analytical, albeit highly personal, retrospectives (part I) with scholarly exploration into aspects of the uprising's aftermath (part II). Part I consists of highly interpretive essays that reflect the range of reactions to and perspectives on the uprising, from the recollections of a Kwangju resident to those of an American missionary. Part II, on the other hand, presents scholarly analyses of the uprising's outcomes, such as its impact on Korean democratization, the condition of the injured survivors, and memories and representations of the event. We believe the volume as a whole offers a balanced and comprehensive reassessment of this seminal event and its effects, the first of its kind available in English.

Prelude

The Kwangju uprising was a ten-day struggle in the city of Kwangju and its vicinity that lasted from May 18 to May 27, 1980. As with other major political events, we need to understand the broader historical and structural context that led to the rise of armed demonstrations in the city. The uprising was the culmination of a series of political crises, opportunities, and challenges that Korea experienced in 1979 and 1980. The assassination of President Park Chung Hee by the chief of the Korean CIA in October 1979, a subsequent military coup led by General Chun Doo Hwan in December, and democratic struggles the following spring were intimately related to the uprising.

To grasp the nature of the fast-moving events of 1979–1980, we need to return to the political context of Korea in the 1970s, especially the autocratic system called Yusin (revitalization). Despite his illegal power grab through a military coup in May 1961, Park Chung Hee enjoyed popular support in the 1960s largely due to successful economic programs. Yet his regime faced growing political opposition as he amended the constitution in 1969 to allow him to run for president a third time. In the 1971 presidential election, the first election held after the constitutional amendment, Park only narrowly defeated the opposing candidate, Kim Dae Jung, despite holding much stronger organizational and financial resources. Shocked and threatened by the election's outcome, in the fall of 1972 Park changed the constitution once again, establishing the Yusin system under martial law. Launching the most repressive regime in South Korean history further restricted human and political rights and also made Park president for life.

This draconian system, however, faced a series of socioeconomic and political crises by the late 1970s. The fast-growing Korean economy showed signs of recession: the growth rate declined, inflation soared, exports slowed, and external debt grew. Politically the regime was losing popular support, evidenced by the outcome of the 1978 general election for the National Assembly in which Park's Republican Party lost to the opposition party by a margin of 1.1 percent, significant because the ruling party had overwhelmingly greater resources in the election. A final trigger was what became known as the "YH incident." In early August 1979, young female textile workers at the YH Trading Company held a sit-in strike at the headquarters of the main opposition party to protest massive layoffs. The government mobilized riot police to suppress their sit-in. One female worker died and tens of protesters were wounded. This excessive use of force by the government displayed the brutality of the Yusin system and greatly alienated the populace. When the regime forced Kim Young Sam, president of the main opposition party, out of the National Assembly, those in his hometown rose up in protest and launched the "Pu-Ma struggle," named after the Pusan and Masan region in which the protests occurred.[5] This protest was a prelude to the Kwangju uprising, which followed a few months later.

Political struggles against the Park regime in the Pusan-Masan area began with student protests at Pusan National University on October 16, 1979. Several hundred students demonstrated on campus, shouting "end the dictatorship" and "destroy the Yusin system," and sought to move their demonstrations off campus and into the streets of the city. All day long, students fought with riot police throughout Pusan. By 7:00 P.M. an estimated 50,000 people had gathered around city hall, demanding an end to the Yusin system, freedom of the press, and reinstatement of Kim Young Sam to the National Assembly. Several public offices, such as police stations, were attacked and an estimated four hundred protesters were arrested, with another six hundred wounded in the street demonstrations. The government declared martial law in the city of Pusan and its vicinity on October 18.

The political struggles spread to Masan, about one hour from Pusan by bus. On October 18 several hundred students of Kyŏngnam University in Masan protested against the Yusin system and sought to advance out of the campus into the streets. Masan was a major city with an export zone that employed many industrial workers. By evening, an estimated 10,000 protesters, mostly students and workers, had joined the anti-Yusin struggles, attacking the police station and city offices of the ruling party. The government imposed a citywide curfew from 10:00 P.M. to 4:00 A.M.

By late October the Park regime was in serious crisis. The ruling bloc was split by schisms, and on the night of October 26, Kim Chae-gyu, chief of the Korean CIA, shot and killed President Park, abruptly ending his eighteen-year reign. Choi Kyu-ha, the prime minister, immediately succeeded Park as the new president. Because he lacked a personal power base (Choi was a career diplomat), however, his capacity to lead the nation through the political crisis was constrained. On December 12, the so-called new military headed by Generals Chun Doo Hwan and Roh Tae Woo seized power in a military coup.

Many Koreans were not sure at the time whether it was a coup or not, as the media was censored by the Chun-controlled military. But in retrospect it was certainly a coup, and this fact was gradually revealed to the populace. The rise of the new military dictatorship provoked frustration and anger among many Koreans, who had expected that the downfall of Park would lead to some form of democratic reform. In the spring of 1980, most college campuses were awash with protests and demonstrations demanding that Chun resign from key positions (such as chief of the KCIA, among others) and calling for immediate democratic reform, including direct presidential elections. This interlude has come to be known in the West as the "Seoul spring." On May 15, just three days before the Kwangju uprising, an estimated 150,000 students and citizens gathered at Seoul station to protest the new military and demand political reform. Hopeful that the government would respond to their pleas, protest leaders on the following day decided to hold off further street demonstrations in order to give the government time to act. On May 16 and 17, most college campuses in Seoul were quiet.

On May 17, however, General Chun and his cohorts decided to extend martial law (already in effect) to the island of Cheju. All of South Korea was now under martial law, which suspended the cabinet and closed the National Assembly. The military was in full control of the republic, exercising absolute power with General Chun as the de facto leader, though Choi remained South Korea's president. The new martial law regime closed down all university campuses across the country and arrested many political leaders, including Kim Dae Jung. The arrest of Kim merits special attention in understanding the Kwangju uprising, as he was a highly popular leader from the Honam region, which includes Kwangju. Many in Kwangju believed that he had defeated Park in the 1971 election but his presidency had been taken away by fraud. They were enraged when they learned that Kim was arrested by the new military regime.

The Uprising

Beginning

Kwangju, the fifth largest city in South Korea with a population of 730,000 at the time, was, like other urban areas, immersed in political struggles for democracy.[6] The center of the movement was Seoul, not Kwangju, though the southwestern city had another day of political engagement after students and activists in Seoul and other cities decided to suspend demonstrations on May 15. On May 16, students in Kwangju organized a torchlight march to "illuminate the darkness" of eighteen years of Park Chung Hee's dictatorship (May 16 was the anniversary of Park's 1961 coup). Then they suspended further demonstrations, as in Seoul. With the extension of martial law to the whole country effective at midnight, however, riot police and paratroopers occupied the provincial government and other key official buildings, as well as universities, and began to arrest student activists and dissident leaders throughout the city. On the morning of May 18, students began to gather in front of the main gate of Chŏnnam National University. Most of them were ordinary students on their way to campus, unaware that the school had been closed by martial law. As the martial law troops blocked their entry to campus, they began a sit-in protest shouting slogans such as "Martial Law Troops Go Away" and "Chun Doo Hwan Must Go!" There was nothing special about such a protest, which had become common on Korean campuses. However, the response by the authorities was very different: a squad of soldiers (paratroopers trained in unconventional warfare, thus hardly qualified for the delicate task of dealing with student demonstrators) charged the students and waded into the crowd swinging their batons. The students were beaten, clubbed, knifed, and bayoneted.

Those students who were attacked and pushed back by the paratroopers retreated, leaving approximately ten injured students, but regathered at Kwangju railroad station with about four hundred people. They marched to the Catholic Center en route to the open plaza downtown in front of the Provincial Building on Kŭmnam Avenue. At about 3:00 P.M. they resumed demonstrations, which were larger and better organized than the earlier sporadic ones. Approximately one hour later, the paratroopers entered the downtown area and embarked on their merciless repression of students and citizens. According to a martial law document, sixty-eight people were injured (including twelve in serious condition) and 405 arrested.

Development

At dawn on May 19, students and citizens began coming out onto the streets, anxious to know what had happened the previous day. Businesses along the main road were mostly closed and all traffic was controlled as martial law soldiers and police patrolled the city. Around 10:00 A.M. between two and three thousand students and citizens gathered on Kŭmnam Avenue and began demonstrations. The martial law troops once again responded with brutality. The soldiers of the Eleventh Brigade, in teams of three and four, searched buildings and houses near the area of the demonstrations and assaulted any young man they found and took him into custody. The captured citizens were forced to strip down to their underwear and were beaten on the streets. Brutal suppression continued throughout the city, and people were shocked to witness merciless acts of violence against even women and the elderly. Now ordinary citizens, many of whom had remained uninvolved during previous student demonstrations, became more involved and increasingly assertive, even fighting with the soldiers. Lee Jae-eui's famous eyewitness account of these fateful days, *Kwangju Diary*, states that "May 19 was the day the torch of the uprising was passed from the students to the ordinary working people of Kwangju" (p. 56).

The next day, May 20, the whole city was in an uproar. Kŭmnam Avenue was packed with 30,000–40,000 citizens, and thousands of leaflets were distributed in the streets of downtown Kwangju. Citizens became more assertive, setting fire to television station buildings for false broadcasting, putting gasoline on trucks and driving them into the soldiers. The martial law troops responded with shots, killing or seriously injuring at least twenty people.

On May 21 a more massive shooting occurred in broad daylight, killing at least a reported fifty-four people, injuring five hundred, and ending the people's hopes for a peaceful resolution. Now citizens began to arm themselves to fight against the troops, and the Citizens' Army was born (see chap. 2). Meanwhile, concerned with the rapidly growing number of casualties, the troops retreated to suburban areas in the afternoon. At around 8:00 P.M. the Citizens' Army entered the Provincial Office building without resistance. The city was now under the full control of Kwangju citizens, who sought to build a kind of commune, which Jung-woon Choi in chapter 1 refers to as an "absolute community."

On May 22 the Citizens Settlement Committee was formed to negotiate with the military. The committee consisted of civic leaders such as clergymen, Catholic priests, lawyers, professors, government officials, and business leaders. The committee presented a seven-point list of demands to the government:

1. Martial law forces shall not be mobilized before negotiations are concluded.
2. All those arrested during the uprising shall be released.
3. The government will officially acknowledge the military's excessive use of violence.
4. A guarantee of no retaliation after the settlement.
5. No charges will be brought against the people for their actions during the uprising.
6. The families of the dead will be compensated.
7. The protesters will put down their arms if these demands are satisfied.[7]

While the committee was continuing its negotiations with the government, resentment was growing against government intransigence, especially its demand that all weapons be unconditionally returned. As Jong-chul Ahn shows in chapter 2, a new group of radicals emerged who favored a fight to the end, offering their lives in suicidal resistance. These radical activists took over leadership of the movement and vowed to fight to the end. Meanwhile, on May 23, Hodding Carter, U.S. State Department spokesperson, announced that the Carter administration had "decided to support the restoration of security and order in South Korea while deferring pressure for political liberalization."[8] Kwangju citizens' hopes for U.S. intervention in support of democracy vanished with this announcement.

During the five-day (May 22–26) period of self-rule, citizens maintained civil order, contrary to government reports of "acts of plunder" and "complete lawlessness." On May 23 markets and stores reopened, local government officials cooperated with the leaders of the uprising to supply food, electricity, and water to social welfare organizations, and citizens volunteered to donate blood and clean up the streets. As Jean Underwood recounts in chapter 3, missionaries and others reported a remarkable degree of order in the city, which seemed to be returning to normalcy. Yet discord within the leadership, especially between the Settlement Committee and the Citizens' Army, increased.

Demise

During the early morning hours of May 27, while it was still dark, troops stormed the city with thirty tanks and guns blazing. The Citizens' Army was not able to match the modern weaponry of the troops. By late morning, the military had retaken the city. The movement was crushed. On June 2, the Martial Law Command announced that 170 were dead (144 civilians, 22 soldiers, and 4 policemen) and 380 wounded (127 civilians, 109 soldiers, and 144 policemen).[9] Yet this official figure omits those missing or dead after May 27 as a result of wounds suffered during the military violence. Even today, two decades after the uprising, it is not certain exactly how many were killed. The best estimates available today suggest about five hundred civilians dead and over three thousand injured.[10] Many injured people still suffer from wounds, both physical and psychological, as Linda Lewis and Ju-na Byun show in chapter 5.

Causes

What, then, led Kwangju citizens to protest? Because motivation to participate in the uprising was not monolithic, and tensions, conflicts, and disputes existed even among protest participants,[11] the causes of the uprising have been the subject of a good deal of debate. In what follows, I introduce and briefly evaluate key explanations for the rise of Kwangju citizens against the government and its armed forces.

Communist Agitation

From the beginning, the government labeled the uprising a communist-agitated "incident." On May 18, the first day of the uprising, President Choi Kyu-ha declared that "North Korean communists' espionage against our nation is causing social chaos. These spies have deeply infiltrated our society and are encouraging and praising the recent campus disturbances. . . . In this very volatile and critical time, some irresponsible and unpatriotic politicians, students and workers are threatening national security. . . . Our nation is in very serious danger."[12] Such an accusation was repeated after the uprising, illustrated by a statement issued by Martial Law Headquarters on June 1980: "We have found traces of North Korean spies and their collaborators who infiltrated Kwangju. They also attempted to enter Seoul to extend their espionage activities. . . . Our claim is based on testimonial by an arrested spy, Yi Ch'ang-yong, and some other evidence we have obtained."[13] However, such charges have proven to be groundless. The Kim Young Sam government (1993–1998), the first civilian administration after three decades of military or semi-military rule, officially rescinded these accusations.

Fight for Democracy

In sharp contrast to the government characterization of the uprising as communist inspired, many Korean activists and scholars have regarded the event as representative of the Kwangju citizen fight for democracy. In fact, the Kwangju uprising occurred in the midst of the Korean democratization movement. As already noted, the spring of 1980 saw the eruption of a nationwide movement that sought to end the military dictatorship, establish direct presidential elections, and enact other political reforms. Kwangju was no exception to this national trend; rather, it was a culmination of this broad democratic movement. Slogans heard during the uprising included "Repeal Martial Law," "Clarify the Democratization Schedule," "Release Kim Dae Jung," and "Chun Doo Hwan Must Go." Today the uprising is officially recognized as the May 18 Democratization Movement (O-ilp'al minjuhwa undong), and the general public seems to endorse such recognition (see note 40).

Yet democracy is a malleable, even ambiguous concept, and what democracy meant to Kwangju citizens who joined the uprising must be specified. It appears that what was most crucial to those who joined the uprising were not abstract ideals of democracy but more immediate concerns with physical survival and human dignity. Han Sang-jin's view of the Kwangju uprising as a "struggle for recognition" to ensure the citizens' survival and to restore their basic human rights and dignity appears to capture this point. Han considers three forms of abuse that provoked the Kwangju citizen struggles for human rights: "first, the barbaric and atrocious treatment of Kwangju citizens as though they were animals; second, denouncing their democratic activism as 'unlawful rioting by the communists'; third, accusing Kwangju citizens of being mobs."[14] The Kwangju uprising was a fight for democracy to the extent that it involved struggles for recognition and human rights (see also chap. 1).

Repression

If Kwangju citizens fought for survival and human dignity, what motivated them? Here, as in other major rebellions and uprisings,[15] repression has been mentioned as a primary factor in triggering collective action. As discussed above, the government deployed special troops trained for guerrilla warfare, which made use of their bayonets from the very first day of operation. Even those who could not defend themselves, such as women, children, and the elderly, became targets of this sort of violence, and these inhuman actions undoubtedly roused the citizens to action. A statement by the Chosun University Committee for Democratic Struggle dated May 22, 1980, captures the essence of this repression-rebellion dynamic:

> Nearly 3,000 paratroopers from Seoul were sent in. These troops began indiscriminately killing people with their clubs and bayonets. Soon the streets were colored with blood. Bodies were thrown into army trucks. . . . Such brutal killing evoked the wrath of the citizens, causing them to rise up to resist. But their empty-handed protests were only an invitation for them, too, to be killed. A 70-year-old woman, protesting the killing of a girl student, was also killed on the spot by the paratroopers. . . . In the city of Kwangju just being young is a crime, and the young are condemned to be crippled for life or to be killed. . . . Alas, the genocide of unarmed people in Vietnam is being repeated upon our own people.[16]

Even the U.S. embassy in Seoul, which did not support the uprising, reached the same conclusion when it stated that "overreaction by Special Warfare troops was the basic cause of the tragedy."[17]

A question still remains: Why and how did Korean troops commit such brutal acts of repression toward their fellow citizens? Here we need to understand the special nature of Korean paratroopers. Paratroopers, also known as Black Berets, were elite troops who had a special loyalty to General Chun, as he was a division commander along the thirty-eighth parallel. But more importantly their training prepared them for behind-the-lines warfare in North Korea and antiguerrilla warfare in the South against North Korean infiltrators in the event of a North Korean attack. If these soldiers had been told that North Korean infiltrators and/or communists had begun an uprising in Kwangju (as the government insisted), they were likely to show no mercy. This would explain their extreme brutality, a brutality that shocked even those unsympathetic to the aims of the demonstrators, triggering citywide collective protest in Kwangju.

Regionalism

While repression triggered the armed uprising by Kwangju citizens, people have speculated on the effects of deep-rooted discontent and resentment in the region. This issue has a particular importance since regionalism has colored modern Korean politics, and since the Honam, or Chŏlla, region (with Kwangju as its center) has been the home of much of the political opposition in the post-1948 period. For instance, the Korean Democratic Party, a major rival to Syngman Rhee's Liberal Party, had its roots in the region, and Kim Dae Jung, the popular opposition leader during the Park regime, also came from the region. The price of this activism was heavy, however, as the region suffered from severe discrimination in virtually all areas of social, political, and economic life.[18] As late as 1978, GNP per capita in Kwangju was only 75 percent of the national average, and agriculture constituted 38 percent of GNP in the South Chŏlla province (compared to only 18 percent for the nation as a whole). In his speech at the USC-UCLA conference held in Los Angeles, "Kwangju after Two Decades," William Gleysteen Jr., U.S. ambassador to Korea at the time of the Kwangju uprising, listed as the first cause of the uprising "the military decision to arrest Kim Dae Jung in the harsh crackdown of May 17 and to accuse him of causing the student turmoil." In his view, "historic resentments in the Chŏlla region intensified the stubborn behavior of the protesting students. Having their national hero singled out by the military as the troublemaker in Seoul tapped into a deep pool of resentment in Chŏlla, where people felt they had been treated as second-class citizens if not outcasts by the rival region of Kyŏngsang and the leadership in Seoul."[19] Kwangju citizens were particularly enraged when they heard rumors that the soldiers killing Kwangju citizens came from Kyŏngsang province (see chap. 3). Although it would be difficult to assess the precise extent of its influence, this regional resentment seems to have played a role in the uprising.

Tradition of Protest

Some may go further to explain the impetus for the uprising by pointing to the tradition of protest in the region. According to this view, what is important is not simply that the Honam region has a history of discrimination, but also that it has a long history of protest. The well-known Tonghak peasant wars of 1894, the anti-Japanese student movements of 1929, and the Yŏsu-Sunch'ŏn armed resistance of 1948 all occurred in the region. This tradition of protest is said to have played a significant role in provoking and sustaining the 1980 uprising. For instance, Son Ho-ch'ŏl, a Korean political scientist, argues that "the Honam region, the granary of the Korean peninsula owing to the fertility of its land, has been a target of exploitation. As a result, the region naturally became the center of *minjung* [popular] movements . . . the Kwangju uprising should be understood in this historical context of the *minjung* movement."[20] A situation report sent to the State Department on May 24 by the U.S. embassy in Seoul also pointed to the significance of "an old Chŏlla tradition" of resistance.[21] During the uprisings such a tradition of protest was frequently invoked to stimulate the spirit and morale of the citizens, and many Citizens' Army leaders, as shown in chapter 2, were seasoned veterans of social activism.

Role of SMOs

Sociological studies of social movements have stressed the importance of social movement organizations (SMOs) in the rise of collective protest: any social movement requires an organization that can mobilize resources for collective action. The Kwangju uprising, however, began as a spontaneous response to government repression rather than a concerted effort by SMOs. There were few SMOs on May 18 that could mobilize citizens for collective action.[22] With the extension of martial law on May 17, most movement leaders in Kwangju were arrested or in hiding. Citizens who came to support the uprising were not organized or systematically mobilized for collective protest; rather, they responded to the brutal repression of the troops in defense of their children, friends, and neighbors. As chapter 2 demonstrates, even the Citizens' Army was hastily organized during the struggle. If there was any organizational base, it consisted of personal networks such as school and neighborhood connections that helped build trust and cooperation among the citizens in protest. Some leaders emerged during the uprising—Pak Nam-sŏn, who took charge of the headquarters of the Citizens' Army, was an example (see chap. 2)—and activists in hiding joined the leadership only in the latter stages of the uprising.

Outcomes and Legacies

The Kwangju uprising ended after ten days of struggle, with tragic outcomes, and subsequently the new military regime consolidated its power. General Chun Doo Hwan, the leader of the new military, arranged to assume the presidency later in the year, declaring his regime the Fifth Republic. The voices of Kwangju were silenced, and most leaders of the democratization movement were arrested and jailed. The Seoul Spring was followed by the darkness of suppression. Nonetheless, the citizens of Kwangju did not shed their blood in vain, for the uprising came to shape the political landscape of the 1980s in many crucial ways.[23]

Legitimacy Problems

First and foremost, Kwangju created serious legitimacy problems for the Chun regime throughout its tenure. Two decades earlier Park Chung Hee had perpetrated a coup on the premise that he would modernize the nation and protect national security against the North Korean threat. Despite its illegal seizure of power, the Park regime gained some popular support largely as a result of its ability to preside over rapid economic growth.[24] In contrast, Chun was widely portrayed as the only ruler in Korean history who mobilized government troops to kill innocent civilians. As Jung-kwan Cho observes in chapter 6, "no other Korean regime in the past was born with such a deficit of legitimacy." To compensate, Chun positioned his regime as "transitional," with a single seven-year term for his presidency. But the transitional nature of the Fifth Republic greatly constrained his political options, and he eventually succumbed to the demand for democratic reform in 1987 (see chap. 6 for details). Scholars of democratic transition have identified economic success or failure as a key to undermining the authoritarianism of a developmental regime. When an authoritarian regime bases its legitimacy on economic performance, Samuel Huntington argues, it can soon face a "performance dilemma," even if it delivers what it promises, since by achieving its purpose, it can lose its purpose. The erosion of legitimacy in authoritarian regimes and the subsequent transition to democracy in Korea have been understood in this way: the consequence of the economic success of authoritarian, developmentalist regimes.[25] In a broad sense, this view makes a valid point. Yet in South Korea, it is more accurate to say that Chun suffered from a legitimacy problem due less to economic performance and more to the atrocities that he committed in Kwangju.

New Strategy for Democratic Activism

While Kwangju presented a legitimacy problem for the Chun regime, it sent a wake-up call to democratic activists. The failure in 1979–1980 clearly taught them a lesson as they reflected on their previous struggles, especially on why they had failed to prevent such a tragedy in Kwangju. In particular, many came to realize that they had fought without a well-articulated strategy and ideology. It seemed clear that first and foremost they needed a "scientific" analysis of Korean society, politics, and economy, and only then could they take concrete action to achieve democracy. It was in this context that the early to mid-1980s saw wide-ranging debates among activists and progressive intellectuals, such as "social formation debates," "debates on Korean capitalism," "debates on modern and contemporary Korea," and "debates on the character of Korean society." It was believed that past mistakes could be avoided by properly specifying the nature of Korean society and articulating a coherent ideology and strategy based on this analysis.[26]

More concretely, the "petty-bourgeois" nature of the earlier democratic movements was criticized, as they were mostly led by students and intellectuals who lacked a grassroots base. Movement leaders felt ashamed that it was largely factory workers, not students or intellectuals, who had fought to the end in Kwangju. A new strategy to build an alliance between students/intellectuals and grassroots citizens was called for, and it was in this context that many students went to factories to work in the 1980s. This new strategy became instrumental in organizing and mobilizing the masses in summer 1987, when millions of people marched together for democracy.

Anti-Americanism

Another important impact of the uprising was the rise and growth of anti-Americanism in South Korea. Before Kwangju, most Koreans viewed the United States as an ally that liberated their nation from Japanese colonialism and then communist aggression. Even many dissident intellectuals and student activists considered the United States a strategic partner in their fight for democracy. Such a view, however, was shattered by the U.S. role during the uprising. Most citizens in Kwangju expected that the United States would and should intervene to stop armed confrontation on their behalf. As Jean Underwood recounts in chapter 3, some Americans worked hard to protect innocent citizens from atrocities committed by the troops. Yet the U.S. government not only failed to prevent bloodshed but also endorsed the redeployment of Korean troops to Kwangju. It insisted that "the U.S. had neither authority over nor a prior knowledge of the movement of the Special Warfare Command

(SWC) units to Kwangju" but admitted that it "'approved' the movement of the 20th division," under the assumption that this army unit specially trained in riot control would be preferable to the SWC.[27] Tim Shorrock, after a careful review of declassified U.S. government documents, has concluded that "senior officials in the Carter administration approved South Korean plans to use military troops against pro-democracy demonstrations ten days before former General Chun Doo Hwan seized control of the country in a May 17, 1980 military coup."[28]

American involvement in Kwangju provoked anger and a sense of betrayal among Koreans.[29] The "families of prisoners in Kwangju" clearly expressed such a sentiment in a letter to Ambassador Gleysteen dated December 1980:

> How long will the US continue to support such a horrible authoritarian government that has no respect for human rights? If this support continues, the US government will be increasingly hated. Please reexamine this situation before it goes beyond the point of no return. Are you going to repeat the same mistake that you have made in many other countries, including Iran, where you have tasted bitter failure? Are you going to sit and do nothing while the same mistake is about to be made in Korea?[30]

The American government did not respond to such pleas, and Koreans increasingly came to question the U.S. role in Korea's quest for democracy. The United States was no longer deemed a potential ally but just another neocolonial power supporting dictatorship.[31] For this reason Korean activists attacked American facilities such as the embassy and cultural centers. In 1982 Mun Pu-sik, a third-year theology student, explained in a letter to the cardinal of the Korean Catholic Church why he set fire to the U.S. Cultural Center in Pusan:

> The reason why we chose this extreme method of setting fire to yet another American Cultural Center in Korea was to chastise the U.S. for the historical crimes it has committed on Korean soil. . . . Just looking at the Kwangju uprising, we must ask how it is that the U.S. gave final power to Chun Doo Hwan, slaughterer of innocent lambs, for his barbarous campaign against the citizens of Kwangju. Even a three-year-old child knows that, based on the Korean-American Defense Pact, all mobilization rights for our army are under the jurisdiction of the Commander of U.S. Forces in South Korea. All generations in this land are aware of the atrocity in our history, whereby these rights were given to Korean forces to kill patriotic citizens calling for democracy and freedom, and front-line troops were sent in to kill citizens of Kwangju. In the tragedy at Kwangju, the U.S. played the role of mother-in-law to the murdering demon Chun Doo Hwan, thus allowing him to accomplish his aims. . . . We chose this method of setting fire to a building in broad daylight because we felt

there was no other way left to chastise the U.S. for acting as the mother-in-law for this dictatorship.[32]

Anti-Americanism became a new form of nationalism that fueled Korea's march for democracy, and Kwangju was the turning point.[33]

U.S. Intervention on Behalf of Democracy

Kwangju's impact was felt beyond Korea, as it reoriented U.S. policy toward Asia as a whole. Charges of U.S. complicity in the Kwangju massacre and the subsequent rise of anti-Americanism in Korea undoubtedly concerned American policy makers. The United States seemed to have learned a lesson from Kwangju when it supported the democratic movement in the Philippines that overthrew Ferdinand Marcos in 1986. As Bruce Cumings has observed, U.S. policy began to shift on a world scale toward support of limited forms of democracy in the 1980s, and Korea was no exception. When James Lilly, a longtime CIA operative, became ambassador to Korea, he augmented the political staff of the embassy and began meeting with opposition forces, something that had not happened since 1980.[34]

The litmus test for American policy came in the summer of 1987, when millions of people filled the streets demanding democratic reform. This time the central site of the uprising was no longer peripheral Kwangju but the nation's capital, Seoul, and the Korean middle class, including white-collar workers and professionals, joined the demonstrations. Furthermore, the democratic movement came to be closely linked to a new nationalism that questioned American hegemony in Korean politics and raised the issue of national division and unification. In sharp contrast to Huntington's claim that "in the 1980s, movements for democracy throughout the world were inspired by and borrowed from the American example . . . the winning model,"[35] Koreans longing for democracy expressed their dissatisfaction with the U.S. role in Korean politics with slogans such as "Yankee Go Home!"

On this occasion, the U.S. government moved decisively by sending Gaston Sigur, an assistant secretary of state, to Seoul to meet with Chun, who was considering mobilizing armed forces once again to resolve the crisis. The United States seemed determined not to repeat the mistake that it had made seven years earlier in Kwangju. Pressured by the Americans, Chun cancelled plans to crush the opposition and granted political concessions that paved the way for a democratic transition in Korea (see chap. 6). Lynn Turk, who was in charge of political affairs at the U.S. embassy in Seoul at the time, concluded that "the Chun regime's mistakes in Kwangju played heavily in its decision in dealing with the massive demonstrations that year (1987)."[36] The memory of Kwangju lingered.

Memory and Representation

The uprising ended on May 27, 1980, but the struggles over how to represent and memorialize it have not. Just as motives for joining the uprising were not monolithic, memories and representations of them are varied, often contested, negotiated, and revisited. In particular, the democratic transition in the late 1980s opened up a space for new civic groups in Kwangju and elsewhere and facilitated public debates over the meaning and representation of the Kwangju uprising. Such contention and negotiation were intensified because the memories and symbols thus produced were not simply descriptive but had prescriptive power. As Don Baker reminds us in chapter 7, by conferring meaning and value on the past, these representations—the product of "interpretation, historicization, and invocation by different groups and individuals for different purposes"—provide guidelines for the present.

Kwangju was a taboo subject among Koreans in the early 1980s. Little was written on what happened in Kwangju other than official stories and accounts of the event. But with the surge of democratic movements in the mid-1980s, Korea saw the growth of what we might call a "5-18 industry."[37] As Baker reveals, Kwangju received a great deal of attention in literature, poems, drama, movies, documentaries, art, and scholarly publications. Such works not only evoked the painful memories of May 18 but also reshaped those memories. In 1990 a collection of testimonials from about five hundred witnesses appeared,[38] and the city of Kwangju published twenty-five volumes of the *General Collection of the Kwangju Democratization Movement* (Kwangju minjuhwa undong charyo ch'ongsŏ). The collection included a massive amount of documents, from leaflets distributed in the streets during the uprising to hearings on Kwangju by the Korean National Assembly to post-uprising writings and recently declassifed U.S. documents. Through these works, participants in the Kwangju uprising were no longer considered mere victims but were recast as heroes or fighters for democracy.

Some products of this "5-18 industry" became very popular nationwide. A case in point was *Morae sigye* (Hourglass), the first dramatic television show to weave the Kwangju uprising into its narrative. When the SBS television network broadcast it in 1995, streets emptied as people rushed home to catch it. *Morae sigye,* consisting of twenty-five episodes of about fifty minutes each, was an ambitious project that sought to retell twenty years of Korean history through an effective combination of painful political history and melodrama. In his paper presented at the USC-UCLA Kwangju conference in April 2000, Min Song compared the narrative and aesthetic tropes of *Morae sigye* to those of such popular American films as *The Godfather, The Untouchables, Kung Fu, Dr. Zhivago,* and *The Sound of Music.*[39]

It became popular even among Korean Americans (I myself watched most episodes in the United States).

As memories and representation were recast in a more positive way, so was the terminology referring to what happened in the city of Kwangju in May 1980. The "Kwangju incident," the term used by the Korean government implying that the uprising had been incited by communists and outside forces, was discarded in favor of a new official term, *Kwangju minjuhwa undong,* the Kwangju democratization movement. Still, there exists little consensus over terminology. Typically "5-18" or "Kwangju" are combined with such terms as "people's uprising" *(minjung hangjaeng)* or "democratization movement" *(minjuhwa undong)* to produce such terms as *5-18 minjung hangjaeng, 5-18 minjuhwa undong, Kwangju minjung hangjaeng, Kwangju minjuhwa undong,* and so on. This varying terminology does not simply reflect semantic differences but more importantly the differences in people's understanding of the event. Some people prefer to call it "5-18," referring only to the date, to avoid ideological and political implications. Such struggles over how to recall the event are far from settled.[40]

The official stance on the uprising also has changed over time. As studies of collective memory and representation show,[41] collective memory changes in tandem with changing social and political circumstances. In the case of the Kwangju uprisings, public perceptions began to change significantly after the June 1987 demonstrations and the subsequent democratization of Korean politics. From November 18 to February 24, 1988, the National Assembly held public hearings on the atrocities. In 1990 the government promulgated the Kwangju Compensation Law for victims and their families. In 1995 the National Assembly passed the 5-18 Special Law that led to the trials of both Chun Doo Hwan and Roh Tae Woo, the leaders of the "new military" at the time of the uprising and subsequent presidents of South Korea. In 1994 the 5-18 Memorial Foundation was established to coordinate various commemorative projects related to Kwangju. Old Mangwŏl-dong cemetery, once a small hill where corpses were dumped by the troops, has been replaced by a huge modern tourist site. May 18 is now celebrated as a national holiday. As Sallie Yea explains in chapter 8, with these changing political circumstances, May 18 has taken on more positive meanings among the public, and these days the city of Kwangju proudly puts on major ceremonies to commemorate what happened in the spring of 1980.

Despite this dramatic turnaround, some victims of Kwangju continue to suffer. Linda Lewis and Ju-na Byun (chap. 5) illuminate the continuing medical problems (both physical and psychological), financial difficulties (including unemployment), and other general hardships experienced by survivors. Some of the victims, their supporters, and others strongly question the institutionalization of the public commemoration of the uprising, which takes place with state support and hence departs from the true spirit of Kwangju as a resistance movement. As Sallie Yea observes, they object to what they view as the commodification of the uprising and choose to visit the old cemetery rather than the new, more grandiose one as "a form of passive protest." As Lewis and Byun remind us, Kwangju remains "a place where public memories and private histories of May 1980 coexist, where the bodies and minds of individual citizens themselves offer a site for resistance to the imposition of a singular 5-18 narrative." Contention over how to remember and represent Kwangju continues today.

Notes

1. See Gi-wook Shin, *Peasant Protest and Social Change in Colonial Korea* (Seattle: University of Washington Press, 1996).

2. Lee Jae-eui, *Kwangju Diary: Beyond Death, Beyond the Darkness of the Age* (Los Angeles: UCLA Asian Pacific Monograph Series, 1999).

3. Henry Scott-Stokes and Jae-eui Lee, eds., *The Kwangju Uprising: Eyewitness Press Accounts of Korea's Tiananmen* (Armonk, N.Y.: Sharpe, 2000).

4. William Gleysteen Jr., *Massive Entanglement, Marginal Influence: Carter and Korea in Crisis* (Washington, D.C.: Brookings Institution, 2000); John Wickham, *Korea on the Brink: From the "12/12" Incident to the Kwangju Uprising, 1979-80* (Washington, D.C.: U.S. Government Printing Office, 2000).

5. For a detailed account of the Pusan-Masan struggles, see pages 11–48 in *Puma esŏ Kwangju kkaji* [From Pusan/Masan to Kwangju], 5-18 Kwangju minjung hangjaeng tongchihoe ed. (Seoul: Saemmul, 1990).

6. My description of the uprising is primarily based on the following sources: Lee, *Kwangju Diary*; May 18 History Compilation Committee of Kwangju City, *The May 18 Kwangju Democratic Uprising* (Kwangju, n.d.); North American Coalition for Human Rights in Korea, "Reports from Kwangju" (1980); and G. Thompson Brown, "Korea: The Kwangju Uprising: May 18–22, 1980," June 30, 1980, both at the UCLA Library, Department of Special Collections, Archival Collection on Democracy and Unification in Korea.

7. Lee, *Kwangju Diary*, 104.

8. Cited on page 21 of "Reports from Kwangju."

9. Brown, "Korea," 5–6.

10. These estimates are based on the information that I received from Dr. Jong-chul Ahn, the author of chapter 2 in this volume, and a few others in Kwangju, including someone at the 5-18 Foundation. Ahn worked at the Kwangju city hall as a specialist on the 5-18 Committee, which published the twenty-five-volume *General Collection*. He is currently working for the Ministry of Administration and Local Autonomy, which is in charge of compensation for the dead or injured from the uprising. In my view, he is the most knowledgeable person in Korea on the uprising. My estimate of the dead include those missing during the uprising.

11. Citizens were said to complain that "students are never to be trusted," "they fled away taking no responsibility," "the educated guys were afraid to die and ran away," and so on. Such distrust of college students was expressed even after the uprisings, when the students were better treated in prisons. See Kim Doo-sik, "'Meaning Construction' of the Kwangju Pro-Democracy Movement and Futuristic Frame," *Korea Journal* 39, no. 2 (1999): 205–37.

12. Cited from Han Sang-jin, "Popular Sovereignty and a Struggle for Recognition from a Perspective of Human Rights," *Korea Journal* 39, no. 2 (1999): 192.

13. Ibid., 193.

14. Ibid., 191.

15. See Charles Tilly, *From Mobilization to Revolution* (Reading, Mass.: Addison-Wesley, 1978).

16. Chosun University Committee for Democratic Struggles, "Chosun University Students' Statement," May 22, 1980, UCLA Archival Collection on Democracy and Unification in Korea, 1–2.

17. "U.S. Government Statement on the Events in Kwangju, Republic of Korea, in May 1980," USIS Press Office, U.S. Embassy, Seoul, Korea, June 19, 1989, 17.

18. For a more detailed treatment of the marginalization of the Honam region, see Sallie Yea, "Regionalism and Political-Economic Differentiation in Korean Development," *Korea Journal* 34, no. 2 (1994): 5–29.

19. William H. Gleysteen Jr., "A former U.S. Official's Perspective on the Kwangju Uprising" (luncheon address, USC-UCLA Conference on Kwangju, Los Angeles, April 21, 2000).

20. Son Ho-ch'ŏl, *Hyŏndae han'guk chŏngch'i* [Modern Korean politics] (Seoul: Sahoe p'yŏngnon, 1991), 362.

21. Cited on page 27 in Tim Shorrock, "The U.S. Role in Korea in 1979 and 1980," www.kimsoft.com/korea/kwangju3.htm.

22. By May 1980, many SMOs appeared in the Kwangju area to resist the Yusin dictatorship. They included the Christianity Group, Constitutional Fellows Group, Noktu Bookstore Group, Modern Culture Institutes Team, Amnesty Group, Good Books Cooperatives Group, Dismissed Professors Group, YWCA Team, Labor Movement Team, Women's Group for Prisoners, Cultural Movement Team, Farmers Movement Team, Evening School Team, Chŏnnam National University Team, and Catholic Team of Justice and Peace. These groups led the pre-May 1980 democratic movements in the Kwangju area, and some of them continued their struggles during the uprising.

23. A 1996 survey shows 31.1 percent of non-Kwangju people believing that May 18 made a "big" impact on Korean democratization (48.3 percent say "some" impact), while 46.5 percent say Kwangju is the Mecca of Korean democratization. See Kim Tong-wŏn et al., *Kungmin i ponŭn 5-18* [5-18 as seen by the Korean people] (Kwangju: Kwangju sahoe chosa yŏn'guso, 1998), 69–70.

24. For a discussion of how Park sought to legitimize his regime, see Gi-wook Shin, "Nation, History, and Politics: South Korea," in Hyung Il Pai and Timothy Tangherlini, eds., *Nationalism and the Construction of Korean Identity* (Berkeley: IEAS/University of California-Berkeley, 1999), 148–65.

25. See Samuel Huntington, *The Third Wave: Democratization in the Late Twentieth Century* (Norman: University of Oklahoma Press, 1991), esp. chap. 2.

26. See Gi-wook Shin, "Marxism, Anti-Americanism, and Democracy in South Korea: An Examination of Nationalist Intellectual Discourse," *Positions: East Asia Cultures Critique* 3, no. 2 (1995): 508–34.

27. "U.S. Government Statement on the Events in Kwangju," 17–18.

28. See Shorrock, "U.S. Role in Korea," 2. Such contrasting views of the U.S. role in the Kwangju uprising were repeatedly expressed by Shorrock and Gleysteen during the USC/UCLA conference.

29. A 1996 survey finds that 82.5 percent of Kwangju citizens believe the United States was involved in 5-18 (50.8 percent for non-Kwangju people). Further, 44.5 percent of Kwangju respondents say the United States should make an official apology for its involvement in 5-18, and 21.8 percent even say the United States should pay compensation to victims. See Kim et al., *Kungmin i ponŭn 5-18*, 94, 99.

30. Families of prisoners arrested in relation to Kwangju, "Letter to U.S. Ambassador Gleysteen from Families of Prisoners in Kwangju," December 1980, UCLA Archival Collection on Democracy and Unification in Korea, 3.

31. See North American Coalition for Human Rights in Korea, *Korea 88: The Bigger Picture* (Washington, D.C., 1988).

32. Moon Bu-shik (Mun Pusik), "Why Did I Commit Arson?" (March 1982), UCLA Archival Collection on Democracy and Unification in Korea, 1–2.

33. See Tim Shorrock, "The Struggle for Democracy in South Korea in the 1980s and the Rise of Anti-Americanism," *Third World Quarterly* 8, no. 4 (1986): 1195–1218.

34. Bruce Cumings, introduction to Lee, *Kwangju Diary*, 17–35.

35. Huntington, *Third Wave*, 286.

36. Lynn Turk, "Why after Nine Years? The 1989 U.S. Government Statement on Kwangju" (paper presented at international conference sponsored by USC and UCLA, Kwangju after Two Decades, Los Angeles, April 20–22, 2000).

37. One of the first public accounts appeared in a 1985 book under the title of *Chugŭm ŭl nŏmŏ sidae ŭi ŏdum ŭl nŏmŏ* (Beyond Death, Beyond the Darkness of the Age), ascribed to a well-known novelist, Hwang Sŏg-yŏng. It was a detailed account of what happened in the ten-day struggle in Kwangju. (I read this book in the late 1980s as a graduate student at the University of Washington.) It was later discovered that Lee Jae-eui was its real author, but Hwang was given credit as a means to help market the book. The publisher believed, Lee recalls, that "if the book were published under a famous writer's name, it would increase both its credibility and sales." Both Hwang and the publisher of the book were arrested and sentenced to prison terms. The book was published in English in 1999 under the title *Kwangju Diary: Beyond Death, Beyond the Darkness of the Age* by the UCLA Asian Pacific Monograph Series.

38. Han'guk hyŏndaesa saryo yŏn'gu, ed., *Kwangju owŏl minjung hangjaeng saryo chŏnjip* [The complete collection of the historical record of the Kwangju May People's Uprising] (Seoul: P'ulpit, 1990).

39. Min Song, "Morae Sigye, Korean Americans, and Historical Knowledge" (paper presented at the USC-UCLA Conference on the Kwangju Uprising, Los Angeles, April 20–22, 2000).

40. Recent public polls show how Kwangju citizens today remember the uprising. A 1996 survey of four hundred Kwangju citizens and eight hundred non-Kwangju citizens asked: "What first comes to your mind when you think of 5-18?" Of the respondents, 31.8 percent said "death/murder/blood," 16 percent "democratization," 12 percent "demonstrations," and 6.5 percent "martial troops." Another survey of 400 Kwangju citizens and 839 non-Kwangju citizens conducted in 1997 showed that 66.8 percent of Kwangju citizens regard the Kwangju uprising as "a democratic movement opposed to the new military," 16.5 percent a "self-defense for survival," and 8 percent a "people's revolution to overthrow the regime." For non-Kwangju respondents, the figures were 46.4 percent, 20 percent, and 14.4 percent, respectively. As is apparent, there was no strong consensus among respondents.

41. See Jeffrey Olick and Joyce Robbins, "Social Memory Studies," *Annual Review of Sociology* 24 (1998): 105–40.

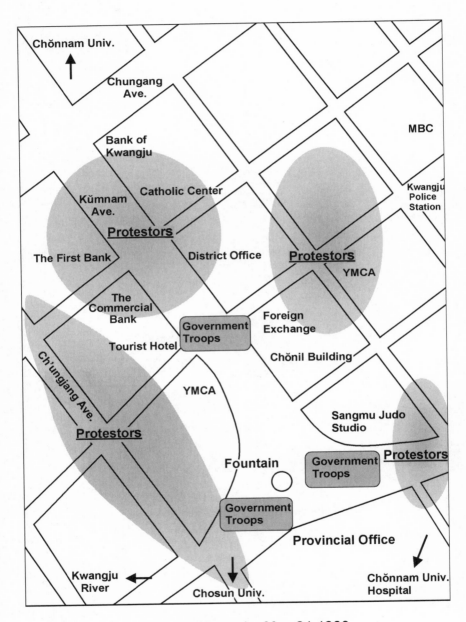

Downtown Kwangju, May 21, 1980

I

ORIGINS AND DEVELOPMENT

1

The Formation of an "Absolute Community"

Jung-woon Choi

A T APPROXIMATELY NOON ON MAY 18, 1980, in the vicinity of Kŭmnam Av-enue, at the center of downtown Kwangju, riot police suppressed student demonstrators demanding democratization and an end to martial law.[1] The number of students, the size of the riot police unit, the precise location and movements of the demonstration—these things did not seem to possess any particular significance. Indeed, such an event had become a common occurrence in large Korean cities during the previous months and years. The significance of such an event was (and still is) conveniently implied in an expression commonly used in Korean society: "student demonstration." Even though martial law had been declared, a student demonstration of this type gave no particular cause for alarm. Citizen response to the demonstration was typically diverse: some expressed their support for the students while others displayed no interest whatsoever. Still others indicated their displeasure with student activism: "It's just because they hate to study."

The events that occurred a few hours later, immediately following the deployment of elite paratrooper units in the Kŭmnam Avenue area, were completely at odds with the norm. Those who witnessed the events found themselves utterly unprepared to comprehend what was happening and, later, to convey it to others. Many could scarcely believe it had actually occurred. The *Dong-A Ilbo* newspaper reporter Kim Ch'ung-gŭn recollected his feelings at the time:

> As I covered the Kwangju uprising, I found myself deploring my own inadequacies as a reporter, my inability to express what was happening. It was then that I

came to the realization, deep down, that there were events that could not possibly be described by means of the spoken or written word. I couldn't find the proper words, as a reporter, to portray the acts I had witnessed. Barbarity, aggression, indiscriminate attack—expressions of this type were utterly inadequate, too smooth around the edges. At my wit's end, the expression that occurred to me was "human hunting." [This expression did not appear in the newspapers due to the censorship in effect under martial law but was frequently used to describe the horrific state of affairs that existed during the uprising.] The violence directed against young women was particularly severe: the prettier the woman and the more care with which she was dressed, the worse it was for her. How do we put into words a situation where a woman's clothes are ripped to shreds, where those parts of her anatomy that distinguish her as a woman become the focus of attack? Expressions such as the following flashed in my mind: rape in broad daylight, outrageous violation, sadistic attack, armed suppression. But none of these could adequately portray the situation in Kwangju.[2]

Bodies clashing against one another, bodies being broken—this was the central characteristic of the Kwangju uprising. People experienced terror, rage, enmity, hostility, solidarity, ecstasy, and inspiration—which in all likelihood they never again felt—an event that later came to be characterized as the "Kwangju syndrome."

In this chapter, I seek to explain how Kwangju citizens rose up and fought off an elite force of three thousand Republic of Korea paratroopers through what I call the "absolute community" *(chŏldae kongdongch'e)*.[3] In the absolute community, there were no private possessions, and citizens did not differentiate their lives from that of others; time ceased to flow. All distinctions between humans disintegrated as disparate individuals joined together as one. Only then could Kwangju citizens risk their lives to band together against the overwhelming force arrayed against them.

The Spark

Events leading to the absolute community began on the morning of May 20, when a corpse was discovered in front of the Chŏnnam Brewing Company. Enraged citizens gathered in front of the Taein market and began to demonstrate. In the afternoon, large numbers of citizens—men, women, the elderly, the young—slowly began to come in from the outskirts of the city and gather in the downtown area. A large demonstration shortly ensued. At approximately 2:30 P.M., the paratroopers began firing flamethrowers at the Sŏbang intersection. Several citizens were burned to death on the spot. The citizens became extremely agitated. Around 3:00 P.M., the Seventh and Eleventh

Brigades were redeployed in the downtown area. An all-out battle between the citizens and the paratroopers broke out.

At this time a new phenomenon appeared in the downtown area. As the paratroopers moved to suppress the demonstrations, several hundred people, engulfed by tear gas, began sit-down demonstrations in various downtown locales. In front of the Hwani Department Store on Kŭmnam Avenue a student gave a speech, led in chanting slogans, and read from leaflets. When it became difficult to hear the student's voice, someone began taking up a collection to purchase a loudspeaker, and a sum of 400,000 won was collected on the spot. The students began to teach the citizens the "songs of the student movement." "We Long for Reunification," "Song of Justice," "Song of the Fighters," and the "Hula Song" were sung again and again. Someone shouted out, "Let's follow those who have gone before us and die together!" The demonstrators were no longer chanting hostile slogans such as "Let's rip Chun Doo Hwan apart and kill him!" Now they expressed the sorrow welling up inside them: "Kill all of us!" and "Let's all die together!" As the demonstration began in earnest, young men armed with pieces of lumber and other weapons moved to the front. The women stood behind, handing the men wet towels, toothpaste, and water to help them withstand the tear gas. Some people brought boards and pipes from construction sites to use as weapons. Gravel and other materials were brought in on bicycles and pushcarts. The paratroopers soon attacked, but the demonstrators were determined not to retreat.

As darkness descended over the city, a large parade of vehicles with headlights turned on was seen coming toward the demonstrators. The citizens trembled in fear, thinking that reinforcements for the paratroopers were heading their way, until someone shouted, "The drivers of democracy have finally risen up!" The vehicles were filled not with paratroopers but with citizen drivers using their vehicles to demonstrate. Buses and large trucks were leading the way, followed by hundreds of taxis honking their horns. The line of cars was slowly heading in the direction of the Provincial Office. The air was filled with shouts of joy, the citizens crying and hugging one another. The paratroopers were terrified and began to break up telephone boxes and large planters on the sides of the streets to use as barricades. Only the day before the citizens had constructed barricades—now it was the paratroopers' turn. As soon as the vehicles in the demonstration reached the barricades, however, a large number of tear gas canisters came flying at them. At the same time, the paratroopers attacked, moving in between the vehicles and engaging the drivers in combat. Many drivers and citizens were hurt, and numerous others were captured. Nevertheless, the citizens had affirmed their unity, and violent demonstrations broke out everywhere in the city. Citizens helped each other in the streets, sharing rice balls, beverages, towels, and cigarettes, as more and more people flowed in from the outskirts of the city to join the demonstrations.

Formation of the Absolute Community

From May 19 to the morning of May 20, citizens fought individual battles against the authorities in order to survive, hoping—as they gave expression to their anger by rushing about, throwing stones, and setting fires—that other citizens would join in the struggle. On the afternoon of May 20, however, on Kŭmnam Avenue and in other locations in the city, the citizens formed a new community—not a traditional community but rather an absolute community. This community was not formed because some leader seized a microphone and began to incite the masses. The absolute community was not an organization, such as the military, that relies on a leader to coerce individuals into combat to achieve a designated goal. Instead, the absolute community was formed by citizens who autonomously overcame their fears, risked their lives in struggle, and came together freely to reaffirm and celebrate their humanity, their true citizenship.

The reporter Kim Ch'ung-gŭn, who was covering the event from the Provincial Office, described a scene of group singing that captured well the atmosphere of the absolute community:

> It was in Kwangju that I first felt myself trembling so vehemently at the singing of our representative folk song, Arirang. Without water and power, all of Kwangju was enveloped in darkness; broadcasting stations and police boxes had been set on fire. Standing alone on top of the darkened Provincial Office, I saw a crowd waving Korean flags coming in my direction. The moment I heard the strains of Arirang, I felt an intense shuddering coursing through my veins. My mind went blank and I began to weep uncontrollably.[4]

The song of Arirang inspired people with the overwhelming feeling of sheer collectivity. The melody of Arirang, inhering the time-honored sensibilities of the Korean traditional community, mysteriously transformed the slow swaying of individual bodies into a single movement of citizens.[5] The sobs and tears of the citizens filling the streets represented a melancholy confession of sin, an expression of the pangs of conscience at not having rushed to the sides of fellow citizens risking their lives. At the same time, these sobs and tears also exuded a warm, embracing forgiveness.

The citizens felt a sense of ecstasy that people from all quarters—men and women of all ages and classes, even bar girls from Hwanggŭm district and prostitutes from the Taein red-light district—were coming together to join the collectivity. As darkness fell, out of nowhere about fifty farmers dressed in white Korean traditional clothes appeared on Kŭmnam Avenue bearing hoes and bamboo spears, looking like warriors from the Peasant War of 1894 who had stepped out of a time machine. The citizens greeted them with thunderous applause. It seemed like a different world. Citizens stood side by side with people they had never met, prepared to fight to the death.

In the absolute community, it became natural to define life and death in terms of the collective rather than the individual. Expressions such as "we are fighting in order to survive" and "we are the ones who must protect the place we were born" indicated that the life of the individual had fused with that of the collective. In the absolute community, there were no private possessions and no separate lives; and because all individuals were recognized as possessing human dignity of the highest order, there were no class distinctions. At the same time, individuals who freed themselves from their fear of death had overcome finitude. In this place, then, time possessed no meaning whatsoever. Indeed, the experience of having overcome the fear of death by means of community engendered a liberation from the sensations and anxieties of the mundane world.[6]

Action and Reaction

On the evening of May 20, the citizens who had formed the absolute community began to appropriate the authority of the state itself. They commandeered all items necessary to do battle. Prior to the afternoon of May 20, some citizens had taken up such items as boards and pipes in order to protect themselves. Now, however, they armed themselves for war, seizing anything they could find, blunt or sharp: pieces of lumber, iron pipes, kitchen knives, charcoal pincers, shovels, pickaxes. Owners of lumberyards fashioned wooden sticks in great numbers and distributed them to the citizens. Citizens captured guns from police stations and armored personnel carriers from Asia Motors, using them to attack the paratroopers. Taking their cue from demonstrations earlier in the afternoon, they mobilized buses, trucks, even fire trucks. They set some vehicles on fire and pushed them toward the paratroopers. Other vehicles were driven by young men who had formed a kind of commando squad, driving flaming cars toward the paratroopers and jumping out at the very last instant. Meanwhile, some others drove around the outskirts of the city, picking up people and bringing them to the downtown area. Having appropriated such authority, the absolute community even passed sentence on public buildings throughout the night of May 20. For airing false broadcasts, the local MBC television station was set on fire, as were the KBS television station and the tax office.[7]

These acts did not simply stem from an "impulse for violence." To be sure, some riotous acts did occur: citizens threw rocks at public buildings, breaking windows, and set fire to police boxes in the city. Nonetheless, most of the targets of violence, destruction, and arson were not chosen at random but selected through citizen debate. Citizens did not lose their sense of morality; they made strong efforts to avoid degenerating into a "mob," a term employed in the paratrooper broadcasts aimed at suppressing the demonstrations.

Into the late hours of May 20, the demonstrators—who now numbered in the tens of thousands—fought in shifts, sleeping for a short time wherever they could on mats in alleys, in inns, in homes. At 4:00 A.M. on May 21, the paratroopers were finally driven from Kwangju station. Dawn seemingly brought victory to the citizens. However, the bodies of two people, killed in gruesome fashion, were discovered at Kwangju station. It was a sign of things to come.

Throughout the morning, people crowded into Kŭmnam Avenue from throughout the city. Citizens rode in trucks and buses, beating on them with sticks, singing songs, picking up others to transport them downtown. Wherever the demonstrators went, fellow citizens provided them with provisions, and food piled up inside of their vehicles. Armed with this support, the demonstrators were filled with new resolve and determination, and about 300,000 of them crowded into Kŭmnam Avenue and surrounded the Provincial Office. Almost the entire population of the city seemed mobilized to participate in the demonstrations.

Tension filled the air as the demonstrators and the paratroopers, positioned a short distance away from each other, entered into negotiations. The negotiations, however, broke down, and around 1:00 P.M. the paratroopers opened fire. Kŭmnam Avenue was transformed into a sea of blood and wailing. Seeking guns, citizens headed to armories in the downtown area and on the outskirts of the city. By midafternoon, guns were distributed in locations such as Kwangju Park. The demonstrators transformed themselves into a civilian militia, a "citizen army" *(simin'gun)*, and began to engage in urban combat.[8] On the evening of May 21, the citizen army penetrated the Provincial Office only to find that the paratroopers had already left. It was an inspiring, if short-lived, victory.

A Question of Dignity

In the final analysis, the citizens of Kwangju risked their lives to recover their human dignity. The essence of human dignity is not found in the pursuit of personal rewards or social standing, but in the acknowledgment of something more valuable than life and in the act of risking one's life for it. For many, this can be the nation or God. In the case of Kwangju's citizens, it was the community, the life of one's fellow citizens. People valued human dignity more than their own lives. Dignity became an issue for the citizens of Kwangju when they saw the paratroopers kick their fellow citizens "like dogs" and found themselves agonizing over not risking their lives in the struggle to stop the violence. In order to affirm their humanity, citizens had to demonstrate both to themselves and to fellow citizens that they would risk their lives fighting for the sake of the community in times of crisis. The absolute community that formed on May 20–21, 1980, solved the question of dignity for Kwangju's citizens.

Notes

1. This chapter is a shortened version of an article published in *Korea Journal* 39, no. 4 (1999). For a fuller account, see Choi Jung-woon, *Owŏl ŭi sahoe kwahak* [The May uprising in the social sciences] (Seoul: P'ulpit, 1999).

2. Korean Reporters Association, *5-18 tŭkp'awŏn ripot'ŭ* [Reports on Kwangju by special correspondents], comp. Mudŭng ilbo and Simin yŏndae moim (Seoul: P'ulpit, 1997), 212–14.

3. Ferdinand Tönnies, distinguishing between "community" *(Gemeinschaft)* and "community of interests" *(Gesellschaft),* states the following: "A case where the affirmation of a social reality occurs for its own sake provides a stark contrast to an instance where the affirmation of a social reality occurs for the sake of an external goal or purpose. I call the former an instance of essential will; the latter is an instance of arbitrary will." Werner J. Cahnman and Rudolf Heberle, eds., *Ferdinand Tönnies On Sociology: Pure, Applied, and Empirical* (Chicago: University of Chicago Press, 1971), 65. Tönnies states the following regarding *Gemeinschaft:* "When a relationship is affirmed through love or affection, or is valorized by custom, mores, or a sense of obligation, this relationship falls under the concept of Gemeinschaft" (p. 67). Tönnies makes no mention of an "absolute community." I employ this term here in order to explain the special circumstances surrounding the Kwangju uprising. For Tönnies, love and affection are the primary attributes of the community, more essential than custom or mores. The community that emerged during the uprising, which I discuss in this chapter, was a social reality affirming itself for its own sake, grounded in a love inextricably linked to life. This community therefore pushes Tönnies's notion of the community to its furthest limits. It is in order to emphasize the exceptional purity of this community that I have designated it in this chapter as the absolute community.

4. *5-18 T'ŭkp'awŏn rip'ot'ŭ,* 215–16.

5. The singing of "Arirang" occasioned a similar effect in other places as well. According to the testimony of Pak Nam-sŏn, who later became commander of a civilian militia, sometime following May 20 (the exact time is unknown), he and others were reading a flyer somewhere near the public transportation terminal when "one of the

citizens began to sing 'We Long for Reunification' and everyone began to sob. People began to chant slogans such as "Filthy Murderer Chun Doo Hwan, Step Down!" "Send the Soldiers Back to the Thirty-Eighth Parallel!" "Bring My Child Back to Life!" Pak Nam-sŏn, *Owŏl kŭ nal: Simin'gun sanghwang silchang: Kwangju sanghwang pogosŏ* [That day in May: Report of the director of operations of the civilian militia on the Kwangju situation] (Kwangju: Saemmul, 1988), 137.

6. Many of those who fought on the front lines have no precise recollection of when, where, and how they fought, or of what happened and where. See Han'guk hyŏndae saryo yŏn'guso, *Kwangju owŏl minjung hangjaeng saryo chŏnjip* [Complete historical records of the Kwangju May people's uprising] (Seoul: P'ulpit, 1990), 486 [2036], 785 [3109].

7. At the time, martial law authorities were continuously broadcasting television reports claiming that large-scale arson was being perpetrated by a "mob." While some claim that citizens did not set fire to the MBC television station, it is clear that citizens intended to set fire to the building by throwing Molotov cocktails at it. The circumstances surrounding the MBC fire are as follows. Citizens facing off against the paratroopers attempted to negotiate with them, offering to engage in peaceful demonstrations. The citizens' attempt to negotiate was rebuffed by the paratroopers. As citizen representatives were returning to their side, an armored personnel carrier started up and headed toward the demonstrators at full speed, killing two small children. The enraged demonstrators attempted to set fire to the MBC building. See Han'guk hyŏndae saryo yŏn'guso, 661 [3058].

8. See chapter 2 in this volume for further details.

2

Simin'gun: The Citizens' Army during the Kwangju Uprising

Jong-chul Ahn

A FTER KOREA WAS LIBERATED FROM COLONIAL RULE, various forms of popular struggles occurred.[1] The 1946 Taegu uprising, the 1948 rebellion that took place on Cheju Island, the Yŏsu-Sunch'ŏn armed struggles of 1948, and the April 19 student uprising of 1960 are key examples of such struggles. The Kwangju uprising of 1980 is similar to these earlier instances of collective protest in that they all were struggles against authoritarian regimes. The Kwangju uprising differs from the other struggles in that ordinary citizens took up arms to directly challenge the armed might of the state. The Cheju rebellions and the Yŏsu-Sunch'ŏn riots involved armed resistance as well. Yet they occurred under the U.S. military occupation (1945–1948) and thus represented clashes over the establishment of an independent South Korean government. The Kwangju uprising, on the other hand, occurred thirty years after the founding of the Republic of Korea, when state power had already been consolidated.

After the martial law troops fired on the crowds at 1:00 P.M. on May 21, citizens began to take up arms, and thereafter they became known as the Citizens' Army *(Simin'gun).* From the start of the uprising on May 18 until May 21, some citizens fought against government troops with primitive defensive weapons (such as sticks, firebombs, Molotov cocktails, etc.). After May 21, when troops began shooting to kill with the M-1 and carbon rifle, the name "Citizens' Army" took on meaning and gained acceptance among the Kwangju people.

The Citizens' Army controlled the city from the afternoon of May 21 to the early morning of May 27. On May 23 markets and stores began to reopen.

Local government officials cooperated with the Citizens' Army to supply food, electricity, and water to social welfare organizations, and citizens rushed to the hospital to donate blood and made meals for the Citizens' Army. No financial institutions or jewelry shops were robbed; in fact, the crime rate during this period was much lower than usual. While the Citizens' Army could not match the superior modern weaponry of the martial law troops, they maintained solidarity until the end and symbolized the Kwangju citizens' fight for social justice.

During the Fifth Republic, established after the uprising, Kwangju citizens were branded as rioters. The Chun government used this characterization to justify suppressing the uprising en route to its illegal power grab. In the official narrative, the bloody oppression of the Kwangju people by military force was justified, while the Kwangju citizens who took up arms were an unlawful mob. This official story has been contradicted since the late 1980s, however, more facts and documents regarding the uprising have surfaced. In this chapter, I seek to restore justice by examining the origins, formation, and character of the Citizens' Army during the uprising.

The Rise

Despite the harsh military repression of student protesters, most citizens did not immediately join them in demonstrations. On May 19 they joined the students in singing protest songs and chanting antigovernment slogans but did not take an active role in leading antigovernment demonstrations. The situation began to change, however, after troops shot at the demonstrators on the night of May 20 at Kwangju station and killed at least twenty people. Most citizens were unaware of the shooting until the following leaflet was distributed that night in the streets of Kwangju:

The Moment of Fight Has Come!
Event Briefing
500 people dead, 3,000 wounded, 3,000 arrested!
The bastards started shooting.
People of Seoul, Taegu, Masan, Chŏnju, Kunsan, Iri, Mokp'o also rose up!
In Chŏnju and Iri police joined the citizens!
The Student Revolutionary Army stole weapons from the *Sangmudae* (army)!

What You Have to Do
Make weapons.
(prepare dynamite, Molotov cocktails, bombs, fire arrows, fire cans, any kind of fuel)

Set on fire any government building.
Get cars.
Organize a special army and steal army weapons.
Ah! Brotherhood! Let's fight to the death!

May 20, 1980
Committee of Citizens for Democratic Struggle, Student Revolution Committee[2]

This leaflet greatly exaggerated the number of casualties but played an instrumental role in the rise of the Citizens' Army. It called attention to the government's merciless violence and the urgent need for citizens to be armed. Demonstrating citizens felt they had little choice but to take up arms. Beyond the bold declaration to fight, however, there was no one to lead the battle. Most social movement organizations and activists were in jail or in hiding. Furthermore, only a very limited organizational base existed to mobilize people for armed resistance. Nonetheless, the declaration to take up arms became a key turning point in the rise of the Citizens' Army.

On the afternoon of May 21 Kwangju citizens began to arm themselves, the day when soldiers fired indiscriminately at the citizens gathered at the Provincial Office, leaving more than fifty people dead. Faced with this massacre, Kwangju citizens hurried to nearby towns such as Hwasun, Naju, Yŏngsanp'o, Changsŏng, Yŏnggwang, and Tamyang to obtain weapons. Since most policemen in neighboring areas had been sent to Kwangju to help suppress the uprising, the citizens were able to acquire weapons from those police stations. From the mines of Hwasun, with the help of miners, citizens even obtained dynamite and detonators. The weapons were brought to downtown Kwangju and distributed to the young men who now were called the Citizens' Army by the Kwangju citizens and regarded as "our army," as opposed to the martial law army. The Citizens' Army set up temporary headquarters at the Citizens Center in Kwangju Park.

The Citizens' Army began a counterattack around 3:15 P.M., two hours after the mass shooting. The street battle moved from the Provincial Office toward Chŏnnam National University Medical School, the Ministry of Labor building, Kwangju Park, and Kŭmnam Avenue. Weapons were brought in from the suburbs, increasing the size and firepower of the Citizens' Army, which even set up a light machine gun on the roof of Chŏnnam University Medical School and pointed it at the Provincial Office. Later in the afternoon the martial law troops, concerned with rapidly escalating casualties in their ranks, retreated to the hills behind Chosun University. In the evening the Citizens' Army entered the Provincial Office without any resistance. Within a few hours after taking up armed resistance, the citizens had driven out the government troops and taken control of most parts of the city.

Organization

On May 22 the Citizens' Army began to regroup, urgently needing to transform the spontaneous armed uprising into a more organized resistance. While their will to fight was strong and morale was high, most members of the Citizens' Army were young and had no formal military training. Responding to the call of a reserve army officer, hundreds of armed citizens gathered at Kwangju Park. A dozen reserve army officers trained the citizens in firearms usage, organizing them into smaller units and making specific assignments to each unit. Some of the units were sent to the suburbs to face the martial troops, while others were given the task of patrolling the suburbs. Other citizens lent a hand by voluntarily cleaning the streets and making meals for those who stood guard. Shops began to reopen, coffins were displayed side by side and covered with white sheets, and a memorial altar was set up at the entrance of the Provincial Office.

On the evening of May 22, the Citizens' Army appropriated the Provincial Office building as its headquarters and used the general affairs office on the first floor as the main control room. There, passes for cars and fuel cards (needed to get gas at the gas stations of the city) and passes to the control room were issued. For maintaining contact with the Citizens' Army in the suburbs, the headquarters used walkie-talkies left by the government troops. High school girls made a list of the dead and informed the citizens of martial troop movements in the suburbs, while other citizens acquired microphones and speakers in preparation for a rally.[3]

The organization of the Citizens' Army developed further on May 23, as Pak Namsŏn, who eventually took charge of the headquarters, assigned close friends and schoolmates to positions such as chief officer, controller, and supervising guard.[4] Yet to a certain extent the Citizens' Army remained a spontaneous gathering. The citizen soldiers usually stayed in the Provincial Office building or slept in cars, and when informed that fighting had broken out in the suburbs, they got into the cars carrying their guns and went to fight. When somebody left a gun and went home, another person filled in.

Among the organized units, the patrols played a key role, functioning partly as police and partly as army units with one car and one radio transmitter per unit. These patrols went through suburban areas informing the citizens of telephone numbers and other ways to convey the movement of government troops to headquarters. They also set up a "communication unit" (*t'ongsin-*

ban) that used walkie-talkies to obtain intelligence information about government forces. Some patrol units also collected weapons, occasionally threatening civic leaders who objected. Most citizens, however, expressed support for the patrols by waving when they passed by. Meanwhile, the mobile strike unit, organized on May 26, symbolized the organization and spirit of the Citizens' Army. Each of the thirteen mobile strike units had five or six people (one leader and four or five members), one jeep, one walkie-talkie, one carbon rifle, and one set of bullets. An official induction ceremony, including an oath of service, endowed the units with solemnity, and all the members, who consisted mostly of workers in their twenties, were issued identification cards and wore clean police uniforms and helmets.

New Leadership

After the martial law forces retreated on May 21, protest leaders set up two committees, the Citizen Settlement Committee and the Student Settlement Committee. The former consisted of civic leaders such as priests, lawyers, and professors, and the latter was represented by students from Chŏnnam University, Chosun University, and some junior colleges in the city. They were set up to negotiate with the government on behalf of the citizens to end the bloody uprising and massacre.

However, most of the Citizens' Army showed a hostile attitude toward these committees, especially the Settlement Committee, as it insisted on unconditionally giving up the citizens' weapons. They thought it was a trap. Nevertheless, many armed citizens began to return their weapons, and the atmosphere at the Provincial Office and around the city cooled rapidly. To reverse the situation, Pak Namsŏn, chief of the headquarters, issued the following statement at a rally to explain why the Citizens' Army should continue to be armed.

"Why We Could Not But Carry Guns"[5]
First of all, we pray for the dead citizens and students who spilled their blood and died to protect the democracy of this city. Why could we not but carry guns? The answer is too simple. Because we could not stand the brutality anymore. On the morning of the 18th they dispatched paratroopers to each school against protesting students, putting bayonets on their guns and rushing the students, and so our students ran out to the streets and denounced the illegal activities of the government. But how could this have happened? The Martial Law government from the 18th dispatched paratroopers to every corner of the city indiscriminately killing students and young men. This was unthinkable, but it happened. Our parents, brothers, and sisters were stabbed by bayonets or run over by cars, and even the breasts of weak women were cut off. They committed an

indescribable, ruthless, and cruel massacre. And we found out later the military sent the 7th Paratroopers from Kyŏngsang province on purpose to provoke regionalism, didn't give food to the troops for three days, and even worse they gave them alcohol and stimulants. Citizens! One other shocking fact: From the night of the 20th the martial troops formally commanded the shooting and started to fire indiscriminately. Democratic citizens who are gathered here to protect this city, what could we do in that situation? What could we have done? We want to ask you. We cannot bear this anymore. This is why we carried guns on our hands to protect this city and our families. Ladies and gentleman, who is the real rioter? Is it the martial troops, who committed brutal and ruthless cruelty, or the Citizens' Army who protected this city? Citizens, in spite of all the obstacles, we the Citizens' Army will protect your safety to the end. Also, if negotiations proceed smoothly we will give up our arms immediately. Democratic citizens, please trust and cooperate with the Citizens' Army.

—5-25-1980, all members of the Citizens' Army

At this point activist leaders who had been hiding or working behind the scenes decided to take over leadership of the armed struggle. They concluded after intense debate that it was their duty and responsibility to give guidance and direction to the resistance that had begun spontaneously among young blue-collar workers. They formed a new steering group named the Kwangju People's Struggle Leadership. The thirteen-member organization consisted of some members of the Student Settlement Committee who were determined to fight to the end, social/labor activists, and those who came to the forefront during the armed struggle (see table 2.1 for members of the new leadership). Most of them were in their mid-twenties to early thirties and had a college education. Some were seasoned veterans who had led previous democratic movements in the city of Kwangju, gaining respect among their peers.

The Struggle Leadership decided to stop returning weapons and organized a division of labor in preparation for the anticipated fight with the martial law troops. As table 2.1 shows, Kim Chongbae, a student activist, was named chairman, and Yun Sangwŏn, a labor activist, became committee spokesman. Their overall strategy was to struggle and negotiate. They called on citizens in the reserve army to form self-defense forces and threatened to detonate dynamite in the warehouses if martial law troops attacked. At the same time, they discussed ways to normalize the lives of ordinary citizens, though they fell short of coming up with concrete programs.

Composition and Character

While the new leadership of the Citizens' Army was largely composed of college students and graduates who had some experience in activism, its members had

TABLE 2.1

Members of the Kwangju People's Struggle Leadership

Name	Age	Education	Occupation	Duty at the Time	Activist Experience	Note
Kim Chong-bae	26	University student	Third-year university student	Chairman	No	Arrested on May 27 at the Provincial Office
Chŏng Sang-yong	30	University graduate	Office worker	Vice chairman, external affairs	Yes	Ran away on May 21 and returned on May 23; taken by the police from Provincial Office on May 27
Hŏ Kyu-jŏng	27	University student	Second-year university student	Vice chairman	No	Taken by the police from Provincial Office on May 27.
Kim Yŏng-ch'ŏl	32	University graduate	Social activist	Director of planning division	Yes	Arrested on May 27 at Provincial Office
Kim Chun-bong	21	Quit high school	Office worker	Research division	No	Arrested on May 27 at Provincial Office
Yun Sang-wŏn	29	University graduate	Labor activist	Spokesman	Yes	Killed on May 27 at Provincial Office
Chŏng Hae-jik	29	University graduate	Teacher	Public service division	Yes	Taken by police on May 27 at Provincial Office
Pak Nam-sŏn	26	High school graduate	Supervisor of lumber mill	Control division	No	Wounded on May 27 at Provincial Office

continued

TABLE 2.1 (continued)

Name	Age	Education	Occupation	Duty at the Time	Activist Experience	Note
Ku Sŏng-ju	24		Dong-a Corporation	Supply division	No	Taken by police on May 27 at Provincial Office
Pak Hyŏ-sŏn	26	University graduate	Teacher	Publicity division	Yes	Taken by police on May 27 at Provincial Office
Yi Yang-hyŏn	30	University graduate		Committee member, planning division	Yes	Ran away on May 21, returned on May 23, and taken by police on May 27 at Provincial Office
Yun Kang-ok	29	University student	Fourth-year university student	Committee member, planning division	Yes	Taken by police on May 27 from Provincial Office
Yi Chae-ho	33	University graduate	Office worker	Commander of task force	No	Taken by police on May 27 from Provincial Office

Note: Tables 2.1–2.3 are based the following sources: Hwang Sŏg-yŏng, *Chugŭm ŭl nŏmŏ ŏdum ŭi sasŏn ŭl nŏmŏ* [Beyond death, beyond darkness] (Seoul: P'ulpit, 1985); Yi Chŏng-no, "Kwangju ponggi e taehan hyŏngmyŏng-jŏk sigan chŏnhwan" [Transformation of revolutionary time through the Kwangju uprising], *Nodong haebang munhak,* May 1989, 21–22; Hyŏndaesa saryo yŏn'guso, *Owŏl minjung hangjaeng saryo chŏnjip* [Complete collection of historical materials on the May people's uprising] (Seoul: P'ulpit, 1990); City Attorney's Office of Kwangju, "5.18 samangja kŏmsi charyo" [Data on the dead from May 18], 1980; unpublished.

more diverse backgrounds. In general, participants in the Citizens' Army fell into three groups: the core student group, action corps members *(haengdong taewŏn)*, and people from various classes. The core student group included student activists and leaders of student associations of Chŏnnam University and Chosun University, the two major universities in the city. They played a pivotal role in planning and carrying out rallies, among other things. Action corps members provided speeches and news reports. They were the ones on the front lines of demonstrations and rallies. Among them was a woman who pleaded for Kwangju citizens to arm themselves as the martial troops attempted to reenter the Provincial Office from late night on May 26 to the early morning of May 27.

The third group mostly consisted of seventeen- and eighteen-year-old boys in occupations such as newspaper delivery boy, shoeshine boy, waiter, factory worker, and peddler. They fought on the front lines, carrying rifles and riding jeeps, and guarded the perimeters of the people's rallies. They wore red headbands and military uniforms and armbands. Because they carried guns they looked fierce, but they were worn down from lack of sleep. The leaders of the boys' group were in their thirties and had military experience. The boys addressed them as "captain," and each captain was in charge of about thirty boys. There were five to six such teams, totaling about 150–80 members. These boys suffered the most, having fought on the very front lines of battle. Table 2.2 presents the class background of members of the Citizens' Army who were arrested. Not surprisingly, most were workers, especially factory workers. The chief of the task force, Yun Sŏngnu, for example, was a furniture carver (pearl inlay of traditional Korean furniture), and the leader of the mobile striking units, Kim Hwaŏng, was a waiter in a restaurant. Table 2.3, which shows autopsy data of the dead from the uprising, presents the same pattern: two-thirds were in their teens and twenties, and over one-third were blue-collar workers. From these figures, it would be fair to say that young workers constituted the core of the Citizens' Army, though students and activists provided leadership for the struggle.

TABLE 2.2
Class Backgrounds of Arrested Members of the Citizens' Army

Class	Number of People	Percentage
Factory worker	19	63.4
Office worker	1	3.3
Service area worker	3	10.0
Student	3	10.0
Small merchant	2	6.7
Farmer	1	3.3
Soldier	1	3.3
Total	30	100.0

TABLE 2.3
Classification by Age and Occupation of the Dead

Age of the Dead	Number of People	%
Under 9	1	0.6
10–19	36	21.8
20–29	75	45.5
30–39	28	17.0
40–49	9	5.5
50–59	7	4.2
60	4	2.4
Other	5	3.0
Total	165	100.0

Occupation of the Dead	Number of People	%
Office worker	19	11.5
Self-employed	12	7.3
Service area worker	9	5.5
Functionary	50	30.3
Farmer/fishery/stock raising	4	2.4
Student	30	18.2
Soldier	2	1.2
Other	39	23.6
Total	165	100.0

The End

At dawn on May 27, the Citizens' Army ceased to exist after the martial troops besieged the Provincial Office and started shooting. Paratrooper units infiltrated the stone walls behind the Provincial Office building and started attacking. Out of the four hundred to five hundred people inside the office building, at least thirty to forty people were killed in the process, including the leader Yun Sangwŏn, mentioned above. The martial law troops also attacked the YWCA building, which was defended by the cultural and public relations unit, high school students, and laborers. The Citizens' Army fought for the cause that other citizens supported—repelling the brutal martial law troops. The solidarity between the Citizens' Army and the citizens of Kwangju was very deep and warmhearted, but this was not enough to achieve their goal. They were simply outmatched by the modern weaponry of the well-trained martial law troops. The Citizens' Army was a voluntary organization composed mostly of ordinary people who had no formal military experience and scarcely knew military tactics. Their strong desire to expel the martial law troops from the city of Kwangju motivated them to continue at the risk of their lives. This was the (un)fulfilled mission of Kwangju citizens.

Notes

1. Paul Chang translated this chapter.

2. City of Kwangju, *5-18 Minjuhwa undong charyo ch'ongsŏ* [General collection of documents of the Kwangju democratization movement] (Kwangju: 5.18 saryo p'yŏnch'an wiwŏnhoe, 1997), 2:23.

3. See Han'guk hyŏndaesa saryo yŏn'guso, *Kwangju 5-wŏl minjung hangjaeng saryo chŏnjip* [Complete historical records of the Kwangju May people's uprising] (Seoul: P'ulpit, 1990).

4. See Pak Namsŏn, *Owŏl kŭnal* [That day in May] (Kwangju: Saemmul, 1988).

5. *5-18 Minjuhwa undong charyo ch'ongsŏ*, 2:63.

3

An American Missionary's View

Jean W. Underwood

Preface

KOREA'S "TIANANMEN SQUARE" INCIDENT OF 1980 occurred not in the capital city of Seoul but in the provincial city of Kwangju, some two hundred miles south of Seoul. Television cameras did not catch the heroic stand of brave men who met the line of oncoming tanks and turned them back.

My husband, John Underwood, and I were among the small group of foreigners living on the Presbyterian mission compound in May of that year. The events that occurred in Kwangju those days are variously referred to as the "Kwangju incident," the "Kwangju uprising," or even the "Kwangju massacre." Koreans say, simply, "5-18" (May 18).

Most of us kept journals.[1] When it was all over, we sat and talked with the tape recorder running. I have John's synopsis of that tape. It has been most helpful in establishing chronology and in separating fact from rumor.

We feared our houses might be searched. Betts Huntley, a Presbyterian missionary, hid his photographs in a place on the compound known only to him. John wrote a fifteen-page summary on the back of other writings and hid the pages among stacks of other papers. He named no names. He labeled some events as "rumor" that we all believed to be true. I have quoted at length from John's summary because of the overall view that it offers, even though he wrote so near the time. I have annotated John's observations with the initials JTU.

Arnold Peterson (the Baptist among us) has written an excellent, detailed account, "5-18: The Kwangju Incident."[2] Arnold's duties included making trips into the center of the city day after day. His eyewitness accounts are invaluable. Again I have quoted at length, although I omitted far more than I included. His remarks are identified by the initials AP.

For background information and knowledge of what was happening outside the city, I referred to *The Two Koreas* by Don Oberdorfer.[3]

And then I have . . . memories.

Sunday, May 18

According to the *Korea Times* of October 7, 1988, the troops used in Kwangju on May 18–19, 1980, were "special airborne troops" commanded by General Chung Ho-yŏng.[4] The same newspaper on October 12, 1988, reported that "the Thirty-third and Thirty-fifth Battalions of Seventh Brigade were stationed at Chŏnnam University and Chosun University campuses at dawn on May 18. The Eleventh Brigade was additionally sent to Chosun at 2:40 A.M. on May 19 and the Third Brigade to Chŏnnam at 7:35 A.M. on May 20. The airborne troops were withdrawn to the Kwangju suburbs on the afternoon of May 21 with the massive protests gradually coming under 'control.'" This description gives a very misleading picture of what we actually experienced.

Martha Huntley dubbed these "airborne troops" the "black berets." Arnold consistently called them "paratroopers." John, after a good deal of research and digging, came up with "airborne troops" as a good translation. This is the term used by the *Korea Times* in its report eight years later. By whatever name, it was the aggressive, needless brutality of these troops that caused the Kwangju uprising.

I walked to the First Presbyterian Church as usual that Sunday morning. Things were quiet, subdued. John drove to a rural church beyond Hwasun, where he preached for the morning service. He returned between 1:00 P.M. and 2:00 P.M. Neither of us experienced anything unusual. It was not until 4:00 P.M. that afternoon when we met for English worship that we learned for the first time of some of the events that had occurred earlier in the day.

Martha Huntley had returned from Taejŏn by bus with a party of "friendship force" guests. (I have no recollection of who these folk were.) They were unable to reach the restaurant where they had planned to eat because of the police.

The Baptists, with their American guests, had split into four groups and attended four different churches. Returning from church, Brant Peterson and his guests smelled tear gas as they neared the hotel. Judy Watts and her party encountered a large demonstration near Chŏnnam University that blocked the streets. They also smelled tear gas. Barbara and Chris Peterson (Arnold's wife and son) and their guest returned by taxi. They had to get out two blocks from the hotel because of military barricades. Arnold wrote, "As they walked toward the hotel they were in a large crowd of pedestrians. A police jeep rounded the corner in front of them and discharged a pepper gas canister into the crowd from very close range. . . . They all received a very heavy exposure on their faces" (AP 14).

Arnold, his guest, and a Korean pastor had eaten lunch in a downtown restaurant. Arnold reported, "While traveling from church to the restaurant we were forced to take an indirect route because many streets were blocked by the military. As we drove, we saw large crowds of students on side streets attempting to march. They were blocked by Kwangju riot police using shields to form a solid wall." Arnold parked about two blocks away from the hotel, and they began walking. "We had to pass through two lines of riot police. The riot police and military were guarding the main street to keep demonstrators off the street. We were allowed to walk down the sidewalk to the front of the hotel only because we were foreigners" (AP 15).

From the hotel's restaurant, which was on its top floor, they were able to observe events taking place on the street below. Students would appear from the side streets and alleys unexpectedly, try to march, and then disappear quickly when police arrived.

At no time did any of us witness any brutality by the riot police. They were trained in riot control and acted accordingly. But many witnessed acts of violence committed by the airborne troops: kicking, beating with night sticks, and other unprovoked attacks. Sometimes citizens tried to intervene. Sometimes they threw stones.

After English worship, Arnold and his guests caught a taxi to return to the hotel. This time they had to get out three blocks away. It was as they were walking toward the hotel that Arnold first witnessed some of the violence. In his words:

> As we got out of the taxi, a young man in his twenties walked past us. He was neatly dressed in casual clothes. . . . He was walking in the same direction that we were headed. We followed about ten yards behind him.
>
> We had walked about one block when this young man came to a group of three paratroopers who were standing in front of a police box. The paratroopers surrounded him and began to question him. Since this took place in the street immediately in front of us, we stopped and watched rather than try to walk through the group.
>
> The paratroopers were each armed with a rifle mounted with a bayonet and were dressed in combat fatigues. They immediately began to hit the young man about the ribs, back, and shoulders with their batons and forced him to his

knees. They questioned him, implying that he was involved in the demonstrations. The young man protested that he was merely on his way home, but his
words fell on deaf ears. . . . They continued to beat him, kick him in the groin,
and lunged at him with the bayonet. The bayonet stopped only inches from his
throat.

While we stood there, a large crowd gathered and watched this confrontation.
Some persons in the crowd threw stones at the paratroopers. Two of the paratroopers chased the crowd away while the other continued to beat their victim.

Arnold and his guests were finally able to sidle past the group and continue
their walk to the hotel. "In the course of walking the next two blocks to the
back door of the hotel, I observed three other incidents in which two or more
paratroopers attacked young men . . . and began to beat them with a night
stick. In each case, there was no apparent provocation by the ones who were
attacked" (AP 17–18).

That evening while heading for the Citizens Hall, where a service for the
Korean Baptist Mission's nationwide crusade was to be held, Arnold again
witnessed paratroopers confronting young men and beating them with batons. He took a taxi.

The driver said, "They are killing our students." "What?" Arnold asked.
"They are killing our students over at Chŏnnam University." A number of his
passengers had reported that students had been injured and killed by airborne
troops that afternoon.

Arriving at the plaza in front of Citizens Hall, Arnold found the entrance
blocked by riot police. He asked to see their commander, told him of the meeting planned for that evening, and wondered if they would be able to hold it.
The commander answered that no curfew had been announced but one probably would be.

Arnold went inside. The crusade choir was just finishing its rehearsal. There
were about a hundred people present, most of them young adults. All wanted
to know what had been happening outside. Arnold and the other pastors discussed the situation. They decided to go ahead with the meeting as scheduled.
The choir members decided to stay and eat in the vicinity rather than risk
public transportation to their homes and back.

At seven o'clock it was announced on radio and television that the martial
law commander had declared a curfew to begin at 9:00 P.M. Phones began to
ring, as Baptist Church members were wondering if they should try to come
out. The pastors held a hurried meeting. Because many would already be on
their way, it was decided to hold a thirty-minute prayer meeting and close at
8:00 P.M. One of the guest speakers would give a brief message. This is what
they did. About two hundred attended that night, and there were a few pro-
fessions of faith. The service ended on schedule and all went home.

That same evening the Underwoods worshiped at the Presbyterian Church. Everything seemed normal, except that the service was held earlier than usual due to the rumored curfew.

May 19

Monday the violence continued. The Huntleys began getting telephone calls early in the morning asking if they knew people were being killed. One man reported that a friend of his wife, walking with her two children, had been beaten until she was unconscious, and he himself had been blinded by tear gas.

An Irish priest at the Catholic Center reported that troopers tied up, hit, and kicked both boys and girls and then took them away.

Someone reported that the pool at Chŏnnam University was full of bodies. Martha phoned the American professor and his wife who lived there in faculty housing. He checked. There were no bodies.

David Miller, our local USIS (United States Information Service) man, called to say demonstrators had tried to set fire to government buildings. Fires set at the Catholic Center and the YWCA were quickly extinguished.

The Baptists were heavily involved in services that day. The men went first to the Christian Hospital and then to the Speer Girl's School. On the trip home for lunch Arnold first saw ordinary citizens coming to the aid of a student (except for the previously noted stone throwing).

When Arnold returned to the hotel after lunch, the team members told of what they had witnessed from the hotel windows. "We watched as hundreds of students were beaten with clubs, kicked, and punched with rifle butts," they said. "They were stripped to their shorts, beaten while their hands were tied with belts. They were loaded into trucks. The riot police watched as the soldiers did this."

The scheduled evangelistic meeting was held at 2:30 that afternoon. About three hundred attended. When the meeting ended at about 4:00 P.M., some who had gone out rushed back, saying, "They are beating our grandfathers and grandmothers!" Soldiers were also boarding city buses, looking for young people and hauling them off. It was deemed unsafe for the choir members to return home by public transportation. Arnold made four trips to various parts of the city carrying carloads of people. He tried to avoid areas of trouble. Even so he reported, "I witnessed many—well over twenty—instances of paratroopers attacking citizens" (AP 25).

The evening meeting was cancelled. Arnold checked the four team members out of the hotel and brought them to his home. Later that day soldiers began searching homes, hunting for young people. The Petersons' cook begged to be allowed to bring her high school–age son and his friend to spend the night. Twelve people slept in the Peterson house that night: four family members, four team members, three Koreans, and another visiting Baptist missionary.

Monday was a day of terror for the citizens of Kwangju. John's summary of that day follows. I've omitted some of the incidents reported earlier:

> Most of the accounts of brutality come from Monday, although there is no doubt that Sunday had its share.
>
> The Underwood family seems singularly exempt from troublesome matters, even at second hand. The Peterson and Huntley families are our source for most of what we know personally. . . .
>
> Reports of severe violence began coming in on Monday morning. Perhaps by coincidence, the first reported riot-type activity was reported on Monday afternoon, when David Miller of the USIS telephoned and said there had been an attempt to set fire to government buildings. . . .
>
> Monday was the first day when we heard reports of airborne unit soldiers entering houses in search of young men. City busses were stopped and young men taken off and beaten; public buildings and eating places were given the same treatment. . . .
>
> A Korean pastor . . . heard the airborne unit personnel speaking with a distinctively Kyŏngsang accent, and reports hearing them say they were going to slay the "no good Chŏlla [local province] rascals." Another witness saw airborne unit troops behaving with a breakdown of discipline similar to what took place with other troops on the train to Taejŏn on Saturday (witnessed by Martha Huntley), and noticed that the men presumably guarding Chosun University looked disheveled, were obviously drunk, and were shouting for food. (There is a rumor current that the men were intentionally underfed and, some add, given drink. Others claim that they were given drugs to make them wild.)
>
> Reports or rumors of girls stripped to their underclothes have turned out to be not from the sources to which they were attributed (the Irish priest), and so far have not been verified by anyone whom we have found.
>
> Both the YWCA and the Catholic Center were entered and searched with a degree of violence better calculated to cow than to flush out people in hiding. . . .
>
> Peace Corps volunteers won a good name for Americans at this time by a sort of non-violent intervention.
>
> It is the spontaneous and unanimous opinion of the missionary community living together here that the Peace Corps volunteers have won a lasting gratitude of great numbers of the citizens of Kwangju for the United States. Sharing the life of the people whom they came to serve, even when it meant sharing serious, perhaps mortal, danger, they made everybody who saw them realize that Americans really care. They identified themselves with the people not by shared animosities but by shared trouble. Missionaries stay as a matter of course, in obedience to a

Master and in a bond of love which leaves no choice; but the Peace Corps volunteers were if anything disobedient to their own master in not leaving the city. It is my personal opinion that if their headquarters had been able to see the situation from the ground as we saw it, headquarters would have hoped that they would stay and do almost exactly what they did. As Americans, we are very proud of our Peace Corps friends.

We heard of no violent or riot-type demonstrations before reports of airborne unit troops' attacks upon students. We heard of no non-violent demonstrations after reports began to circulate. Again, we heard of no violent or riot-type activities after the withdrawal of the forces of law and order from the city. . . . There was definitely absolutely no looting.

May 20

All seemed quiet Tuesday morning. John went to the bank, as did Arnold later. The military was in complete control. Soldiers stood guard at all of the major intersections and at the river, but they were not the black berets. These were new troops said to be from North Chŏlla province. Young men were ignored as they strolled the streets with other pedestrians. Arnold noted that there was "very little vehicular traffic."

Earlier that morning the Baptists had again worshiped at the hospital chapel. Arnold writes:

> After the opening hymn, the worship leader called on one of the doctors to lead in prayer. The doctor prayed for the city of Kwangju and for its people. He asked God to guard and protect their young people and students. He said, "Dear God, what kind of an event is this when our own soldiers kill our brothers and sisters and our children?" He broke into tears and most of the congregation also wept. For several minutes he was silent. The chapel was filled with the sound of crying. His prayer continued by expressing his deep anguish and distress over the behavior of the military on the previous two days and over the innocent suffering of the students and young people. His prayer expressed the concerns of the hearts of everyone in attendance. I have never seen such a spontaneous expression of deep emotion as was shown by these doctors, nurses, and hospital employees as they shared their grief with one another and with God.
>
> Many young people, including some family members and friends of those in attendance, had disappeared in the previous two days.

On Monday paratroopers began breaking into houses searching for young men. Tuesday frantic pastors and doctors began appearing at the mission compound with their sons, begging us to hide them. It was rumored that there would be more house-to-house searches. Wednesday even

more young men came. The Peterson house was already filled to overflow-
ing. The Underwood-Dudley duplex was deemed to be too exposed by
those who looked it over. The Huntleys took in an attic full, carefully warning the young men to keep their shoes with them. (According to Korean
custom shoes are removed at the door. If those in hiding had done so, this
would have been a dead giveaway to searchers.) By far the largest number
hid out in the Dietrick house. Some hid in the woods. Sisters of the young
men at the Huntley house brought food from home for them every day. I
don't know how the others managed.

We discussed what we should say if soldiers came to our doors. Most
thought it would be best to say nothing. Fortunately no searchers came.

That afternoon Arnold picked up a carload of young people at one of the
Baptist churches and drove them to safety outside the city. On the way home
he learned that a large, peaceful demonstration was planned for that evening.

One of the Baptists first heard gunfire around 3:00 P.M. During supper
Arnold reports that "we began to hear gunfire, the sound of honking horns
and the rumbling noise of a crowd. After supper, the noise was much louder.
As the evening progressed, the noise level continued to increase."

Nevertheless the demonstration began peacefully enough. The crowd
protested the wanton brutality of the black berets. They demanded to talk to
the mayor or the governor. Both had already fled the city. They then demanded to talk to the martial law commander. They wanted an apology.

At some point the peaceful demonstration turned violent. It lasted all night.
Estimates of the size of the crowd range from 150,000 to 400,000. Before the
night was over they had burned the MBC television building. The Baptists
watched the flames from their homes. By morning most of the troops had
withdrawn to the edge of the city.

Lying in bed that night I heard the roar, like the roar of a stormy ocean,
hundreds of thousands of voices raised in fury. Whenever I awoke during the
night I heard it. John heard nothing. Martha reported hearing gunfire.

Tuesday evening telephone communication was cut off between Kwangju
and the rest of the nation. Lines within the city remained open.

May 21

Wednesday we awoke to chaos. Students careened down the streets in commandeered vehicles, cheering, shouting, honking. Onlookers cheered too.
John and I watched as a group entered the grounds of Speer School and broke
into a bus. They knocked out all of the windows, presumably to be able to lean
out. The bus then careened down the drive to join the others.

Arnold, hearing loud sounds of gunfire, horns, and crowds in the streets, went down to see what was happening. He witnessed an unrestrained celebration of joy and victory. There were many city buses, flatbed trucks, pickup trucks, and jeeps driving back and forth carrying students and other citizens. They were brandishing sticks and pipes, carrying placards and banners, shouting and rejoicing over the results of the demonstration the night before. Their signs read, "Abolish Martial Law," "Kick Out Chun Doo Hwan," "Kill the Murderer Chun Doo Hwan," and "Release Kim Dae Jung."

People told Arnold that during the night the military had withdrawn from the city except for a small group still holding the provincial capitol building. All around him people were yelling, "We have won! We have forced them out!" Arnold reports that "the mood of the people was almost carnival-like."

At about 9:00 A.M. Pastor Kim phoned the Petersons. Two young adults in his church wanted to leave the city. Could Arnold help? He agreed to take them to Namp'yŏng, a nearby town where they could get a bus. Three of the Florida team members went along. Arnold describes what happened next:

> We picked up the two students and drove toward the south side of the city. We came to a large intersection where the road to Namp'yŏng crosses some railroad tracks. A large crowd was gathered in the intersection. A pile of automobile tires was burning in the middle of the street. Beside it was a city bus whose windows had been knocked out. These created a barricade across the road.
>
> In front of the barricade was a large group of people. As I drove up to this group, I leaned out of the car window and asked them to move aside so that we could get by. A man in his thirties came over to talk to me. In less than a minute our car was completely surrounded by the crowd. Many of the people were obviously angry. I explained to the man that I was a missionary who lived in Kwangju and that I had with me in the car two students who wanted to leave Kwangju and return to their hometowns so as to get away from the military. By the time I had been able to make him understand this in Korean, the crowd had begun to bang on the car and make threatening gestures. One young man was approaching the rear window with a crowbar in hand, threatening to smash the window.
>
> I urged the man I was talking with to let us go. I said that we were friends who agreed with their anger toward the soldiers, and that I was trying to help these two students get away from the soldiers. After what seemed like a very long time, the man understood what I was saying. He called to the crowd saying "these people are our friends, let them go. They are helping two students get away." The crowd moved back slightly and the way opened in front of the car so that we could move. We drove past the fire and the bus and left the city. (AP 40–41)

On the return home, going by a different route, they saw blood in the streets. They were again threatened but escaped by telling their story.

Sometime that same morning Arnold, accompanied by the Dudleys, was told by a crowd of people that bodies were lying on the walk in front of the Catholic Center. They wanted him to take pictures. He drove as close as he could to the spot but was afraid to leave the car unguarded. The Dudleys did walk over and did see bodies.

Around noon several of us observed citizens giving buns and bottles of soda pop or cans of fruit juice to the students in the busses and other vehicles. We were told that several supermarkets also gave food away free.

Early that afternoon looking from their balcony, the Baptists saw a fire burning in the city. Several went to the roof of the seminary to get a better view. The government tax office was burning.

Around 2:00 P.M. a helicopter flew over the city dropping leaflets warning the people to get off the streets or there would be dire consequences. It was also around 2:00 P.M. that a group of young working men broke into the military arsenal at Hwasun. The "citizen fighters" had become armed.

A large rally had been planned for 3:00 P.M. The people did not get off the streets. Helicopters began circling around the city, shooting into the crowds from the air.

Kwangju Christian Hospital began receiving casualties early that afternoon. Martha Huntley and John immediately headed over to the hospital hoping to interview some of the wounded. It was shortly after 3:00 P.M. when the wounded began pouring in. More than an hour later it began to dawn on me that the hospital would certainly be needing blood. I got ready and headed over.

I made my way down the road from the wooded hill where we lived to the street. Many were coming and going. Overhead two helicopters were circling. Suddenly a third appeared, flying so low that I could clearly see the soldier sitting in the open door with his machine gun pointing down. The street immediately emptied. We all got as close as we could to the walls and shops, trying to find shelter under the eaves. The copter circled two or three times, not shooting, and then moved on. Slowly we came out, looked up, and then continued on our various ways.

As I walked up the drive leading to the hospital, Betts Huntley met me coming down.

"I'm going to give blood," I said. "Can you tell me where to go?"

Betts laughed. Laughter and tears are not that far apart.

"The hospital is swamped with people trying to give blood," he replied. "They're turning people away. You'd just add to the confusion."

Betts and I returned to our wooded hill. As we walked, he filled me in on the situation. There were ten dead and more than fifty wounded at our hospital alone, and ours was not the largest in the city. The first of the wounded was a middle-aged man who had been bayoneted in the back. He had gone into the city because he was concerned for his daughter who worked in an office there. The first of the dead was a middle school girl. She had been shot. Of the five missionaries who had tried to give blood that afternoon, only Katherine Dudley had succeeded in doing so. She somehow found a gap in the line, squeezed into it, and patiently waited her turn.

Late that afternoon foreign correspondents made their way into the city. They ate supper with the Petersons and then moved on. Judy Watts moved in, swelling the number who slept there to thirteen. She reported hearing shooting coming from the hill above.

Martha Huntley had walked with the children from her house to the Petersons and then home again. She recalled later, as the tape recorder ran, "We were just dodging bullets . . . just there on the street, coming in this direction."

For some reason we met at our house for prayer that evening. Our usual night was Thursday, as some in our group liked to attend Korean church services on Wednesday evenings. Before we finished, Barbara Peterson phoned, warning us to turn off our lights because of the sound of approaching gunfire.

The Marks spent the night at our house. Most slept in their clothes.

John reported, "Wednesday darkness brought a large increase in gunfire, much of it seeming to be in the immediate vicinity. The latter part of the night was much more quiet, despite a supposedly sure word that the city was to be reoccupied during Wednesday night."

May 22

Before Kwangju was cut off from the outside world, it had been agreed that the team of Florida pastors should be sent to Taejŏn on May 22. Now that we were cut off, getting them to Taejŏn would be difficult to accomplish. Foreign correspondents had gotten into the city by putting big "Foreign Press" signs on their vehicles and bribing their way through road blocks. Arnold hoped that a similar strategy might work for us. They took magic markers and wrote big signs reading "Foreigner's Car" and put them on the vehicles. Each vehicle also flew an American flag. Two vehicles were to go, one driven by Arnold and one by John.

It was decided that we should try to get the children out. The older Huntley and Peterson children were already at boarding school in Taejŏn and would be worried that they could not call home. The younger children with us had been exposed to a great deal of tear gas, and now stray bullets seemed to be flying all through the woods around us. Judy Watts, who had just finished her term as teacher of the missionary children, and Barbara Peterson decided to go with the group. Barbara could also act as interpreter if the group ran into any trouble. David Dudley also went, expecting to return with Arnold and John.

They left at about 7:30 that morning. According to John, students directed them until they got outside the city, and then the military told them where they could get a train, as the Songchŏngni station was now in citizens' hands and the trains were no longer running. At some point one of the Baptist pastors foolishly took out his camera and began taking pictures. Angry soldiers confiscated the camera and exposed the film. Eventually they were permitted to proceed to the nearest train station. The group boarded the train a little after 10:00 A.M. John asked one of the officials to phone us that everything was all right. Then the three men started back.

Those of us who were left behind began gathering at the Huntley house. No one wanted to be alone. Around 10:30 A.M. the call came. Betts took it. He came back with a puzzled look on his face and reported, "It was in Korean. He said we were to come." Come? How? And where? We decided to stay. We later figured out that the colloquial pronunciation of "come" and "all right" are so similar in sound that anyone of us could have made a similar misinterpretation.

Arnold, David, and John tried to return by the same route that they had taken out, but the entrance to the city was now blockaded. Soldiers refused to let them pass. "We are about to attack the city. No one can go in," they said. The men pleaded, "We've just taken foreign guests out. We have families in the city. You must let us get back to them." They were finally permitted to proceed.

Years later in America I read Arnold Peterson's account of the events of that day. I discovered it had been a much more eventful and frightening trip than I had first believed.

That same morning a small group of Christian ministers had met at the Central Presbyterian Church. The minister of the First Presbyterian Church (which we attended), Reverend Han Wan Suk, was among them. The group consisted of three Baptists, three Presbyterians, one Methodist, and one "Evangelical" (Arnold Peterson's term). They discussed the problem. The city could not exist in isolation. The government takeover, when it came, was sure to be bloody. Could normalcy be restored by negotiation? They prayed that it could.

An angry mob of armed students now controlled the provincial capitol. The three Baptist pastors, Park Young Bok, Shin Soon Kyung, and Chang Sei Kyun, agreed to talk with the students. Reverend Park later said, "We were not trying to tell the citizens what to do, but we were following the command of Christ's love and tried to bring peace between the people and stop the flow of blood" (AP 49). The students listened. They agreed to begin negotiations.

A committee was formed. Officially they called themselves the "5-18 Incident Kwangju Countermeasures Committee." Among ourselves we referred to them as the "Reconciliation Committee." The committee consisted of the original eight ministers, one priest, two lawyers, one professor, one student representative, one citizen fighter, and two citizen supporters. They drew up a series of demands that were carried to the military forces surrounding the city. After some delay, the martial law commander agreed to the following:

1. The entrance of the military into the city would be delayed.
2. It was admitted that there had been "excesses."
3. The wounded would be cared for and the dead provided for.
4. Prisoners would be released.
5. There would be an accurate reporting of events.
6. As a precondition to any agreement, the citizens must collect and turn in all weapons.
7. Regret was expressed to the families of the dead.

The committee reported this reply to some 100,000 who were gathered at the Provincial Capitol plaza. Printed fliers were circulated throughout the city, and terms of the agreement were broadcast on both radio and television. The collection of arms and ammunition began that afternoon. They were stored in the basement of the Provincial Capitol, guarded by citizen army veterans. By Saturday it was estimated that 95 percent of all the weapons had been turned in.

Days later, when a line of tanks began entering the city, members of the Reconciliation Committee met them. They tied a white rag to a stick and approached the tanks. When the column stopped, they talked with the commander and persuaded him to turn back. Reverend Han later told John that the military postponed its invasion four times because of pleas from the Reconciliation Committee. Radio news at noon Thursday reported that the newly appointed prime minister was on his way by helicopter to talk with the city leaders. In actual fact, when he reached the city, he looked down and saw some 30,000 people gathered in front of the Provincial Capitol and decided it was too risky. His copter returned to Seoul without trying to land. The message was broadcast over radio and television.

Arnold heard from Pastor Choi that "a few communist spies had been captured by the citizens. They had instigated the setting of the fires and were carrying photocopied citizens registration cards. They were taken to the edge of the city and turned over to the military" (AP 51).

It was rumored that the American embassy staff had fled the city. Others reported they had entered the city, flags flying. As there was no American embassy in Kwangju, the rumors probably stemmed from Arnold and John's flag-flying auto trip with the party going to Taejŏn.

At 5:00 P.M. Arnold received a call from David Hill, a friend who was a first sergeant at the Kwangju air base at Songchŏngni. Arnold writes, "He told us that the U.S. Air Force was considering making a forced entry of Kwangju to rescue the Americans in Yangnim Dong (the area of the city in which we lived). I said that there was no need for such action. The idea for the 'rescue' was the result of false fears created by David Miller, the American consular representative in Kwangju who had left the city and gone to the air base" (AP 51).

We had been told to evacuate on Tuesday. Many Americans sought shelter at the base—some two hundred they told us. This surprised us. None of us had thought there were that many Americans in the city!

John concluded his summary of Thursday with these words:

> Rumors again confidently foretold the occupation of the city Thursday night. From 11:00 P.M. until 12:30 the Underwoods (but not the Huntleys) heard sustained and heavy firing, including weaponry larger than small arms. There was a discernable progression from the vicinity of the military unit halfway to Songjŏngni in the west, in a southward arc and around to a point sounding in the night like the neighborhood of the Provincial Capitol.
>
> In the morning there was no sign of any such action having taken place, so far as observations possible to us revealed.

May 23–26

A great quiet settled over the city. There was no traffic. Shops and stores had closed their doors, but anyone who needed anything could always go to a side door to buy. Now shopkeepers were opening their doors again. The police had disappeared, "melted into the woodwork," as Martha Huntley observed. Yet no one looted.

We went for long walks, John carrying his camera. I still have the photos, fading and yellowed. The six-lane avenue that led to the Provincial Capitol plaza was unbelievably empty. Some, like us, walked; a few rode bicycles. Here and there the remains of wrecked vehicles could be seen.

Arnold made a walking tour of the city. All was quiet and calm. Some worked at clearing the streets of debris and rubbish. As he walked, he talked with people and found them "amazingly" hopeful and optimistic.

The Reconciliation Committee was hard at work pleading with the radicals to turn in their weapons. Baptist Pastor Chang Sei Kyun (Chang Se-gyŏn), though not officially head of the committee, seemed to be the one always on the spot and was most active in the many forum-like meetings that occurred.

In the absence of David Miller (USIS), Arnold became the U.S. embassy's contact man. Communication was complicated:

The method of contacts with the embassy was strange. During the predawn hours on Wednesday, May 21, all long distance telephone lines between Kwangju and the rest of the nation were cut off by the military. The American Military base at SongJeong Ri (Songjŏngni) was outside the perimeter which surrounded Kwangju. However, their telephone system was a part of the Kwangju local phone system. As a result, our friend, Dave Hill, a First Sergeant in the Air Force, was able to telephone us.

However, the telephone system on the American base was subject to the control of the Korean military. The Korean military tried to prevent calls between the American military and Kwangju citizens as a method of limiting the flow of information into and out of Kwangju. However, the American commander protested sufficiently that the Korean military agreed to allow the American base to make calls to our telephone number. After some additional negotiation, the Korean switchboard operator was also allowed to accept calls from my telephone and connect me through to the American base. In this way, we were able to communicate one or two times a day.

The embassy contacted me several times through the American Air Base. Each time they gave me the name, phone number, or other information about persons whose safety they wished to confirm. I then called or otherwise tried to contact these persons to gain information to pass along to the embassy. Altogether, I made contact with eight other foreigners in Kwangju at the request of the American embassy. (AP 53)

Saturday Arnold rented a bicycle. On one of his trips to town he met Judy Chamberlain, who led him to Associated Press reporter Terry Anderson (of Lebanese hostage fame). Anderson had bicycled in. They talked for about an hour, Arnold sometimes acting as interpreter.

I remember another day sitting on the Huntleys' lawn with missionaries, Peace Corps volunteers, and a few foreign correspondents. I can no longer recall what was said.

Sunday we walked to church as usual. Conversation before and after the service was subdued. People appeared numb, wondering what would happen next, wondering when the blow would fall. I suppose we met for English worship that afternoon as usual. I have no recollection of it.

Arnold reports that David Hill phoned him Sunday afternoon, strongly urging us to leave. The air force would send helicopters to airlift us out, he said. This was the last contact we had with the American air base. The men talked it over and decided to stay. Nevertheless, we all agreed to meet at the Huntley home Monday morning and discuss the situation.

Monday morning Arnold again reported David Hill's urgent message. No one thought we should go. We all felt that any impact we might have made by our presence would be lost if we left now. David later told Arnold that the Korean military had considered bombing the city and feared for our safety.

Monday morning an American CBS camera crew arrived. We all gathered at the Huntleys' front door. Arnold did most of the talking. We later learned that the program was broadcast Monday evening in the States, just twenty-two hours after it had been taped!

Hope for a peaceful reconciliation between citizens and the military seemed bleak that Monday morning. For an analysis of what went wrong, I'm going to turn to John:

> Baptist pastors took a lead in seeking the formation of an effective delegation to deal with the martial law command. The Presbyterians led in the formation of a Kwangju City Emergency Relief Committee composed of about sixty ministers from many denominations. There also came into being an amorphous body of concerned citizens, including students, which was in almost constant fluid session in what appears to have been the office of the Provincial Governor. The delegations which dealt with the martial law command were in large measure an extension or instrument of this group of concerned citizens. The interrelation of these bodies is confused because the bodies themselves were almost completely without organization or structure.
>
> The concerned citizens achieved and maintained a very clear consensus which the Reconciliation Delegation then carried to the Martial Law Command.
>
> The Martial Law Command was quoted to us as having made a statement on the radio which was very conciliatory and asked only the turning in of weapons of the citizens. This is probably the same as an almost identical set of promises broadcast by leaflet as the fruit of the reconciliation delegation.
>
> The leaflet listed eight promises:
>
> 1. Troops not to enter the city without prior notice.
> 2. Excesses acknowledged.
> 3. Those in custody to be (for the greater part) released.
> 4. Indemnification and medical treatment for dead and wounded.
> 5. Broadcast resumption with factual reporting.
> 6. Discontinuance of use of defamatory vocabulary.
> 7. Free passage for unarmed pedestrians on signal of raised hands in motion.
> 8. Absolutely no retaliation, pledged on personal honor. Citizens' matching obligation only the turning in of arms.
>
> Apparently from this point when everything was achieved, things began to go wrong.
>
> If this report of mine is in error, it is an error not of malice. I did not easily believe what I do believe to be the case, and I am unhappy about the reflection these facts [or distortions?] make on a group which I regard more highly than this report will indicate. Recognizing, then, that my efforts to be fair may have faltered or my information betrayed me, my understanding of what happened next is as follows.
>
> Up to this point there appears to have been one broad category of people not represented on the amorphous committee of concerned citizens. There appears to

have been no representation of the so-called Social Activist community of Christians; nobody from the ROK Presbyterian Church, from the YWCA (or YMCA?), or from the Roman Catholic social action organization. By an unhappy coincidence, people representing these bodies began appearing in the concerned citizens' committee soon after the eight-point settlement was reached, and by the same unfortunate coincidence, the former consensus did not continue. The committee of concerned citizens was no longer united in willingness to welcome reoccupation of the city on the agreement reached, but became divided on the question of whether some material political concessions ought not also to be demanded.

Another factor now became evident. This was the existence of three schools of thought among the students. Dr. Hahn Wansuk [Han Wan-suk] defined them this way. One group, which consisted largely of local Kwangju students, was the conciliatory group. Another group, composed chiefly of students not in Kwangju institutions and mostly from Seoul, was the hard-line group. A third group, not to be identified with anything except their shared position, was the suicide group. The conciliatory group was in agreement with the settlement worked out by the delegation. The hard-line group wanted to secure some kind of political concessions as a price for the bloodless readmittance of the forces of government. The suicide group wanted nothing to do with any settlement, but simply to die and by their death to wake Korea to the intolerable situation in which they felt her to be lost, so that the nation would awake and save itself.

By and large the hard-line students did not refuse to accept the settlement achieved, but some of them felt with the social activist newcomers on the concerned citizens' committee that a little tougher bargaining would be better. The suicide group, of course, was the major problem.

With the breaking of consensus, the delegation could no longer speak for the city in dealing with the Martial Law Command.

On Sunday night we received a message indicating that only military security forbade telling us outright that military action would begin on Sunday night or Monday. Since there had been no notice given the city, Mr. Peterson, Mr. Huntley, and Mr. Underwood agreed to seek members of the reconciliation delegation and suggest that they ask enough delay to keep the promise made before.

On Monday morning we set out on this errand; and saw posted on the street new posters of an inflammatory nature, over a name almost but not exactly like that used by the reconciliation procedures committee. The committee member whom Mr. Underwood approached seemed to Mr. Underwood to have felt that he had done all he could do, and that the breaking of the consensus had resulted in the breaking of the city's side of the achieved settlement, so that the promises were already void. The fabricated posters were clearly the work of others, and would not be believed by intelligent people. Mr. Peterson's contact was out of touch at the moment, but we met some others, and were taken by them to the meeting of concerned citizens, not to speak but to listen.

There had been a deadline announced, and in fact the martial law troops did not come until after that deadline passed, so either our interpretation of the information we received was wrong or somebody took action after all.

The occupation of the city came on Monday night, or more properly in the early hours of Tuesday morning, May 27th.

The military operation was swift and neat. The gunfire we heard was far less than we had heard on the Thursday when it had been so noisy.

We think it clear that the occupation of the city was as relatively bloodless as it turned out because in fact the city did not oppose it. The only actual opposition, we believe, was from the suicide group and some tragic high school children who joined them. (JTU 10–12)

May 27 and Aftermath

Government forces began their attack on May 27 at 3:00 A.M. I awoke during the night and heard a low rumbling that I assumed to be tanks passing on the road below. By morning the radio and loud speakers were playing martial music interspersed with announcements that the government was now in control of the city. Someone phoned asking if the foreigners were safe. I assured him that we were.

Relatively few lives had been lost. Some young people had been holding an all-night prayer meeting at the YWCA. The girls had gone home because of curfew, but the men stayed. They were armed. When soldiers entered the Y and found armed young men, they shot. One youth and a Y worker were killed. Marian Pope went to the YWCA later that morning. I still remember the look of horror on her face as she described the scene.

Another fatality that night was Moon Yong Dong (Mun Yong-dong). Moon, an army veteran, studied at the Honam Seminary and also served on the staff of the First Presbyterian Church. During the demonstrations and fighting he helped transport the wounded to hospitals. On the night of the takeover he was at his post guarding the recovered weapons and explosives. They killed him on the spot.

Negotiations had broken down Monday. People wanting to fight on, or at least gain some political concession from the government, had joined the Reconciliation Committee. The committee was no longer united and had no way of controlling all of Kwangju's citizens. Some gave up early. Baptist Pastor Chang Sei Kyun worked in vain until late Monday night. Midnight was the deadline given by the government for a peaceful settlement. Then he too left the provincial capitol building. Moon was at his post, sleeping.

We attended Moon's funeral on Thursday, May 29. It was the second mass burial that day. The plain wooden coffins were loaded onto a truck; the mourners rode in three buses provided by the city. A hillside some miles from the city had been provided for the dead. Families were not allowed to use their own family burial plots.

When we arrived, the caskets were unloaded. The sound of wailing was overpowering. There was also a strong smell of death. An entire mountainside was covered with new graves. Those at the top were newly filled from the morning burial. From about two-thirds down the mountainside they were empty. John joined the other men of the seminary faculty in carrying Moon's coffin to the properly numbered grave site. We held a brief burial service. Moon's family and friends threw in handfuls of earth. His fiancée stood quietly by. The city would later finish filling in the graves and make the appropriate mounds.

At least two other Christian funerals were held at the same time, and the sounds of a Buddhist gong and chanting could be heard. At one grave a woman was scolding, "I told you not to go out. Now see what's happened. I told you. I told you!" At another a woman poured a soft drink over the mound with the words, "Eat well." We climbed back on the bus for the ride home.

Arnold Peterson went to Taejŏn to bring his family members home. When they returned, he learned that Pastor Chang Sei Kyun had been arrested on May 30. Arnold, with Pastor Chang's wife and some of the Baptist ministers, began a fruitless search to find out where he was being held and what the charges against him were. Finally on June 4 Arnold made contact with the commanding general's office. He threatened to go to the foreign press unless he could talk with the general and find out what was happening to Pastor Chang. That night at 10:00 P.M. he was released.

Epilogue

Koreans hold memorial services on the anniversary of a death. The government's insistence that all of the victims of the Kwangju massacre be buried together means that every May 18 all of those who suffered most are gathered together in one place. Outsiders now join them. The gravesite has become almost a place of pilgrimage.

Wounds continue to fester. The people want an apology. Most of all they want the truth to be known. Perhaps now the truth will be allowed to come out and the wounds begin to heal.

When we prepared to leave Korea in the early summer of 1993, we were treated to the usual farewell ceremonies: seminary, hospital, and several churches. The city presented John with its symbolic "keys." At each of these ceremonies the usual flattering things were said, tailored by the nature of the institution. There was one common thread: "You stayed with us during the Kwangju incident." How glad I am that we did.

Notes

1. John's journal was the basis of his summary and Arnold Peterson's journal presumably became the basis of his written account (see below). Both are quoted extensively in this chapter. I never saw the journals but I remember the conversations about them.

2. Unpublished manuscript, 1990.

3. Don Oberdorfer, *The Two Koreas* (New York: Basic Books, 1997).

4. The Korea Baptist Mission had planned a nationwide evangelistic crusade for May and engaged a team from Florida: Reverend Dewitt Matthews as speaker and musicians Reverend Billy Souther, Dr. Edward Lyon, and Dr. Louie Bailey. Arnold and the local Baptist pastors had worked for weeks to reserve the necessary facilities and get the required government permission to hold the meetings. The crusade was scheduled to begin May 18.

The four Florida ministers arrived in Kwangju on May 16. Arnold checked them into the Tourist Hotel, which was located in the center of the city. The hotel also served as crusade headquarters. This placed the Baptists right in the middle of the turmoil, mobs, and violence. Of the Presbyterians stationed in Kwangju at that time, the Dietricks and Nieusmas were on furlough. The Nieusma house was occupied by the Marks, an American professor, and his wife; the Dietrick house was unoccupied except for a sleep-in guard. The Underwoods and the Dudleys, short-term educational missionaries, occupied the two sides of a duplex.

Although the Huntleys lived farthest in, their house became the center of most of our activities. Martha had been a journalist before her marriage and still wrote regularly for the *Korea Times* and other publications. Betts served as hospital chaplain. He also took excellent photographs. Mary and Susan Huntley were at boarding school; Jenny and Michael were at home. Of the Huntleys John wrote:

> The May Eighteenth Incident has demonstrated dramatically the place which the Huntleys had won in the hearts of the Christian community as a whole. It is the Huntleys who receive telephone messages of information or distress, who are asked for help or shelter, who are counted on by people in trouble. Whatever good opinion the rest of us may receive from those around us, when the chips are down it is the Huntleys on whose love and help they count.

Canadian missionary nurse Marian Pope was also in the city. She lived below Sajik Park in a Korean house.

Though not living on the mission compound, two Peace Corps volunteers, Judy Chamberlain and Tim Warnberg, became part of our community. The Peace Corps volunteers had been caught downtown when soldiers began their brutal attacks on unarmed civilians. When these young people—Dave Dollinger may also have been there—saw someone being beaten, they interposed their bodies as shields between the soldier and the victim. It did no good. The soldiers simply moved on and began beating someone else. The courage of these young people was unbelievable!

4

Has Kwangju Been Realized?

Keun-sik Jung

W HEN I CHARACTERIZED THE DEMOCRATIC POWER SHIFT of 1998 in Korea as a delayed realization of "Kwangju" at the Second International Conference on Peace and Human Rights in East Asia (held in Cheju, Korea, in August 1998), one of the participants disagreed and stated that it could not be a "truthful" realization of the Kwangju spirit. In response to his objection, with which I partly agreed, I modified my characterization to a "partial" realization of Kwangju.

The answer to the question, Has Kwangju been realized?[1] depends first on whether the dignity of those who were sacrificed in the 1980 Kwangju uprising has been restored and whether their goals and causes have been fully realized. It is a simple yet pregnant question that involves the past, present, and future of Kwangju. If we take the main goal of the victims of Kwangju as liquidating military authority and achieving procedural democracy in Korea, we could say that it was realized through the 1997 election. The victory of the opposition party led by Kim Dae Jung, the most prominent symbol of opposition to military oppression, could be seen as a substantiation of the Kwangju spirit. The main issue is how we characterize the Kim government and the complicated relationship between "Kwangju" and the politician Kim Dae Jung.

But if we take the spirit of the Kwangju uprising as something beyond a call for procedural democracy—such as national reunification or strengthened national autonomy and integration—we clearly would understand the power shift of 1997 as only the beginning—a meaningful but introductory step toward reaching the ultimate goals. Despite the improvement of democracy in

Korea, we cannot avoid answering "no" to the question of whether the spirit of Kwangju has been realized, given the persistence of a divisive regionalism and what Koreans call a "red complex,"[2] both of which constitute driving forces of modern Korean politics.

We must also examine the multidimensional context of the Kwangju uprising. Major historical events or social movements are rooted within a larger structural framework of the times, beyond their own internal dynamics. In South Korea, significant historical events such as Kwangju should be discussed in three contexts: (1) the local scene, (2) national circumstances, and (3) the international environment. The geopolitical significance of the Korean peninsula following the Korean War (i.e., as one of the fronts in the Cold War) meant that major political events in South Korea often were affected by municipal, national, and East Asian or international conditions.

Development and Topology of the Kwangju Uprising

The Kwangju democratization movement covers two periods: the "Kwangju uprising,"[3] which refers to the ten-day struggle in Kwangju and its vicinity on May 18–27, 1980, and the time since then, during which the "May movement" has been mobilized to counter state terror and restore the dignity of the Kwangju victims. The former was a collective citizen struggle for democracy in Kwangju and neighboring cities. The latter was a long-term and continuous movement for democratization designed to unveil the facts surrounding the event and thereby revive and perpetuate the spirit of Kwangju.[4]

The Kwangju uprising, I would argue, should be studied as a comprehensive process. Of course, the ten days in May 1980 are most important.[5] But we should examine the preliminary stage before the uprising as well as the final stage, which opened up the possibility of a future struggle for democratization.[6] What political demands were raised in the massive rallies by Kwangju citizens before the uprising occurred? What were the aspirations and hopes of those who, at dawn on May 27, risked their lives to bring about justice? This analysis should include an exploration of the political visions presented before, during, and after the uprising, as well as of the sociopolitical system that produced the state terror. Given the national division and the authoritarian military government that denied basic freedoms to the Korean people during and after Kwangju, we need to dig up many things hidden beneath the surface.

The Kwangju uprising, which began on May 18, can be traced as a continuum of three consecutive events: (1) from May 18 to 21, the callous beating and killing of peaceful demonstrators by the army and the ensuing formation of a collective civil resistance; (2) from May 22 to 26, the strengthening of the collective resistance and the formation of a civil defense force after the retreat of government troops; and (3) on May 27, the violent suppression of the Citizens' Army and the people of Kwangju by the military. During the first phase, most of the victims were citizens enraged at violent attacks perpetrated by the special military units, mostly in the downtown area. In the second phase many innocent bystanders, caught in the crossfire between the government forces and the Citizens' Army, were shot and killed on the outskirts of the city. In the final phase, the victims came from the young group of Citizens' Army volunteers led by Yun Sang-wŏn, who, though few in numbers, defended the provincial hall to the end in the face of the assault.

Throughout this period, hundreds of thousands of citizens from Kwangju and neighboring towns joined in the uprising. The citizens drew close together and developed a collective mentality, which grew out of their rage against the violence of the martial army, out of the jubilant sense of liberation and ensuing anxiety over an uncertain future, and finally out of heroic sacrifice.

Only when we recognize the totality of the "spirit of Kwangju" can we understand how the 1980 Kwangju uprising made an important contribution to the democratization movement in Korea, as the collective efforts to commemorate the Kwangju uprising evolved into the May movement. The democratization movement in Korea entered a new era after the Kwangju uprising. First, the movement was able to expand its base from the students to many more sectors of society. This expansion resulted in, for example, the formation of a youth movement and prompted stronger participation from the older generation. Second, the student movement moved beyond a few elite schools and expanded to include most colleges and universities in the country. Third, the grass roots were energized, as local activities led to nationwide alliances among diverse social movement groups. Fourth, there was a rejuvenation of the *minjung* (masses) movement, which mobilized workers and farmers and helped raise their class consciousness. Fifth, in the 1980s mass social movements in Korea came to be organized around the three dominant conceptions of *minjok* (nation), *minju* (democracy), and *minjung* (masses), although fierce debates arose about the ordering of priorities.[7]

While the May movement was initiated through the efforts of the families of those killed and injured in the uprising, following the June 1987 democratic transition the May movement began to draw support from diverse sectors of society, as long suppressed civic movements began to revive. These developments opened the door for the truth behind Kwangju, which began to come to light gradually in the mid-1980s and then exploded into public consciousness in the closing years of the decade. Eyewitness testimonies, pictures, and other pieces of evidence vividly revealed what happened in Kwangju and proved critical in stripping the military government of credibility. The public hearings in the National Assembly in 1988–1989 provided the turning point in the politics of memory surrounding Kwangju. While these hearings fell short of uncovering the complete story, they provided an accurate outline of the events and gave birth to a new official term for the uprising: the "Kwangju democratization movement" instead of "Kwangju incident."

In 1990 the government for the first time sought to provide restitution to the victims of the uprising through the Kwangju compensation law, a major breakthrough in the democratization movement. Still, complications accompanied this step. The government of Roh Tae Woo, one of the top generals in the military group that had taken power in 1980, hoped to mollify the citizens of Kwangju through economic incentives, but many people were wary. In response, the leaders of the May movement in Kwangju came up with the "five principles for the resolution of the Kwangju matter": (1) revealing of the truth, (2) punishment of those responsible for the massacre, (3) compensation, (4) restoration of the victims' honor, and (5) commemoration and maintenance of the Kwangju vision. These principles were developed in 1988 and agreed on in 1992.[8]

The 1993 inauguration of Kim Young Sam's "civilian government" produced only a partial, perhaps even distorted realization of the spirit of Kwangju. Although the compensation project was reestablished and the memorial service for the victims was institutionalized under his administration, Kim opted to forgo any legal action against the responsible figures. The May movement pushed very hard for the government to resolve these ambiguities. Pressured by nationwide rallies, the government decided finally to legislate the 5-18 Special Law in 1995 and put the former presidents on trial—a move almost unprecedented in developing countries.[9] Near the close of Kim Young Sam's presidency in 1997, May 18 was officially designated as a national memorial day.

Enlarging the Scope of Public Awareness

The Kwangju uprising in 1980 has recast and energized not only the Korean democratization movement but also the movement for Korean reunification as well as human rights campaigns in East Asia. When viewed in the context of Korea's national division, the Kwangju uprising made it possible to consider the reciprocal relationship between Korean politics and the divided system in a more fundamental way. People gained a better and clearer understanding of the forces ruling Korea, and this stimulated a public outcry against repressive state practices as well as calls for the formation of new social movements.

First, Kwangju clarified how the Cold War system in East Asia and the post–Cold War world order contributed to South Korean authoritarianism. The role of the U.S. government and the position of the Japanese government in May 1980 exposed important mechanisms of the Cold War system in East Asia. The image of the United States as a supporter of democracy began to crumble after the revelation that it approved the deployment of Korean military forces before and during the Kwangju uprising. The United States began to be seen as a public supporter of Korean military authorities and the divided system in Korea. Such an image stimulated radical social and political movements to criticize and attack anything related to America. After June 1980, for example, numerous arsons were committed against American targets protesting the U.S. role in the suppression of the Kwangju uprising. This anti-American sentiment led to a formation of an anti-American national autonomy movement and a "knowing North Korea" movement within student activist circles.

The Kwangju uprising and the May movement made a significant contribution to a reconsideration of the nation's contemporary history. The movement in the 1980s was divided into two strands—one prioritizing democratization and the other emphasizing national autonomy. The leaders of the May movement tried to distance themselves from the latter until the mid-1990s, when many similarities were recognized between the brutal exercise of state terror in the Kwangju uprising and other massacres in the earlier years of the divided-state system (such as the Cheju uprising of 1948).[10] Furthermore, the official national commemoration of Kwangju gave social activists a chance to reconsider honoring and compensating the victims of the democratization movements during the 1970s and 1980s, and to look into other civilian massacres in South Korean history. Whereas some of the earlier massacres occurred during the Korean War, later ones took place in the process of the democratization movement. Both represented the brutal exercise of state terror and the annihilation of human rights.[11] The 5-18 Special Law in 1995 provided a stepping-stone to the passage of the 4-19 Special Law in 1999, commemorating the April 1960 student movement, and the honor restoration law in 2000 commemorating democratic sacrifices.

Through these efforts, the May movement has served as a signpost that encourages endeavors all over the world to reveal the truths about the victims of dictators and authoritarian regimes. The success of the May movement showed that democracy is possible in Korea and other authoritarian East Asian nations. The trajectory of democratization movements in Korea has garnered respect and interest from progressive movements in Southeast Asia. Striving for democracy and human rights under extremely adverse situations, these groups have been encouraged by democratization in contemporary

Korea and have developed a special kind of camaraderie with the citizens of Kwangju.[12] These events have encouraged the reinterpretation of the Kwangju uprising in terms of human rights and thus furthered the project of making Kwangju a symbol of Asian democracy.

Remaining Challenges

The democratization of Korea might have seemed too slow in the eyes of people who wanted to resolve all problems in May 1980, but it has taken a distinctive path of step-by-step development. The year 2000 was the fiftieth anniversary of the Korean War and the twentieth anniversary of the Kwangju uprising. These two eruptions still shape the politics and culture of Korean society, and by extension they influence the geopolitical order of East Asia. While the half century since the Korean War has structured the geopolitics of the Korean peninsula and Northeast Asia, the two decades since the Kwangju uprising have provided a means to break this structure from the inside.

But the realization of the Kwangju spirit still has a long way to go. On the level of national politics, Koreans still suffer from the destructive effects of regionalism and other antidemocratic ideologies propagated during the uprising by the military authorities to legitimatize their activities. Regionalism and the lamentable divisions among the democratization groups have been major forces in shaping the political geography of South Korea. In order to get elected, Kim Dae Jung established a coalition with conservative groups and furthermore formed a truce with the two former presidents, Chun Doo Hwan and Roh Tae Woo, who were the mainstays of the 1980s military group. Because of such compromises, Kim's presidential project for political and social renovation oscillated and was distorted. Korean politics still faces the challenges of overcoming regional, factionalist ideology and solidifying democracy. Even so, the spirit of Kwangju promises to continue to guide Koreans and non-Koreans alike in the new millennium.

Notes

1. Discussion of Kwangju leads to another question, Is May 18 over? The question was included in the title of the annual symposium on the Kwangju uprising held in May 1999 by the Academic Association of Critical Scholars in Korea. This raises the question of whether it is still feasible for any social movement to pursue the vision of the 1980 Kwangju uprising, and whether enough social energy remains to evolve into the making of new history.

2. "Red complex" refers not to anticommunism but to the fear and stigma, imposed through decades of state-led anticommunist campaigns, of being labeled as a communist or leftist or being suspected of it.

3. Strictly speaking, what happened in Kwangju during May 18–27, 1980, was a mixture of various elements such as civilian massacre, resistance, uprising, and so forth. Calling it simply "Kwangju uprising" may not do justice to the entirety of events.

4. There have been disagreements as to the naming of the event, and about the key groups in the brutal suppression of and resistance to it. Consequently, some people speak symbolically of "May 18," referring to the first day of the uprising. But this term does not do justice to the fact that even before the explosive events on May 18, Kwangju was the site of many major antigovernment rallies and sit-ins on May 14–16. Similar to the large demonstrations by university students in Seoul between May 13 and May 15, 1980, a series of mass demonstrations on May 14–16 occurred in Kwangju. But these demonstrations in Kwangju, unlike those of Seoul, brought in many nonstudent participants and were peaceful. The leaders circulated a list of what to do and where to gather in case the schools were shut down, confirmation that the preparations were already very concrete. See Jung Keun-sik, "Minjuhwa wa owŏl undong: Chipdan-jŏk mengt'allit'ae ŭi pyŏnhwa [Democratization and the May movement: Change in collective mentality]," in Na Kan-ch'ae, ed., *Kwangju minjung hangjaeng kwa owŏl undong yŏn'gu* [The Kwangju people's uprising and the May movement] (Kwangju: 5-18 yŏn'guso, 1997).

5. Two of the better studies on the Kwangju uprising are Choi Jung-woon's work on absolute community (see chap. 1) and Han Sang-jin's interpretation of it as "a struggle for recognition." See Han Sang-jin, ed., *Hyŏndae sahoe wa inkwŏn* [Contemporary society and human rights] (Seoul: Nanam, 1998). Whereas the former focuses on the earlier phase of the Kwangju uprising, the latter focuses on its midpoint.

6. For a radical interpretation with too much emphasis on the final stage, see Yi Chŏng-no, "Kwangju ponggi e taehan hyŏngmyŏng-jŏk sigak chŏnhwan [A revolutionary shift in perspective on the Kwangju Uprising]," *Nodong haebang munhwa* (Liberation culture of labor) (1989), 5. He evaluates the Kwangju uprising as a revolutionary movement of workers, focusing on the role of one leader of the Citizen Army, Yun Sang-wŏn.

7. For a more detailed discussion, see Pak Hyŏn-ch'ae and Cho Hŭi-yŏn, eds., *Han'guk sahoe undongsa* (History of Korean social movements), vols. 1–4 (Seoul: Chuksan, 1990).

8. In a similar step in 1993, the principle of reparations for past state terror was established by Theo van Boven, who was a UN Human Rights Committee special rapporteur. See Sŏ Sŭng, "Tongasia esŏ ŭi kukka t'erŏ e ŭihan hŭisaeng ŭi myŏngye hoebok kwa paesang e kwanhan pigyo yŏn'gu [A comparative study on reparations and the restoration of honor for victims of state terror in East Asia]," M.A. thesis, Seoul National University, 2000.

9. There are many critical evaluations from inside the movement concerning the resolution of the Kwangju matter. For example, some argue that the truth of 1980 has not been completely revealed, and that the amnesty given to the convicted principal figures responsible—Chun Doo Hwan and Roh Tae Woo—was motivated by political expediency.

10. This kind of historical recognition might have made room for the psychological alliance between the civilian victims of Kwangju and other provinces. Since 1997, the East Asian Conference on Peace and Human Rights has been held with participation by representatives from Taiwan, Okinawa, Japan, and Korea, with the fourth annual conference held in May 2000 in Kwangju. Another sign of this alliance can be found in the participation of representatives from Cheju and Pusan in the conferences of the May 18 Foundation.

11. Although the Kwangju uprising had a relatively smaller number of victims— about 170—than did some other civilian massacres during the formative years of the Cold War system, its effect and influence could be much stronger because (1) it did not directly challenge the Cold War ideologically and instead appealed to the universal values of democracy; (2) it took place at the moment the Cold War system was on the brink; (3) it occurred in a major city; and (4) it quickly became an international issue due to the mass media coverage.

12. This was confirmed at the International Youth Camp organized by Kwangju Citizen Solidarity in Kwangju in 1996 and Bangkok in 1999. Recently the May 18 Foundation developed an international network of the victims of democratization struggles.

II

LEGACY AND REPRESENTATION

5

From Heroic Victims to Disabled Survivors: The 5-18 Injured after Twenty Years

Linda S. Lewis and Ju-na Byun

WITH THE REALIZATION OF CIVILIAN RULE IN 1993, and especially with the election of President Kim Dae Jung in 1997, the Kwangju uprising, reinscribed as the "5-18 Kwangju democratization movement" *(5-18 min-juhwa undong),* has been written into the newly constructed national narrative of democratization. In Kwangju during the annual May anniversary observances, *minjung* evocations of struggle against oppression stand uneasily beside the new chronicle of the triumph of democracy. Kwangju after twenty years is also, however, a place where public memories and private histories of May coexist, where the bodies and minds of individual citizens offer a site for resistance to the imposition of a singular 5-18 narrative.

This chapter will explore some of these juxtapositions of alternative (and shifting) representations of the event itself, and their articulation with the lives and experiences of those who bear witness to it. The transition to a democratic society in South Korea in the 1990s opened up a space for the emergence of new civic groups in Kwangju and for public contestation over the meaning and future direction of the 5-18 movement. One result has been the renewed marginalization of the 5-18 victims (bereaved family members, the injured, and those who were detained/tried/convicted) themselves. This analysis will focus on the response of the victims at the turn of the century to these changing circumstances; in particular, it will consider the ongoing, emergent transformation of the Kwangju injured.

From Heroic Victims to Disabled Survivors

A Record of Suffering

In the past twenty years, scant public attention has been paid to the physical, social, and psychological suffering of the 5-18 victims and their families. Throughout the 1980s, the emphasis on the political aspects of the Kwangju uprising overshadowed issues of ongoing human pain. Although victim groups claim that the number of 5-18 victims—dead, missing, injured, or detained—now reaches over four thousand and point out that injured survivors constitute 80 percent[1] of them, little was done to systematically document (or address) their problems. Testimonials published by the bereaved families association(s) in the 1980s frequently referred to the tragic life events that befell relatives of 5-18 victims, following in the wake of their loss. Like a pebble dropped in a pond, the death of a child or parent in May 1980 caused ever widening ripples, shattering the lives of family members as well. Until recently, however, empirical evidence of the increased risk for social and psychological problems, and even early death, for 5-18 victims and their relatives has remained largely anecdotal, only hinted at in the literature.

In the *Kwangju People's Uprising Memorial Book*[2] (published by the Bereaved Families Association and available at the Mangwŏl-dong cemetery), for example, brief memorials to each victim recount the details of his or her death. These victim stories often include, in the (sometimes graphic) narrative of suffering, the impact on the family. The record of a child shot while playing beside a reservoir concludes with the statement that "afterwards, his father, Pang Tu-hyŏng, who had embraced his eldest son's corpse and rolled on the floor kicking and screaming like the world had collapsed, couldn't pass a day without drinking and finally, unable to get over his son's gruesome death, he became mentally deranged."[3] A young widow "goes with her two young children to Mangwŏl-dong cemetery whenever she is reminded of the uncertainty of her life,"[4] while a bereft eldest son "still suffers from a phobia of soldiers and policemen because whenever he sees them, he remembers all the horror connected with his father's death."[5] Siblings and parents suffer nervous anxiety,[6] depression,[7] and lingering illnesses and death.[8]

While these memorial accounts intentionally focus on both the innocence of the 5-18 dead and their suffering in May 1980—primary issues for 5-18 movement groups in the Chun era—they also offer insight into the real-life circumstances of the bereaved families themselves, including (in at least one instance) the constant harassment they endured from the authorities. In particular, these families were subject to preventive house arrest, detention, and even abduction by the police whenever there was some reason to fear they might cause trouble.[9] A memorial piece refers ironically to this practice of abduction and detention, comparing such "trips" to "filial piety excursions," in which children send their parents on vacation. In remembering Hwang Ho-göl, a high school student, the text states that

> His parents couldn't believe their child was dead. . . . His words, telling his mother Ch'oe Sun-ja that he would earn money to send them on a "filial piety excursion," still ring in her ears. And now, as Ho-göl was killed, this "filial piety excursion" has become a disgraceful act of oppression, in that every time Chun Doo Hwan comes to Kwangju, the bereaved families are taken elsewhere, by force.[10]

Elsewhere, testimony by the 5-18 injured and detained reveals post-1980 life histories of ongoing medical problems, financial difficulties (including unemployment), and general hardship. The *Complete Collection of the Historical Record of the Kwangju May Peoples Uprising,*[11] an encyclopedic record of 5-18 compiled by the Korean Modern Historical Materials Research Institute (1990), contains testimony from almost five hundred witnesses, many of whose narrative accounts of the events of May 1980 carry forward their story into the present, bringing to light a pattern of continued suffering. Typical is the comment of one woman—once a *hagwŏn* (cram school) teacher, now a peddler—who was a street broadcaster during the uprising. She said of her life since then that "in nine years of oppressive existence, I have had many devastating experiences."[12] In a survey conducted in 1988 by the Catholic Church's Kwangju Diocese Peace and Justice Committee,[13] researchers found that among the injured and the bereaved, the majority (70.2 percent) identified themselves as working class. These victims, as a group, suffered significant downward mobility in the 1980s: 40.9 percent were unemployed (including housewives) in 1988, compared with 23.9 percent at the time of the uprising. The survey states that many of the respondents believed they had lost their jobs because of their involvement in 5-18, although no other details are given.[14]

As it turns out, the ongoing life difficulties and physical distress of the 5-18 victims alluded to in the uprising literature is very real. In 1994 the Injured Peoples Association appointed a medical anthropologist/nurse, Dr. Ju-na Byun, to be their research adviser. Her study of sixty-seven injured victims and fifty nonvictims in Kwangju was the first systematic attempt to fully document the physical, psychological, and sociocultural problems of the victims. Using standardized tests, medical records, and case reports, Byun found that over 91.7 percent of 5-18 victims evince posttraumatic stress disorders. Among the survivors, 42 percent suffer from physical ailments, 19 percent from mental problems, and 31 percent from both; in addition, their degree of life change events (7.1 times), anxiety (3.2 times), and depression (2.7 times) is higher than for nonvictims in Kwangju.[15] Many suffer chronic pain from bullet splinters and fragments left in their bodies, for which the only relief is ever larger dosages of drugs; another common problem is lead poisoning.[16] Survivors are at higher risk for drug addiction, alcoholism, and suicide; in addition, the disabilities of over six hundred of the injured are classed as first (100 percent) through ninth (50 percent) degree, which means they are either completely incapable of, or at least severely limited in their ability to find, suitable employment.[17] Needless to say, caring for the victims is stressful for their families, who may in turn need financial and psychological support.[18] Family members of the 5-18 dead and missing are in fact more likely to suffer associated deaths, often from *hwabyŏng*.[19]

Subsequent research (much of it conducted and presented in the context of the three annual Injured Peoples Association scholarly symposiums, held in 1996, 1997, and 1998) supports Byun's initial findings that the 5-18 survivors suffer from a complicated array of problems, and that "the injured victims' physical and psychological well-being and their family and social life have been harmed" in the years since May 1980.[20]

On the basis of survey data from research done in 1997 (see appendix at the end of the book) Byun argues that the 5-18 injured victims have led miserably unhappy lives and do not expect that their life will ever be as satisfying as before the uprising. Using international standardized instruments for measuring happiness[21] with a sample group of 156 members of the 5-18 Injured Peoples Association, Byun analyzed the uprising's impact on the life satisfaction and happiness of the victims, comparing changes from before May 1980 through December 1997.

Byun found that for the answers on life satisfaction, 97 percent of the subjects answered "not satisfied," with 45.1 percent rating themselves "very unsatisfied"; no respondents were "satisfied." Major unhappy feelings reported by the victims were (in order) perplexity, sick feeling, painfulness, misery, exhaustion, sense of aggravation, loneliness, helplessness, and depression. Further, the scores for unhappiness were greater among those with less access to clinics, with higher degrees of disability, and with mental and physical illnesses, as well as among the unemployed. Indeed, illness and employment factors account for as much as 78.7 percent of their unhappiness. Life satisfaction scores also varied over time, with lower ratings after the 1990 period of compensation and the 1995 special compensation law enactment, and the highest scores before May 1980.

Byun's findings support the contention that the rights of the 5-18 injured victims to happiness have been severely and permanently violated as a result of the May uprising and their life experiences since 1980. The right to happiness is stipulated in the Korean constitution as an inviolable right of Korean citizens; article 10 states that "every citizen has dignity and value as a human being and has the right to seek happiness." Further, "the Nation is responsible for assuring and guaranteeing this inviolable right to every individual."[22] Not only have the 5-18 victims and their families suffered physical, social, and psychological harm in the past two decades, but their unhappy state constitutes a violation of their basic human rights as Korean citizens.

The Victims and the 5-18 Movement's "Second Stage"

National public recognition of the Kwangju uprising as the "cornerstone"[23] of South Korean democracy and the official valorization of its martyrs in the 1990s have resulted in mixed blessings for many of Kwangju's survivors. The decade-long struggle to uncover the "truth" of May 1980 has been brought to an end, and the civic honor of the city and its citizens has been restored (at least symbolically). During the Chun era, 5-18 victims endured political and social ostracism, and openly seeking help for their physical and mental problems carried the risk of self-stigmatization. Systematic government measures and treatment plans for the injured—including medical care cards[24]—date from the early 1990s,[25] and obviously the newly altered political climate has made it easier for them to come forward.

It also, however, has made it more difficult for them to be heard. One effect of the memorialization of 5-18 (and certainly of the 1996 trial and conviction of former Presidents Chun and Roh for their roles in the "Kwangju massacre") has been to bring a sense of closure to this particular episode in Korean history. Even in Kwangju itself, where until May 1995 anniversary slogans still proclaimed that "even now, Kwangju continues"[26] and discussions about "resolving" 5-18 were part of the civic agenda, a few years later public sentiment clearly favored a renunciation of the "so-called anti-government struggle style of the past."[27] The 5-18 movement was portrayed by its own leaders as "approaching a second stage, changing to a spirit of universal humanity,"[28] and an official Kwangju city account of the May uprising, published in 1997, ends with the statement that

> In order to prepare for the coming 21st century, we must realize our community and our history, and let go of the pain and distress of the past. Through realization of our community, which helps and trusts in each other and lives and lets live, the spirit of the Kwangju Democratic Uprising should shine brightly into tomorrow.[29]

But exactly whose pain, and whose distress, is now to be part of the past? In Kwangju, the symbolic center of oppositional politics throughout the 1980s, there is growing public weariness with the noisy "drama of dissent" and little patience with or sympathy for the continuing clamor of 5-18 victims with complaints and unsatisfied claims against the government. Further demands are generally dismissed by Kwangju citizens as the "exaggeration of some shameless victims who are greedy for more money," and some even suggest that the campaign for additional compensation and aid for the victims is contrary to the "May spirit" itself.[30] The public perception, in short, is that everyone has gotten his or her due, and it is time to move on.

Advocates for the injured victims, however, argue that government efforts on their behalf are, thus far, a case of "too little, too late." From the very start, the fact that victims did not receive compensation until a decade after the uprising has meant that many of the injured missed the best opportunity for treatment, and their conditions are now much worse than would have been the case had they received better medical attention immediately, in the early 1980s. Even those few of the most seriously impaired who got government subsidies for individual treatment, under what Byun terms a "downright makeshift policy," were provided "only with wheelchairs and narcotic painkillers in the name of special medication, on which they are now totally dependent."[31]

Moreover, it is also assumed that many of the additional 120 victims who have died since 1980[32] might have been helped by earlier intervention. Over half (sixty-nine) were gunshot victims in their twenties and thirties, and surprisingly few (only seventeen) were older people in their sixties and seventies.[33] The Association for the Bereaved Families of 5-18 Wounded Who Died Later *(Oilp'al sangihu samangja yujokhoe)* attributes many of these untimely deaths to the despair the injured feel over their inability to work and their financial difficulties.[34] As the chairman of the group pointed out,

> Among the wounded who have died it is clear that the many mysterious or accidental deaths at a young age are from mental illness and suicidal depression resulting from injuries caused by such things as bullet wounds, beatings, and torture. Wouldn't they be able to live a bit longer if their living conditions were good, and they received continuous medical treatment? . . . Those who died afterwards suffered many times the pain of those who died at the time—and then they died.[35]

Victim advocates further contend that the medical subsidy paid to the injured under the 1990 compensation law, made as a lump sum payment, has in most cases been inadequate. As the director of a family counseling center in Kwangju noted, in attesting to the ongoing needs of the injured,

> In the case that the victim was originally from the lower class, or that the victim was not capable of supporting the family due to death, injury, or aftermath of in-

jury, the compensation for his physical injuries, which was paid 10 years after the Incident, was naturally used to pay the debt that he had owed for treatment and livelihood in the meantime.[36]

The medical insurance cards issued to them in 1993 have not solved their on-going problems, since the coverage is limited, and the victims themselves feel they cannot expect good medical care because the cards reveal their status as 5-18 survivors.[37] Although in the 1990s government funding poured into 5-18 memorial enterprises in Kwangju—most notably the monumental $32 million May 18 cemetery completed in 1997,[38] victims groups point out that these projects are by and large symbolic ones honoring the dead or com-memorative activities that celebrate the history of the May uprising[39] itself. They have not included significant medical and social welfare programs tar-geting the ongoing life problems of 5-18 victims. Advocates for the injured have suggested that what is needed is a specialized treatment center for 5-18 victims, which would be equipped to handle their complex multiple physical, psychological, and social problems by providing not only medical but also re-habilitation and counseling services. Plans for a comprehensive care facility were unveiled in 1997 at the second annual scholarly symposium sponsored by the Injured Peoples Association,[40] but the project has not won widespread public interest or support.[41] In sum (and in the words of one advocate), "the seriousness of their injuries, the political atmosphere that made them miss the proper time for treatment, and the lack of life relief programs have made it harder for the victims to recover from their physical problems."[42] At the same time, in the climate of a newly democratic South Korea at the turn of the century, victims groups in Kwangju who attempt to speak out about their continuing problems and needs risk renewed marginalization and restigma-tization. The class-based political *minjung* (people) movement dominant in the 1970s and 1980s has all but disappeared, replaced by the *simin* (citizens) groups of an emergent civil society, in which the trend is toward constructive engagement with, rather than opposition to, the state. The election of Kim Dae Jung in 1997 made it difficult for them to place responsibility for their continued suffering at the feet of an unjust and brutal regime; lacking the counterpoint of an illegitimate government, they have lost legitimacy as op-pressed victims per se. With the waning of the *minjung* movement,[43] they can no longer successfully frame their grievances in the oppositional political dis-course of decades past. Even in Kwangju, the rhetoric of protest and dissent is, at the turn of the century, passé—a civic embarrassment, out of step with the new readings of the "May spirit" and the officially sanctioned character of the 5-18 movement itself. Local leaders, who once linked arms with radi-cal students, labor and democracy movement activists, and 5-18 victims and their families to defend the honor of Kwangju's May martyrs, now distance themselves from acts of resistance and continuing expressions of discontent.[44]

Repositioning 5-18 Victims in the 1990s

If 5-18 victims—bereaved family members, the injured, and those who were detained in 1980—are to make themselves heard and successfully press their claims, they must find a way to reposition themselves in the context of a newly democratic South Korean society. Abelmann suggests, in examining the farmers movement in the 1990s, that while "many of the old activisms continue . . . the aesthetics of the age are certainly new."[45] Further, "1990s activism fashions itself through the public discourses on and the memory of the 1980s"[46]—a discourse that in Kwangju posits triumph over the military authoritarian state and a vision of the city as an international "Mecca of democracy" and human rights.[47] In line with this civic agenda, by the close of the 1990s, the contours of a new position for 5-18 victims were beginning to emerge in the arguments being made by a small circle of supporters on their behalf.

This reimaging of the victims for the twenty-first century appears most coherently in a book published in conjunction with twentieth anniversary commemoration events in May 2000.[48] The book collects research on the status of the victims (previously presented at the three scholarly symposia sponsored by the Injured Peoples Association in 1996, 1997, and 1998), together with articles by various 5-18 leaders, government officials in Kwangju, and nationally known human rights activists, as well as essays by other specialists, in a single edited volume. The primary goal of the editors is "inducing more attention to the life-threatening conditions of the victims, so that further research efforts will be made to verify their problems presented here, and to prepare effective countermeasures for these problems."[49]

Part 2, "The Wounds," documents the physical, social, and psychological difficulties of the injured, and part 3, "Victims' Testimonies," contains individual narratives of suffering. Part 4, "Counter Measures," considers, in the abstract, the issues of reparations (from an international human rights perspective) and rehabilitation (from the point of view of treatment of the disabled) and concludes with a detailed proposal for the establishment of a "5-18 Memorial Human Rights Clinic." "It is time," these advocates proclaim, "to achieve a true humanitarian recovery in Kwangju and Korea by helping the May disabled people to completely rehabilitate themselves."[50] The most appropriate first step in achieving this, the book suggests, is to build the victims a rehabilitation/treatment center.

In this volume the case for additional aid for the injured is made in two significantly new ways. First, they are, on the whole, positioned in the text as disabled survivors of political abuse rather than as 5-18 victims per se. Second, the authors by and large utilize the language of universal human rights and health, rather than governmental oppression and injustice, to legitimate their continuing needs. The primary emphasis is on the status of the 5-18 victims not as the survivors of a particular event (the Kwangju uprising), but as exemplars of a more general category: the casualties of political violence and ongoing human rights violations. The "human right" that they are being denied, twenty years after the Kwangju uprising, is the right to a healthy, happy life. "Healthy living is a basic right of every human being,"[51] the editors assert. Further, according to the World Health Organization, health is "not just a state of being disease-free, but of being secure physically, emotionally, and socially."[52] Thus (the argument goes), the Korean government, through its failure to provide adequate care and rehabilitation services for the 5-18 survivors, is perpetuating their abuse by not ensuring their right to a healthy existence.

Contributors to the book construct the category of "victims of human rights abuses" variously and in broadly inclusive terms. From a chronological perspective, the 5-18 survivors are positioned in the context of Korean history—a history that has been, in modern times, "the history of mass killing, torture, and detention."[53] Many of these past victims (and perpetrators) are either dead or forgotten, and it is too late to recover justice for them; it is not, however, too late for the victims of the brutality in Kwangju. Thus addressing the issue of past injustices "can start with the realistic reparation of the 5-18 Massacre."[54] At the same time, humane treatment of the Kwangju disabled serves by extension to rectify the inhumane and callous national neglect of the many casualties of the past. The human rights lawyer Won-soon Park, in making this point, evokes the suffering of torture victims in the 1970s and 1980s (in both political and ordinary criminal cases), as well as those who died in the 4-3 incident in Cheju and in the Kŏch'ang, Sanch'ŏng, and Hamyang massacres as examples of forgotten victims of twentieth-century Korean political history who are linked to Kwangju's survivors. Justice for 5-18 victims would serve as the means to "open up" other "long-buried conspiracies."[55] The contributors imagine the victims of the future: a commitment to the well-being of 5-18 survivors "will eventually serve as a model policy for the welfare of North Korean refugees and torture victims around the process of unification."[56]

The 5-18 victims are represented in this volume as suffering from a particular type of human rights violation—political violence—a category extended (as noted before) to include victims of torture. But mention is made, as well, of victims of "social disasters," and in the conclusion the editor suggests that "efforts to look at health issues from a human rights perspective are not necessarily limited to the health problems of the survivors of political violence."[57]

She goes on to point out that in the United States human rights clinics deal with political refugees and even the "human rights of the dead," through such functions as forensic exhumations and identification of the missing. In the broadest sense, human rights clinics could deal with such "victims" groups as AIDS patients and poor women and children.[58]

By detaching the 5-18 disabled from the specific details of the Kwangju uprising, the contributors sidestep the contentious issues that remain around it—compensation already paid, kinds of victims, the politics of the 5-18 movement, responsibility for the massacre, and so on. Victim advocates make the key point that "underneath the glitter of historical meanings of the uprising, it is difficult to deny the facts of the incurable suffering of the victims up to today."[59] The contributors emphasize these "undeniable facts" of survivor disability by situating them as "victims" in the broadly inclusive categories of Korean (political) history and human rights abuses.

This represents a change from the arguments made by victim advocates in the mid-1990s, when a medical center for Kwangju's injured was first publicly (and unsuccessfully) proposed—in the context of a national discourse on "resolving" the wounds of May 1980—as a facility solely for 5-18 victims. In contrast, at the Fourth International Scholarly Symposium for the Establishment of a 5-18 Memorial Human Rights Clinic and Book Publication Ceremony,[60] sponsored by the Injured Peoples Association and held on May 20, 2000, many of the eight panelists who offered comments on the proposed clinic emphasized the "universal" nature of the center. "This is not just for you," one speaker reminded the 5-18 victims in the audience; it is dedicated to the memory of Kwangju's survivors but is not intended for their exclusive use.[61]

Perhaps, twenty years after the event, the repositioning of the 5-18 injured as generic historical and/or social "every victims" may successfully elicit renewed popular sympathy and support for them. Public attitudes toward and treatment of the disabled are relatively recent concerns in Korea and as yet remain free of political overtones. Sangkyu Kim, an advocate for the disabled, claims that Koreans feel guilty about the disabled and places the blame for this attitude on government neglect. "Kwangju," Kim suggests, "can become the city of the disabled as well as the city of human rights if the Government shows faithful and reliable efforts to resolve the problems of the 5-18 injured victims."[62] Certainly, representing the problems of the victims as an issue of health and human rights, rather than politics, appears to be a promising strategy in an era when most Koreans would prefer to put the turmoil of the 1980s behind them.

As for the injured themselves, in the vast new 5-18 cemetery in Kwangju there are empty spaces waiting to accommodate them[63] after death. Given the choice, however, most would prefer to live longer as disabled survivors, rather than hasten their posthumous glorification as heroic victims. In order to do so, they will have to find a new voice for the twenty-first century, one that articulates (in an acceptable manner) a counterhegemonic narrative of ongoing human suffering and pain. After more than twenty years, "Kwangju continues," inscribed on the minds and bodies of its victims.

Notes

1. Min-ho Lee, "The Occurrence of Physical Disease among 5-18 Victims," in Ju-na Byun and Linda S. Lewis, eds., *The Kwangju Uprising after 20 Years: The Unhealed Wounds of the Victims* (Seoul: Dahaes, 2000), 167. Estimates vary. As of 1998, 4,540 people had been paid compensation under the 5-18 compensation law, which included 154 dead, 66 missing, 94 dead after injuries, 3,059 injured, and 1,168 detained (Ju-na Byun, introduction to Byun and Lewis, *Kwangju Uprising*, 31). Other groups calculate the numbers higher; for example, there are 107 "unofficial" missing, and the Association for the Injured claimed 4,326 in 1990 (as quoted in Ju-na Byun, "5-18 minjuhwa undong p'ihaejadŭl ŭi changaehyŏn kwa taech'aek [5-18 democratization movement victims' current obstacles and countermeasures]," a lecture presented at the Second Annual 5-18 Injured Association's Scholarly Meeting, Kwangju, May 24, 1997). In addition, some claim that 120 victims died between 1980 and 1997 (as quoted in a report on "*5-18 minjung hangjaeng sangihu samangja* [Those who died after 5-18]," presented by Sŏng Su Kim at the same event). This number does not include victims' families, who are also recognized as being at increased risk.

2. 5-18 Kwangju minjung hangjaeng yujokhoe (5-18 Kwangju Peoples Uprising Bereaved Families Association), *Kwangju minjung hangjaeng pimangnok* [Kwangju peoples uprising memorial book] (Seoul: Tosŏ, 1989).

3. *Kwangju minjung hangjaeng pimangnok*, 207.

4. *Kwangju minjung hangjaeng pimangnok*, 199.

5. *Kwangju minjung hangjaeng pimangnok*, 190.

6. *Kwangju minjung hangjaeng pimangnok*, 286.

7. *Kwangju minjung hangjaeng pimangnok*, 288.

8. *Kwangju minjung hangjaeng pimangnok*, 232, 247.

9. *Kwangju minjung hangjaeng pimangnok*, 357–59.

10. *Kwangju minjung hangjaeng pimangnok*, 230.

11. Han'guk hyŏndaesa saryo yŏn'guso (Korean Modern Historical Materials Research Institute), *Kwangju owŏl minjung hangjaeng saryo chŏnjip* [Complete collection of historical records of the Kwangju May peoples uprising] (Seoul: P'ulpit, 1990).

12. *Kwangju owŏl minjung hangjaeng saryo chŏnjip*, 911.

13. Ch'ŏnjugyo Kwangju taegyogu chŏngŭi p'yŏnghwa wiwŏnhoe [Catholic Church, Kwangju Diocese Peace and Justice Committee], *Kwangju simin sahoe ŭisik chosa* [A study of Kwangju citizens' social consciousness] (Kwangju: Pit koŭl, 1988).

14. *Kwangju simin sahoe ŭisik chosa*, 52–53.

15. Ju-na Byun, "Kwangju 5-18 minju hangjaeng p'ihaeja 15 chunyŏn hŭisaengyang chŭnghugun [15-Year aftermath-victim-syndrome of the 5-18 Kwangju

civil uprising]," presented at the First Annual Injured Peoples Association Scholarly Symposium, Kwangju, May 25, 1996.

16. Byun, "Kwangju." See also Min-ho Lee, "Physical Disease," 12. Because domestic doctors lack skill in treating bullet wounds, several of the more critically ill would benefit greatly from care at U.S. trauma centers. Unfortunately, they cannot afford to travel overseas for treatment.

17. Byun, introduction, 29.

18. Many victims have been abandoned by their families. See Lee Chae-hŭi, "Sŏng-gonghan k'udet'a sinŭm hanŭn Kwangju minju simin [Kwangju's democratic citizens bemoan successful coup d'etat]," *Modern Praxis* 14 (1995): 84, for accounts of wives who have received awards for their devotion to bedridden husbands.

19. Causation as explained by the survivors' families. *Hwabyŏng* is recognized in Korean culture as death due to excessive *hwa*, or pent-up anger, frustration, and resentment.

20. Ju-na Byun, "15-Year Aftermath Syndrome" (English version).

21. The Cantril life satisfaction ladder. See H. Cantril, *The Patterns of Human Concerns* (New Brunswick, N.J.: Rutgers University Press, 1965); and the Memorial University of Newfoundland Scale of Happiness (MUNSH). Also see A. Kozma and M. J. Stone, "The Measurement of Happiness: Development of Memorial University of Newfoundland Scale of Happiness," *Journal of Gerontology* 35 (1980): 906–12.

22. From the preamble to the Korean constitution, vol. 10, pt. 2. Available at www.koreanpolitics.com/korean/constitution.html.

23. See the May History Compilation Committee of Kwangju City, *The May 1980 Kwangju Democratic Uprising,* trans. Lee Kyung-soon and Ellen Bishop (City of Kwangju, 1998), 5.

24. For free treatment. See Min-ho Lee, "Physical Disease," 105–6.

25. On August 6, 1990, a law regarding 5-18 compensation was passed, stipulating that victims be paid compensation, a medical subsidy, and a living subsidy. See Won-soon Park, "International Law Perspective," in Byun and Lewis, *Kwangju Uprising,* 251, for discussion of issues surrounding compensation.

26. Compare materials published by the Fifteenth Anniversary Committee *(Oilp'al minjung hangjaeng sibo chunyŏn haengsa wiwŏnhoe),* which frequently displayed the slogan *Chigŭmdo Kwangjunŭn kyesok toego itta.*

27. Chŏng Su-man, chairman of the Bereaved Families Association, as quoted in the *Chŏnnam ilbo,* May 19, 1997, 20.

28. Chŏng Su-man, 20.

29. *May 18 Kwangju Democratic Uprising,* 179.

30. Byun, introduction, 31.

31. Byun, introduction, 32.

32. As of May 1997, as cited by Kim Sŏng-su, "5-18 pusanghu samangja silt'ae (Condition of those who died after being injured in 5-18)," unpublished paper presented at the Second Annual 5-18 Injured Peoples Association Scholarly Meeting, Kwangju, May 24, 1997.

33. Kim Sŏng-su, "5-18 pusanghu samangja silt'ae."

34. Kim Sŏng-su, "5-18 pusanghu samangja silt'ae." See also Lee Jae-eui, "Sŏng-gonghan k'udet'a sinŭm hanŭn Kwangju minju simin [Kwangju's democratic citizens bemoan successful coup d'etat]," *Modern Praxis* 14 (1995), for accounts of the lives (and deaths) of the injured.

35. Kim Sŏng-su, "5-18 pusanghu samangja silt'ae."

36. Ch'oe Sŏn-nyŏng, "Kwangju minjung hangjaeng p'ihaejadŭl kwa kŭ kajokdŭl ŭi simnisahoejŏk munje e taehan sahoe saŏpjŏk chŏpkŭn [A social work approach to the sociopsychological problems of the Kwangju peoples uprising injured and their families]," paper presented at the Second Annual 5-18 Injured Peoples Association Scholarly Meeting, Kwangju, May 24, 1997, as quoted in Won-soon Park, "International Law," 250–51.

37. Byun, introduction, 32–33.

38. Constructed at a total cost of 26.1 billion won (*Korea Times*, May 17, 1997, 3), it covers about 165,000 square meters and includes a photographic memorial hall, a memorial tower, and commemorative statues and sculpture. The bodies of the 5-18 dead were moved there from the nearby Mangwŏl-dong plots and the space was consecrated in May 1997.

39. Plans include a May 18 memorial park and theme park. The old *Sangmudae* military courtroom and jail, in which citizens were detained and tried, will be preserved as a historical site. See Kwangju City, *Oilp'al yujŏkchi annae* [Information on 5-18-related historical sites], pamphlet published in 1997. Memorial funding has also supported 5-18 historical documentation projects.

40. See the unpublished proceedings of the Second Annual 5-18 Peoples Uprising Injured Peoples Association Scholarly Meeting, May 24, 1997, which was entitled "5-18 p'ihaeja ch'iryo mit chaehoebokcha sent'ŏ kŏllibŭl wihan simp'ojium [A symposium on the establishment of a 5-18 victims' treatment and welfare center]."

41. Until May 2000, when a prospectus for establishing the 5-18 Memorial Health and Human Rights Center was drawn up and a committee was formed to promote the project.

42. Byun, introduction, 34.

43. See, for example, Nancy Abelmann, "Reorganizing and Recapturing Dissent in 1990s South Korea," in Richard Fox and Orin Starn, eds., *Between Resistance and Revolution* (New Brunswick, N.J.: Rutgers University Press, 1997), 253. Abelmann notes that *minjung* activism had all but disappeared from view in the 1990s, although there is speculation and disagreement about the future of the movement. Some focus on the development of civil society in a newly democratic Korea (see Sunhyuk Kim, "Civil Society in South Korea: From Grand Democracy Movements to Petty Interest Groups?" *Journal of Northeast Asian Studies*, Summer 1996) or, more broadly, state–society relations in Korea (see Hagen Koo, "Strong State and Contentious Society," in *State and Society in Contemporary Korea* [Ithaca, N.Y.: Cornell University Press, 1993]). Others suggest that democratization opened a space for participation by the middle class, which then deserted the *minjung* movement. Remnants of the *minjung* movement continue in the labor movement, for example, and in the more moderate agendas of other social groups (see Jang Jip Choi, "Social Movements and Class in South Korea," paper presented at the Association for Asian Studies Meeting, Honolulu, 1996).

44. See Linda S. Lewis, *Laying Claim to the Memory of May: A Look Back at the 1980 Kwangju Uprising* (Honolulu: University of Hawaii Press, 2002), for a more complete discussion of the impact of the transition to democracy on the 5-18 movement in Kwangju and the marginalization of radical student groups in the anniversary commemoration events in the late 1990s.

45. See Abelmann, "Reorganizing," 251.

46. Abelmann, "Reorganizing," 253.

47. As first coined in a brochure published by the citizens group Kwangju Citizens Solidarity in 1995. On the eighteenth anniversary of the uprising, in May 1998, Kwangju was a venue for the declaration of the newly drafted Asian Human Rights Charter (see Kwangju Citizens Solidarity, "Program: Declaring the Asian Human Rights Charter," available at www.ik.co.kr/kcs), and the anniversary slogan that year was "Human Rights and Peace, Toward a Harmonious Future."

48. Ju-na Byun and Won-soon Park, eds., *Ch'iyu toeji anŭn owŏl: Isip nyŏn hu Kwangju hangjaeng p'ihaeja silsang mit taech'aek* (Seoul: Dahae, 2000). Published in English (with fewer chapters) as Ju-na Byun and Linda S. Lewis, eds., *The 1980 Kwangju Uprising after Twenty Years: The Unhealed Wounds of the Victims* (Seoul: Dahae, 2000).

49. Byun in Byun and Lewis, *The 1980 Kwangju Uprising*, 37.

50. Byun and Lewis, *The 1980 Kwangju Uprising*, 37.

51. Byun and Lewis, *The 1980 Kwangju Uprising*, 28.

52. Byun and Lewis, *The 1980 Kwangju Uprising*, 22.

53. Won-soon Park, "International Law," 253.

54. Won-soon Park, "International Law," 253.

55. Won-soon Park, "International Law," 252–53.

56. Byun, conclusion to Byun and Lewis, *The 1980 Kwangju Uprising*, 303.

57. Byun, conclusion, 300.

58. Byun, conclusion, 300.

59. Byun, introduction, 30–31.

60. "Oilp'al kinyŏm inkwŏn pyŏngwŏn kŏllibŭl wihan kukche haksul taehoe mit ch'ulp'an kinyŏmhoe."

61. The prospectus for the 5-18 Memorial Health and Human Rights Center envisions a facility with three parts: a hospital, a research center, and a welfare center. The medical clinic will be a "general hospital system where the political violence victims and their families receive inclusive medical and rehabilitation treatment." The research center will investigate and document human rights abuses, while the welfare center will function as a "shelter for human rights victims and their family members and as a general welfare and rehabilitation services center." From unpublished prospectus, summer 2000, 4.

62. "The Government's Responsibility and Role in the Victims' Rehabilitation," in Byun and Lewis, *1980 Kwangju Uprising*, 275.

63. Those who are classified up to the fourth degree (80 percent) disabled; "Government's Responsibility," 32.

6

The Kwangju Uprising as a Vehicle of Democratization: A Comparative Perspective

Jung-kwan Cho

S TUDIES OF DEMOCRATIZATION ACROSS COUNTRIES often reveal critical incidents of mass uprising and/or massacre that decidedly affect the course of events. The Kwangju uprising was one such incident, facilitating Korea's democratization in the 1980s and 1990s.[1] Although the uprising lasted only ten days, its impact on Korean politics lasted more than fifteen years, changing the ideology and features of the antigovernment movement, restructuring the relationship between the authoritarian regime and the democratization movement, functioning as a symbol of the struggle for democracy, and conditioning other major political processes.

Drawing on theoretical achievements from comparative democratization studies, this chapter explores how the Kwangju uprising influenced the protracted process of political democratization in Korea. The analysis is divided into four sections. The first section discusses the way in which the legitimacy deficit created by the Kwangju massacre damaged the authoritarian regime and induced the regime to the path of democratization.[2] The second section deals with how the legacy of the Kwangju uprising empowered the opposition in the 1980s to challenge authoritarianism, with a focus on cultural framing. The third section, which utilizes the elite survey data I collected in 1996, analyzes the influence of the Kwangju uprising in deterring military involvement at a critical juncture in June 1987. The fourth section shows why and how the legacy of the Kwangju uprising facilitated the democratic consolidation of Korea.

The Weakening of Authoritarian Legitimacy

What makes a country that once had political equilibrium under an authoritarian regime[3] move toward the "uncertain" world of democracy? A common thread among a vast literature of studies on democratization is the change of relative power between regime and opposition. Among the various factors that contribute to a change in the relative balance of power[4] is an occurrence (or occurrences) of an explosive collective action and/or a subsequent brutal repression or massacre. Such an incident weakens the authoritarian regime, most of all, by undermining its legitimacy. Legitimacy is defined as a belief that "in spite of shortcomings and failures, the existing political institutions are better than any others that might be established, and that they therefore can demand obedience."[5] All political regimes, democratic or authoritarian, are more or less dependent on their legitimacy.[6] No political regime in the world is able to sustain itself only through repression and coercion. If the grounds for legitimacy are weak, a regime cannot last long.

Like most contemporary bureaucratic authoritarian governments, the Chun Doo Hwan regime in Korea based its legitimacy primarily on the need for safeguarding national security and stability. However, unlike its immediate predecessor, the Chun regime was not able to base its legitimacy on that premise alone. Both the demise of the preceding government by an assassination of its leader, and the popular yearning for democracy clearly expressed from March to May 1980, convinced the new military leaders that a mere repetition of the Yusin system would not work. The Kwangju uprising in particular demonstrated the people's potential for the highest form of revolt against an unjust state power, while the unprecedented massacre reflected the illegitimacy of the new military in power. No other Korean rule in the past was born with such a high legitimacy deficit.

However, a legitimacy deficit incurred by a massacre does not necessarily lead in the long run to the serious weakening of a regime. For instance, after a series of massacres that killed thousands of demonstrators in 1988–1990, the Burmese military junta, State Law and Order Restoration Council (SLORC), still maintains a firm grip over the country. More than a decade after the Tiananmen Square massacre of 1989, the Chinese Communist Party (CCP) also remains strong. How did the Kwangju uprising differ from these other massacres? The main clue lies in the difference in the nature of the political regime.

As apparent from table 6.1, the Chun regime began with a much lower degree of legitimacy than the CCP regime, which, being founded on revolution, gained a powerful source of enduring legitimacy.[7] The blame for the Tiananmen massacre could be diffused to the military or to individual CCP leaders

TABLE 6.1
Comparison of Political Regimes

Characteristics	The Chun Regime in Korea	The CCP Regime in the PRC
1. Method of establishment	By a military coup	By social revolution and a civil war
2. Organizational base of leadership	Nonhierarchical military	Communist Party (military subject to the party)
3. Ideology (facade)	Liberal democracy	Communism
4. Level of pluralism allowed	High	Low
5. Level of institutionalization	Low	High
6. External dependence	High	Low

such as Li Peng, but in Korea criticism was directed to the center of the regime. The Chun regime itself became identified as a "butcher." Only a part of the military, rather than the military as a whole as in Chile, Uruguay, and Brazil, formed the political regime in Korea. As a result, some in the military who claimed no involvement in the massacre could challenge those former generals in power.[8] The National Polytechnic massacre in November 1973, which led to the decline, and ultimate demise, of a nonhierarchical military regime in Greece provides a good reference.[9]

The Chun regime, whose legitimacy was based on the promise (however nominal it may have been) of defending liberal democracy against the communist threat, could not help but allow a relatively high level of political pluralism and individual freedom. Over time, this condition allowed the discourse on the Kwangju uprising to spread and deepen across the nation, and it facilitated the strengthening of the opposition, which we will examine in detail in the next section. In the PRC, where communist doctrines were officially maintained, political pluralism and individual freedom were very limited; room for diffusion of the Tiananmen discourse was small.

When the massacres took place, the Chun regime was in its initial phase of formation, while the CCP regime was already highly institutionalized. As a result, the Chun regime was in a much weaker position to defend regime legitimacy. True, China in 1989 was undergoing rapid change in terms of policy orientation and social configuration that picked up speed after the mid-1970s. However, the CCP regime's institutional control over society was relatively strong and cohesive, while China's civil society was immature.[10]

Given the high level of international exposure of the massacres in both Kwangju and Beijing, the extent of regime dependence on external power is another key factor in the degree to which a regime may be pressured to defend its legitimacy after being wounded by the incidents. The PRC as a great power is independent in terms of political-military relations with foreign countries.

Economic sanctions on human rights issues have been viewed as impractical, given China's size, because sanctions are more likely to hurt the sanctioner than the sanctionee. On the other hand, maintaining smooth foreign relations with Western countries, especially the United States and Japan, is in the vital interest of any South Korean regime in terms of national security as well as the economy and even the growth of domestic approval for the new regime. Furthermore, both Washington and Tokyo, which share strategic interests with Korea, have leverage to influence policy in Seoul.[11] While condemning the atrocities in Kwangju, foreign governments at first were reluctant to recognize, and even considered sanctioning, the new military junta.

Therefore, unlike the regime in Beijing after June 1989, which turned to coercive measures, the new military regime in Seoul after May 1980 had to make a gesture to compensate for its wounded legitimacy. In order to legitimate itself, the CCP regime did not have to promise democratization. Legitimation through economic nationalism and political conservatism appears to have been sufficient to maintain political stability.[12] In contrast, the emerging Korean military regime had to pledge democratic reform in the years to follow. It did not, however, advocate establishing a permanent form of limited democracy, such as "a Korean style of democracy," which its predecessor pushed. Instead, the Chun regime attempted to establish legitimacy by proclaiming itself a "transitory" regime toward full democracy. Institutionally, for the first time in Korean history, the new constitution of 1980 incorporated a single, nonrenewable tenure for the president, making it certain that a governmental transfer would take place at the end of Chun's term in seven years.[13] Moreover, the presidential election system, which had almost guaranteed the incumbent president's victory under the preceding Yusin constitution, was revised to introduce more competitive elements by enlarging the size of the electoral college[14] and by allowing party identification of electoral college candidates. Provided that elections were held in a reasonably free atmosphere, the rules would limit the advantages of the ruling party.

Throughout the political process in 1981–1988, this claim for a "transitory" regime greatly constrained the range of political options for Chun. First, it paved the way for the regime's liberalization. An authoritarian regime that identifies itself as temporal or transitory loses the grounds for its own existence, once the exigent circumstances (such as guerrilla warfare and economic crisis) that invited it are overcome. In Korea, when the national economy in 1983 showed clear signs of recovering from the crisis situation of 1979–1980, Chun's claim for an authoritarian system as a vehicle of economic recovery was expected to weaken soon. At the same time, economic success enabled the power holders to be more confident in taking risks in managing the regime. Feeling confident in power,[15] Chun relaxed political repression in December

1983. Contrary to his expectations, however, this political opening drove his regime into a more difficult situation. Civil society as well as political opposition was promptly resurrected and grew into a formidable alliance that soundly defeated the ruling party in the general election of 1985.

Second, the "transitory" nature of his regime with a clear time limit constrained Chun in his preparations to select his successor. When a personalistic dictator of an authoritarian regime is bound to leave the office according to a set timetable, succession increasingly becomes a contentious issue. Without a properly legitimated institutional mechanism for succession, such a situation is likely to bring about a lame-duck president, a division among elites within the regime, or a chaotic situation. Obviously Chun did not favor any of these scenarios and was eager to devise a succession mechanism under his command that would ensure a safe succession and preserve his influence over the successor after he left office. Toward this goal Chun tried to amend the constitution toward a parliamentary system in early 1986. But his scheme provoked strong resistance from the democratic forces that rallied around the call for a democratic constitution which would allow a direct presidential election.

Empowering the Opposition

While the role of the democratic movement in Korea's transition to democracy in 1987 is widely recognized, attention has rarely been given to the question of how a relatively recent movement could effectively wage a protracted struggle against a strong, cohesive authoritarian regime. This section examines how the legacy of the Kwangju uprising helped strengthen the infant mass movement, with a focus on "cultural framing," which comparative studies suggest is one of the three most important factors that determine the power of a social movement.[16]

Despite wielding strong influence at key junctures of Korean political development, the organized mass opposition movement, outside university campuses, did not have a long history. In the 1970s, it had consisted mostly of intellectuals, professionals, religious leaders, and independent political notables retired from electoral politics.[17] This *chaeya* (literally, "out in the field") opposition movement relied mostly on moral appeals and did not challenge the hegemonic discourses of the authoritarian regime, such as pro-Americanism, developmentalism, and anticommunism, but simply called for a restoration of democracy. With this petty-bourgeois nature, it focused more on voicing political protests in the street than attempting to build an organizational support base among the masses. When political opportunities opened following the breakdown of the Yusin regime in October 1979, the opposition movement was unable to lead and coordinate the explosive waves of the spontaneous mass actions. As a result, the new military effectively tore down and gagged this old-style movement after Kwangju's demise.

The foundation for building the new opposition movement[18] in the early 1980s was laid by an assessment of what went wrong during the Seoul Spring. Most prominent in the analysis of movement leaders were three aspects of the Kwangju uprising. First, the fact that the people's own armed forces killed the very citizens whom they were supposed to protect led to questions about the nature of the repressive state in Korea. Second, the United States, conventionally viewed as a promoter of liberal democracy and an ally, was now condemned for its complicity in the bloodshed. Third, the Kwangju uprising was viewed not just as a massacre but also as a heroic struggle against the repressive state.

The foremost influence the Kwangju uprising exerted on the new movement was on the formation of a sustainable, militant set of "collective action frames"[19] around which the populace could be mobilized. The bloody suppression of the uprising led the movement to discard its past reliance on the conventional discourse of "voice protest" and "responsive care from a Confucian state." Just as in the Tiananmen Square massacre, any hope that "the people's voices will be heard" had been ruthlessly trampled down. In the PRC, where the repressive regime is dependent, at least formally, on communist ideology, this experience led the post-Tiananmen movement to discard its hope in the CCP and to rely more on liberal ideology. In a reverse parallel, Korean democrats, under a repressive regime with the facade of liberal democracy, discarded their hope in liberal democracy and sought a radical solution.

A fad of radical social theories ranging from dependency/world system theory, neo-Marxist theories, Marxism-Leninism, and Maoism to even the North Korean ideology of Juche-ism swept through the movement's leadership.[20] The leaders now designated Korean society as (colonial) state monopoly capitalism in the service of foreign and domestic monopoly capital, and the Chun regime as a fascist state that repressed the masses, or *minjung*. The United States, as the representative of world capitalism and protector of foreign capital, was portrayed as the sponsor of the military dictatorship. Alleged U.S. complicity in the Kwangju bloodshed was seen as proof. Therefore, a revolutionary change, not reform, was deemed necessary. From a reading of the heroic saga of the Kwangju *minjung*, who fought against the state until being slain, new movement leaders, now baptized with radical theories, confirmed the revolutionary potential of the *minjung* and focused on organizing and mobilizing labor, peasants, and the urban poor.

The collective action frames of the new movement quickly gained support among young activists in the early 1980s and became a handy resource in fighting the regime, as well as in recruiting supporters. Since the government concealed the real story behind the uprising, a revelation of what happened in Kwangju turned out to be a powerful instrument to arouse action. Under the harsh repression of 1980–1983, this process of enlightenment powered underground organizations and the inversionary discourse summarized above. The name "Kwangju" came to symbolize righteousness against the repressive dictatorship.

While consensus formation produces a collective definition of a situation, for collective action to occur, "consensus mobilization" is necessary, consisting of deliberate attempts to spread the views of the movement among parts of a population.[21] The regime's turn from outright repression to liberalization after December 1983 provided a timely environment for consensus mobilization. From campuses to streets, churches, and workplaces, activists enthusiastically staged campaigns to mobilize consensus for the collective action frames. Again "Kwangju" was utilized as a living text to show how cruel and illegitimate the Chun regime was and what the nature of the United States was. Consensus mobilization was also facilitated by the ritualization of "Kwangju." Each year in May, nationwide student demonstrations were held in memory of the Kwangju uprising. Important sites of the Kwangju saga, such as Kŭmnam Avenue and Mangwŏl-dong cemetery, became sacred places. Kwangju turned into "symbolic capital" that could be invested against the hegemonic discourse of Chun authoritarianism.

Such a consensus mobilization based on the legacy of Kwangju had several important effects on the democratization movement. First, it provided the movement with strong symbolic power to resist waves of repression and fueled extreme forms of protests, including seventeen self-immolations and four persons who leaped out of tall buildings to their death.[22] Second, the new consensus supported the movement's efforts to build mass-oriented organizations, including Mint'ongnyŏn, or "Popular movement coalition for democracy and reunification," and facilitated linkages among them for a unified front, such as Kungmin undong ponbu, or "Headquarters for the national movement." In fact, these were the central forces behind a series of mass mobilizations in post-1985 politics, including the June 1987 Struggle. In a highly symbolic move, the last march by a crowd of more than a million, on July 9, 1987, was a funeral procession for Yi Hanyŏl, a student from Kwangju killed by a tear gas canister. At the end of the procession, Yi was buried in the Mangwŏl-dong cemetery alongside those killed during the Kwangju uprising. Finally, the anti-Americanism of the movement compelled Washington to encourage gradual democratic reform in Korea and to prevent the Chun regime from implementing another authoritarian regression.

Deterring a Military Solution in June 1987

As already noted, the relative power between regime and opposition is crucial in determining the outcome of a prolonged struggle in an authoritarian polity. If the power of an authoritarian regime, measured in both physical and political power, does not overwhelm the opposition, the cost of repression in the eyes of authoritarian leaders exceeds the cost of toleration. In such circumstances the regime tends to try to extricate itself from governmental power as soon as possible. If the power of an authoritarian regime is perceived to be equal to that of the opposition, a deadlock emerges and mutual incentives to negotiate grow. In this case, conventional theories contend that a split between hard-liners and soft-liners within the regime elite facilitates the choice of a negotiated transition to democracy.[23] If the power of an authoritarian regime is perceived to be weaker than that of the opposition, the opposition would be inclined to opt for a rupture strategy rather than a negotiated reform.

The situation in June 1987 in South Korea resembled the second type, stalemate. Researchers, however, have not found a meaningful division within the regime bloc.[24] Rather, the general understanding so far has been that top regime leaders, including Chun and his hand-picked successor Roh Tae Woo, did not disagree over the policy turn toward a negotiated exit from the standoff in June 1987.[25] The question then turns to what made them change their minds.

TABLE 6.2
Elite Perception of Relative Power, June 1987

Q: "There are many different opinions about the relative power between the regime and opposition in June 1987 before the June 29 Statement. Which of the following three opinions is the closest to yours?"

Response	Regime Elite	Opposition Elite	Total
The regime was strong enough and could have continued for a long time.	13 **(52.0)**	1 (3.8)	14 (27.5)
Neither was the regime in the condition of continuance, nor was the opposition in a position to overthrow.	7 (28.0)	10 (38.5)	17 (33.3)
The opposition was very strong and could have overthrown the regime.	5 (20.0)	15 **(57.7)**	20 (39.2)
Total	25 (100.0)	26 (100.0)	51 (100.0)

Chi-square = 15.80; DF = 2; P = 0.00037.
Numbers out of parentheses = number of cases; numbers in parentheses = percentage.

In the summer of 1996, I conducted a survey of sixty-one top political leaders from 1987 in both the government and opposition movement. They were senior government officials, national assemblymen from the opposition party, government ministers in charge of interior and political affairs, high-ranking Blue House staffers, heads of the National Security Planning Agency and Defense Security Command, and democratic movement leaders.[26] Table 6.2 shows that in June 1987 a majority of the regime elite were fairly confident about the regime's likelihood of surviving the crisis while a majority of the opposition elite also had a high level of confidence in their power to overthrow the regime.[27] The confidence on both sides suggests that each side was likely to pursue all-or-nothing strategies rather than attempt to extricate themselves from the deadlock.

In a situation in which protesters overpowered riot police in the street, the regime's choice of repression depended on the availability of the military option, as well as on how much confidence the power elite had in using such a method. Given the absence of a crack within the regime, Chun should have had little problem in calling troops onto the streets. The military solution, however, did not win a consensus among the power elite. As table 6.3 shows, more than one-half of the regime elites believed that military suppression was not a viable alternative. Among those who thought a military solution could be a way to restore law and order, none had strong confidence in it. Under these circumstances, Chun was unlikely to depend on the military to solve the crisis. Although he did attempt to deploy the armed forces to crack down on

TABLE 6.3
Elite Perception of Military Suppression as an Alternative

Q: [a] "Now please be reminded of the situation in June 1987. Do you think such a forceful suppression by the military could have been one way available to the government to maintain law and order during that period of social unrest?"

Response	Regime Elite	Opposition Elite	Total
Strongly yes	0	4	4
	(0.0)	(15.4)	(7.8)
Yes	12	10	22
	(48.0)	(38.5)	(43.1)
No	11	9	20
	(44.0)	(34.6)	(39.2)
Strongly no	2	3	5
	(8.0)	(11.5)	(9.8)
Total	25	26	51
	(100.0)	(100.0)	(99.9)

[a]In the survey, this question came immediately following a question asking for a personal evaluation of the regime's military suppression of the Kwangju uprising in 1980.

protests on June 19, he cancelled these orders hours later and turned to negotiation with the opposition.

One might argue that the sheer power of the democratic forces prevented
the Chun government from using the military.[28] Nevertheless, however strong
it may be, the people's power alone is not sufficient to explain a cohesive,
strong authoritarian regime's decision to abstain from a military mobilization. There are many cases in which greater people's power was effectively broken down by military action. The Tiananmen Square massacre in 1989 and
the Burmese massacres in 1988–1990 are recent examples. Hence we need to
consider more direct causes for elites' hesitation to mobilize the military.

The survey results suggest that the legacy of Kwangju contributed to the
regime elites' reluctance to use the military option. First, the projected negative consequences of the use of the military were amplified by what the Korean leaders learned from Kwangju in 1980. As noted earlier, the Kwangju
massacre, as a "birth defect," continued to plague Chun Doo Hwan throughout his rule. The regime tried to defend itself with the logic that the military
suppression of Kwangju was necessary to ensure national security and political stability. Nevertheless, it was not able to convince even some of the
regime's core elites. Table 6.4 shows that only twelve among twenty-three
regime elites agreed that the bloody suppression of the Kwangju uprising was
necessary.

In addition, given radical protest tactics such as suicides and violent attacks,
soldiers, once in the streets, would respond violently. That not only would
have violated Chun's pledge of a peaceful transfer of power, but perhaps more
importantly would also have spoiled the 1988 Olympic Games in Seoul. It is
noteworthy that at every critical moment in the post-1985 politics of liberalization, Chun repeatedly emphasized that he was able and ready to use military force to settle matters, but he never actually mobilized the forces.[29] In a
personal interview with the author, he mentioned that once the military in-

TABLE 6.4
Elite Opinion on the Regime's Justification for Suppressing Kwangju

Q: "The Kwangju incident of 1980 had a strong impact on the political process in the
1980s. Some argue that the violent suppression of the Kwangju uprising was necessary
to ensure national security and stability. Do you agree or disagree with that argument?"

Response	Regime Elites	Opposition Elites
Strongly agree	3 (13.0)	NA
Tend to agree	9 (39.1)	2 (8.0)
Tend to disagree	8 (34.8)	1 (4.0)
Strongly disagree	3 (13.0)	22 (88.0)
Total	23 (100.0)	25 (100.0)

truded into the civilian realm, it would become difficult to control their abuses of power.[30] He particularly seemed to have Kwangju in mind as he calculated the potential cost of repression when dealing with the popular demand for democratic reform.

Second, Kwangju affected the manner and extent of the U.S. government's intervention to deter a military solution. From the early period of the June crisis of 1987, Washington was actively involved in inducing both the Chun regime and the opposition to the negotiating table. On the one hand, the United States attempted to enhance the option of toleration on the part of the Chun regime by assuring Washington's support for the government and for its promises of political liberalization. At the same time the United States sought to deter repression by pointing to the improbability of the hard-line solution and by appealing directly to Korean military leaders to refrain from political intervention. As a result, after a meeting with U.S. Ambassador James Lilley on June 19, Chun canceled his order to deploy the armed forces to the cities. The United States also urged the opposition not to resort to extremist positions but to negotiate with the regime.

Washington's stance lay in part in its policy of encouraging the democratization of friendly nations, which it pursued successfully in Haiti and the Philippines. However, the primary reason was obviously related to U.S. interests in maintaining stability and in preventing the growth of anti-Americanism in Korea. The opposition's accusation of U.S. complicity in the suppression of Kwangju fueled anti-American sentiment among Koreans, dramatically demonstrated when the U.S. Cultural Center in Pusan was burned down in March 1982 and the U.S. Information Service in downtown Seoul was seized in May 1985. A further expansion of anti-Americanism in Korea would have posed a major problem for U.S. strategic interests in the region even beyond Korea. It is noteworthy that American officials in June 1987 took visible action to demonstrate to the Korean people that the United States was on the side of democracy[31] and sought preventive measures to avoid losing control of the flow of events, as they did in 1980. The U.S. government seemed to have learned from the past.

The Legacy of the Kwangju Uprising in Democratic Consolidation

Literature on comparative democratization has shown that regime transition is path dependent.[32] The types of transition, determined by the power of the authoritarian regime relative to the opposition, constrain the post-transition process toward democratic consolidation. Among the three main types of transition—collapse/defeat/withdrawal, extrication, and reform/transaction, in the order of the authoritarian regime's relative strength from weakest to strongest[33]—the South Korean case belongs to the "reform/transaction" type.[34] Similar cases include Spain in 1975–1976, Hungary in 1989, Poland in 1989, Brazil in the 1980s, Taiwan in the 1990s, and Chile in 1990.[35] Countries that have experienced this type of democratic transition exhibit strong continuity between the outgoing authoritarian regime and the incoming democratically elected regime. Democracy tends to be limited within a certain range, such as the introduction of competitive elections alone, while both the widening and deepening of democratic reform are likely to stall or be postponed. Therefore, to consolidate democracy, the necessary next step is to remove (or at least reduce the extent of) nondemocratic elements that undermine the operation of democratic politics. Of course, the first elected government, in affinity with the defunct dictatorship, tries to impede such a process. Hence, *protracted* struggle can be expected during the post-transition process between the government and the resurgent democratic opposition, which claims that democracy has yet to be achieved.

In Korea's post-transition politics following 1987, the legacy of the Kwangju uprising exerted strong influence over this protracted struggle. First, as in the pre-transition period, Kwangju continued as a rallying point from which the opposition pressured the new government to implement more democratic reforms. With more and more details concerning Kwangju unveiled by the liberalized press in the post-transition environment, the government became further and further constrained by the opposition's demand for investigating the government's suppression of the uprising and for punishing those responsible. A series of congressional hearings in late 1988 on the Kwangju massacre along with other wrongdoings of the defunct Chun regime was the culmination of the opposition-led National Assembly's attempts to seize the political initiative and force the incumbent Roh Tae Woo government toward reform. The opposition was able to force the resignation from the National Assembly of ex-General Chung Ho-yŏng, the former special war commander and army chief of staff who was strongly suspected of having directed the paratroopers in Kwangju in May 1980.

Second, the legacy of the Kwangju uprising was instrumental in Roh's attempt to sever links with Chun and other authoritarian allies and to push the "forward legitimacy" of democratic reform. The aforementioned congressional hearings on the Kwangju uprising in late 1988 and the subsequent congressional inquiries, which ended with Chun's testimony to the National Assembly on December 31, 1989, provided Roh with the decisive momentum to disassociate himself from his former boss, who had anointed him as successor. Cultivating the heightened public mood against the former regime through a vivid display of political theater on the massacre and other evils, Roh not only forced Chun into self-exile at a remote Buddhist temple but also purged his cronies from powerful posts. The removal of General Ch'oe P'yŏng-uk from the Defense Security Command in November 1988 served as a representative example. Such an effort to uproot pro-Chun forces facilitated the subordination of the military to the elected government, without which the bold purge in 1993, undertaken by the next president, Kim Yong Sam, would have been much more risky and difficult, if not impossible.[36]

The legacy of the Kwangju uprising also played a big part in bringing ex-presidents Chun Doo Hwan and Roh Tae Woo to trial in December 1995. Both the conspicuousness of Kwangju in Korea's democratization struggle and the temporal proximity of May 1980 generated a high level of grievance among Koreans against the authoritarian perpetrators. When, in the summer of 1995, the Kim Yong Sam government decided not to prosecute the leaders of the past regime, it fueled nationwide protests, ultimately forcing Kim to reverse his decision.[37]

Comparative studies of democratization caution against such a trial of previous authoritarian leaders because it may invite instability or breakdown in the incipient democracy.[38] Such action may arouse considerable discontent from a portion of the population, including the elite, that sympathizes with the former regime (as in Spain after Franco), or the military might consider the legal proceedings a serious threat to its own existence (as in Argentina under Alfonsin). Neither happened in South Korea, where the "trials of the century" invited not a high degree of political instability but rather a greater consolidation of democracy by firmly bringing to a close the legacy of military rule and political violence.[39] Korea showed that it had advanced toward a mature democracy.[40]

Conclusion

South Korea has experienced a dramatic democratization over the last two decades, and the legacy of the Kwangju uprising has been one of the main facilitating factors in the process. It weakened military dictator Chun Doo Hwan's legitimacy to the extent that he had to resort to the claim of a "transitory" regime that promised an ultimate return to democracy. This constrained the range of alternatives at his disposal. On the other hand, Kwangju furnished the opposition movement with ample resources for a strong, militant collective action to resist waves of authoritarian repression. It was in this context that the Chun regime refrained from using military force to quell the popular demand for democratic reform in the mid-1980s.

Despite the reformist path of the Korean democratic transition, continued progress in democratic consolidation after the first competitive election in 1987 was in no way guaranteed. In this context, the legacy of the Kwangju uprising again turned out to be a main facilitator of democratization. Through a protracted process of investigation and punishment of those responsible for the Kwangju tragedy, the opposition was able to grasp reform initiatives in 1988–1989, while the authoritarian-turned-civilian government under Roh Tae Woo utilized these circumstances to sever its link with the past. In the 1990s, the authoritarian past was discredited through the trials of previous authoritarian leaders, made possible in large part by the emotionally charged memory of Kwangju, while the democratic consensus was consolidated.

Notes

1. English-language surveys of South Korea's democratization process include, among many others, Hyug Baeg Im, "Politics of Transition: Democratic Transition from Authoritarian Rule in South Korea" (Ph.D. diss., University of Chicago, 1989); James Cotton, "From Authoritarianism to Democracy in South Korea," *Political Studies* 37 (1989): 244–59; Sung-joo Han, "South Korea: Politics in Transition," in Larry Diamond, Juan J. Linz, and Seymour Martin Lipset, eds., *Democracy in Developing Countries: Asia*, vol. 3 (Boulder: Lynne Rienner, 1989); Wonmo Dong, "University Students in South Korean Politics: Patterns of Radicalization in the 1980s," *Journal of International Affairs* 40 (1987): 233–55; Doh Chul Shin, *Mass Politics and Culture in Democratizing Korea* (Cambridge: Cambridge University Press, 1999); Larry Diamond and Byung-Kook Kim, eds., *Consolidating Democracy in South Korea* (Boulder: Lynne Rienner, 2000); and Jung-kwan Cho, "From Authoritarianism to Consolidated Democracy in South Korea" (Ph.D. diss., Yale University, 2000).

2. The Tiananmen Square massacre is selected for comparison on the grounds that it showed considerable similarity with the Kwangju uprising in the cultural context as well as striking parallels in the process of collective action. For details, see Karen Eggleston, "Kwangju 1980 and Beijing 1989," *Asian Perspective* 15, no. 2 (1991): 33–73.

3. Juan J. Linz defined authoritarian regimes as "political systems with limited, not responsible, political pluralism, without elaborate and guiding ideology, but with distinctive mentalities, without extensive or intensive political mobilization, except at some points in their development, and in which a leader or occasionally a small group exercises power within formally ill-defined limits but actually quite predictable ones." "Totalitarian and Authoritarian Regimes," in Fred I. Greenstein and Nelson W. Polsby, eds., *Handbook of Political Science*, vol. 3, *Macropolitical Theory* (Reading, Mass.: Addison-Wesley, 1975), 264.

4. The literature on democratization is too large to summarize. To briefly survey the factors identified by social scientists to date, see Samuel P. Huntington, *The Third Wave: Democratization in the Late Twentieth Century* (Norman: University of Oklahoma Press, 1991). For representative works of theoretical and comparative treat-

ments, see Guillermo O'Donnell, Philippe C. Schmitter, and Laurence Whitehead, eds., *Transitions from Authoritarian Rule*, 5 vols. (Baltimore: Johns Hopkins University Press, 1986); and Juan J. Linz and Alfred Stepan, *Problems of Democratic Transition and Consolidation* (Baltimore: Johns Hopkins University Press, 1996).

5. Quote from Juan J. Linz, *The Breakdown of Democratic Regimes: Crisis, Breakdown, and Reequilibration* (Baltimore: Johns Hopkins University Press, 1978), 16.

6. Regime legitimacy should be distinguished from performance legitimacy, or efficacy. While regime legitimacy refers to a level of belief among the ruled and rulers in the way in which a political system is institutionalized, performance legitimacy is more or less a level of belief in the policy outcomes and is subject to temporal fluctuation. Although the continued low performance of a political regime or an extreme level of crisis resulting from a policy failure may lead to the erosion of regime legitimacy, the distinction between efficacy and regime legitimacy is necessary for an analysis of regime change. Individual governments fall due to policy failures and the consequential decline of popularity. However, the demise of political regimes needs further erosion of public belief in the institutions itself. See Linz, *Breakdown of Democratic Regimes*, 18–22.

7. A classic argument on the importance of revolutionary legitimacy as a confining condition is found in Otto Kirchheimer, "Confining Conditions and Revolutionary Breakthroughs," *American Political Science Review* 59 (1965): 964–74. Mexico under the PRI and Cuba under Castro are other examples of strong regimes established through revolution.

8. For extensive theoretical and empirical treatment on the distinction between a hierarchical and a nonhierarchical military regime, see Linz and Stepan, *Problems of Democratic Transition*, especially 66–68.

9. P. Nikoforos Diamandouros, "Regime Change and the Prospects for Democracy in Greece: 1974–1983," in O'Donnell, Schmitter, and Whitehead, *Transitions from Authoritarian Rule: Southern Europe*, 153.

10. For an extensive treatment of China's civil society, see Barrett L. McCormick, Su Shaozhi, and Xiao Xiaoming, "The 1989 Democracy Movement: A Review of the Prospects for Civil Society in China," *Pacific Affairs* 65 (1992): 182–202.

11. For a comprehensive treatment of the U.S.-Korean relationship, see Baeho Hahn, "Major Issues in the American-Korean Alliance," in Youngnok Koo and Dae-Sook Suh, eds., *Korea and the United States: A Century of Cooperation* (Honolulu: University of Hawaii Press, 1984), 91–110; and Wookhee Shin, "Geopolitical Determinants of Political Economy: The Cold War and South Korean Political Economy," *Asian Perspective* 18, no. 2 (1994): 119–40.

12. Yang Zhong, "Legitimacy Crisis and Legitimation in China," *Journal of Contemporary Asia* 26, no. 2 (1996): 201–20.

13. From the beginning, ideologues of the Chun Doo Hwan regime justified the establishment of the Fifth Republic by stressing its contribution to political development through the introduction of a presidential term limit. Hur Mun Do, interview by author, Seoul, July 8, 1996.

14. The size of the presidential electoral college under the *Yusin* regime was 2,359 in 1972 and 2,583 in 1978. The first and only electoral college of the Fifth Republic was more than double this size, consisting of 5,278 in February 1981.

15. A ruling party's opinion survey conducted from October 29 to November 13, 1983, found that Koreans gave high approval to the economic performance of the government while retaining considerable distrust of the government's pledge for a single presidential term. Jong Ryul Rhee, *Chŏnhwan'gi ŭi nolli wa hyŏnsil* [Logic and reality of Korean politics in transition] (Seoul: Pagyŏngsa, 1988), 13–29.

16. A few exemplary works (among others) in regard to framing issues on the Korean democratization movements include Chulhee Chung, "Structure, Culture, and Mobilization: The Origins of the June Uprising in South Korea" (Ph.D. diss., State University of New York at Buffalo, 1994); and Joon-Oh Jang, "Discourses on the Korean Student Movement in the 1980s: Democracy as a Master Frame" (Ph.D. diss., University of Kansas, 1994).

The other two most important factors in the movement's power are political opportunities and mobilizing structure. Major works in this paradigm of "political process theory" include Sidney Tarrow, *Power in Movement: Social Movements, Collective Action, and Politics* (Cambridge: Cambridge University Press, 1994); and Doug McAdam, John D. McCarthy, and Mayer N. Zald, eds., *Comparative Perspectives on Social Movements: Political Opportunities, Mobilizing Structures, and Cultural Framings* (Cambridge: Cambridge University Press, 1996).

17. For details on the opposition movement in the 1970s, see Hak-Kyu Sohn, *Authoritarianism and Opposition in South Korea* (London: Routledge, 1989).

18. I do not mean that there was a break or a quantum leap between the old style and the new movement, however. The seeds for the new movement were already growing in the late 1970s. As protests continued to deepen against the *Yusin* regime, the *chaeya* expanded in number and in the variety of occupations and social statuses. It gradually changed into a kind of a peak organization over the sectoral movement organizations led by young activists. The young leaders with a background mostly as student movement dropouts in the late 1960s and the early 1970s became more inclined to a strategy of building mass mobilization than to relying on verbal and symbolic protests from prominent figures alone. However, under the accelerating repression of the *Yusin* regime, such a transformation was slow and did not produce substantial outcomes. The only exception (though it was premature and quickly defeated by the authorities) that attempted to substantially organize a mass movement under a strong elite leadership was the case of *Namminjŏn*, short for *Namjosŏn minjok haebang chŏnsŏn* (National liberation front for South Korea). For a study of *Namminjŏn* and other movements, see Hee Yeon Cho, *Hyŏndae han'guk sahoe undong kwa chojik* [Contemporary social movements and organizations in Korea] (Seoul: Hanul, 1993).

19. For details on collective action frames, see Tarrow, *Power in Movement*, 22–23, 118–34.

20. An excellent study in English on the evolution of the Korean movement's discourse is found in Gi-Wook Shin, "Marxism, Anti-Americanism, and Democracy in South Korea: An Examination of Nationalist Intellectual Discourse," *Positions* 3 (1995): 508–34.

21. Hank Johnston and Bert Klandermans, eds., *Social Movements and Culture* (Minneapolis: University of Minnesota Press, 1995); and Tarrow, *Power in Movement*, 124.

22. In contrast, only one case of protest by self-immolation (by Chŏn T'aeil) was reported in the 1970s. The numbers are based on "O'ilpal wanjŏn haegyŏl kwa chŏngŭi silhyŏn hŭimangŭl wihan kwagŏ ch'ŏngsan kungmin wiwŏnhoe" (National committee for the purge of the past in order to completely resolve the May 18 problems and to realize justice), *Minjok minju yŏlsa, hŭisaengja, ŭimunsa myŏngye hoebogŭl wihan che-ich'a haksulhoe ŭi charyojip* [Proceedings of the second conference on the restoration of honor for martyrs, victims and those who suffered suspicious deaths] (Seoul, 1997), 140.

23. O'Donnell and Schmitter assert that "there is no transition whose beginning is not the consequences—direct or indirect—of important divisions within the author-itarian regime itself, principally along the fluctuating cleavage between hard-liners and soft-liners" (see *Transitions from Authoritarian Rule*, 19).

24. For a representative work that argues the existence of the hard-line/soft-line split, see Hyug Baeg Im, "Politics of Transition: Democratic Transition from Authoritarian Rule in South Korea." However, many empirical studies conducted in the 1990s, when more data became available, found a stronger cohesion within the regime and an absence of a meaningful split over policies. For instance, see Dae Hwa Chung, "Han'guk ŭi chŏngch'i pyŏndong 1987–1992 [Political change in Korea, 1987–1992]" (Ph.D. diss., Seoul National University, 1995).

25. Sŏng Ik Kim, *Chŏn Tu-hwan yuksŏng chŭngŏn* [Real voice testimony by Chun Doo Hwan] (Seoul: Chosŏn ilbosa, 1992); and Cho Kap-je, "No T'ae-u yuksŏng hoegorok" (Real voice memoirs of Roh Tae Woo), *Wŏlgan chosŏn*, June 1999, 207–20.

26. Sixty-one political elites (twenty-eight regime and thirty-three opposition elites) in 1987 were personally interviewed by the author between May and June 1996. The total number of responses reported in this paper is not sixty-one, however, because the time limit, which varied from interview to interview, often prevented the author from asking all the questions in the prepared interview questionnaire. For more details on the elite survey, including selection methods and full questionnaire, see Jung-kwan Cho, "From Authoritarianism to Consolidated Democracy in South Korea."

27. The sources of such confidence on the regime's side were, first of all, confidence in achievements by the regime, a high level of internal cohesiveness within the regime, availability of powerful and disciplined military forces, existence of a considerable proportion of conservative, stability-oriented people, and weakness in the organized opposition. The sources of the opposition's confidence lay in, first, the lowest level of legitimacy of the authoritarian regime at the point, the cohesiveness of the opposition converged into the *Kungmin undong ponbu* (Headquarters for national movements for a democratic constitution), and a high level of spontaneous visible support for democracy from the middle and lower classes, growing in quality and quantity through increasingly affluent economic conditions.

28. Most accounts by individual regime elites of 1987 emphasize this point. For example, see Kim Yong-gap, *Kojiga paro chŏginde yesŏ mal sunŭn ŏpta* [So close to the top of the mountain, we cannot stop here] (Seoul: Muae, 1991); and Jong Ryul Rhee, *Tae-gwŏn ŭi chubyŏn* [Around the presidential power] (Seoul: Naeil, 1991).

29. Sŏng Ik Kim, *Chŏn Tu-hwan yuksŏng chŭngŏn*, passim.

30. Interview at his house in Seoul on August 22, 1998. I am grateful to Dr. Sang-Hyon Yoon for arranging the interview, and to the NEAC Council on Korean Studies of the Association for Asian Studies for a travel grant.

31. In regard to the elite consensus on Korean policies in Washington at the time, it is helpful to see Stephen Solarz, "Applying Leverages on South Korea," *New York Times*, May 17, 1987. Solarz was chairman of the House Subcommittee on Pacific and Asian Affairs.

32. Representative works calling for path dependency include Terry Lynn Karl, "Dilemmas of Democratization in Latin America," *Comparative Politics* 23, no. 1 (1990): 1–21; Terry Lynn Karl and Philippe Schmitter, "Modes of Transition in Latin America, Southern and Eastern Europe," *International Social Science Journal* 128 (1991): 269–84.

33. For details of the tripology, see J. Samuel Valenzuela, "Democratic Consolidation in Post-Transitional Settings: Notion, Process, and Facilitating Conditions," in Scott Mainwaring, Guillermo O'Donnell, and J. Samuel Valenzuela, eds., *Issues in Democratic Consolidation* (Notre Dame, Ind.: University of Notre Dame Press, 1992), 73–78; and Scott Mainwaring, "Transitions to Democracy and Democratic Consolidation: Theoretical and Comparative Issues," in *Issues in Democratic Consolidation*, 317–26. Samuel P. Huntington adopted the same categorization but with different terminology: replacement, transplacement, and transformation (*Third Wave*, 114).

34. The South Korean case does not fit into the first category because the outgoing authoritarian rulers held on to power significantly beyond the crisis that set off the transition. Nor does it belong to the "extrication" category because this category requires much weaker power of the outgoing rulers than that of Korea. In the case of extrication, the outgoing rulers should be more or less trying to negotiate a minimal set of terms for their retreat. In 1987 Korea, the authoritarian regime could impose terms and conditions with relatively powerful strength and confidence. It did not have to install a safety outlet, such as reserved domains and military prerogatives, as shown in Uruguay in 1985 and Peru in 1980. During the transition the Korean case showed no sign of breaking the formal rules and framework of the outgoing authoritarian regime. For details on the definition of the Korean path to democratic transition, see Jung-kwan Cho, "From Authoritarianism to Consolidated Democracy in South Korea."

35. The comparatively stronger imposition of an authoritarian legacy to the next democratic government made the Chilean case an exceptional one even in the "reform" category, however.

36. On the taming of the Korean military after the democratic transition of 1987, see Jung-kwan Cho, "Taming the Military to Consolidate Democracy: The South Korean Experience," *Pacific Focus* 16, no. 1 (2001): 117–48.

37. For details, see Sunhyuk Kim, "From Resistance to Representation: Civil Society in South Korean Democratization" (Ph.D. diss., Stanford University, 1996), chap. 6.

38. Huntington, *Third Wave*, 211–31; and Alexandra Barahona de Brito, *Human Rights and Democratization in Latin America: Uruguay and Chile* (Oxford: Oxford University Press, 1997).

39. Survey results reported by Doh Chul Shin show evidence of increasing democratic consensus through the trials. See Shin, *Mass Politics and Culture*, 216–18.

40. However, the trials also carried negative effects on democratic development, especially in terms of the rule of law, which should be consolidated to develop a stable democracy. For details, see James M. West, "Martial Lawlessness: The Legal Aftermath of Kwangju," *Pacific Rim Law and Policy Journal* 6 (January 1997): 85–168.

7

Victims and Heroes: Competing Visions of May 18

Don Baker

IN ORDER TO APPRECIATE THE SIGNIFICANCE FOR KOREAN HISTORY of that tragic event known as "May 18" *(Oilp'al),* we need to investigate not only the general contours of what actually happened in Kwangju between May 18 and May 27, 1980, but also how what happened has been remembered and interpreted in the decades since. Two decades is not a very long period of time, as historians usually measure it. Nevertheless, it is long enough for the way the events of two decades ago have been perceived and remembered to have changed significantly, including significant changes in the way I personally remember and interpret those events.

For example, in 1988 I presented a paper at a Canadian Asian Studies conference that I rather arrogantly subtitled "What Happened in May 1980." If I tried to present such a paper today, there would be a couple of important differences. First, the local Republic of Korea consulate general would not contact the panel organizer to demand that the consulate be allowed to send someone to present a contrary view. (Someone at the consulate general in Toronto made such a telephone call in 1988.) As the conference that led to this publication clearly shows, no longer is the Korean government afraid of scholars putting the events of May 1980 under a scholarly microscope. In fact, with Kim Dae Jung as president, there was a 180-degree turn in the official attitude toward the tragic events that transpired twenty years ago in the largest city in southwestern Korea. Rather than a stain on Korea's reputation, the resistance of the people of Kwangju to the military coup of Chun Doo Hwan and his *Hanahoe* (Society of unity) co-conspirators is now seen as an event of historic import in the democratization of Asia. Events once labeled a riot and a threat to Korea's national security are now described as a righteous uprising of brave citizens who risked their lives to resist oppression and bring democracy to Korea. Visitors to Kwangju today are even encouraged to visit "the May 18 democratic uprising historic sites" with the aid of a map and guidebook, available in both Korean and English, distributed by the Kwangju city government.

This change in how May 18 is perceived in official circles in Korea (and in the United States as well) is the first significant change affecting how I now discuss and analyze the events in Kwangju. I no longer have to argue with the South Korean government. The other significant change is in how I personally interpret May 18, how I try to make sense of what I saw and heard that May and how I convey my understanding of May 18 to my students.

No longer do I claim to know what really happened in May 1980. First, I was in Seoul on May 18 and didn't arrive in Kwangju until May 28, the day after the army reentered the city. I was not an eyewitness to the events I have described and analyzed in lectures. Moreover, by the time I arrived in Kwangju, the most active resisters, those who formed the Citizens' Army *(sim-in'gun)*, were either dead or hiding. The people I observed and talked with in Kwangju were traumatized and depressed. I saw no proud heroes there. I saw only victims, such as the mother chasing her son's coffin down the street crying "don't go," or the long line of grandmothers lined up outside the Sangmu Judo Studio to see if the bodies of their grandchildren were inside. The young men I talked to told me how frightened they had been. No one bragged about risking all for democracy. In fact, some confessed that they had been too paralyzed by fear to leave their homes on the morning of May 27, when the army began its final assault, though they clearly heard the pleas of the young woman who rode through the streets of Kwangju in a sound truck pleading for them to come to the Provincial Office building to help the young men who were making a last stand there.

If I relied on my own experience in Kwangju in the aftermath of those terrible ten days, I would have an incomplete, even distorted, picture of the events that now go under the label "May 18." Obviously my personal experiences, and those of the people I talked to in Kwangju in late May 1980, provide only a glimpse of what occurred throughout the city and its surrounding area and how those events would be interpreted later. For example, no one told me at that time about Yun Sang-wŏn and the dispute between his group of hard-liners and the more moderate members of the Settlement Committee during those few days when Kwangju was facing the imminent return of Chun Doo Hwan's martial law forces. Nor did any of us know at the time that the apparent defeat of democratic forces in Kwangju was temporary and that fifteen years later Chun Doo Hwan and Roh Tae Woo would be punished for their crimes.

When I, as a historian, attempt to reconstruct and impart meaning to the past, I need to take into account what others say about why and how Kwangju was attacked and why and how the people of Kwangju responded the way they did. Moreover, as someone who cares deeply for this city whose citizens introduced me to Korean culture, I have to be careful not to allow my personal experiences and the emotions they evoke to undermine the scholarly objectivity both teaching and academic writing require.

Creating a Usable Past

In trying to integrate my personal experiences with what other eyewitnesses and scholars have said and written about May 18 in order to obtain a more reliable, more complex and nuanced, and hopefully more objective understanding of May 18 and its significance, I found a recent book by Paul Cohen about a traumatic event in modern Chinese history to be quite useful. In *History in Three Keys: The Boxers as Event, Experience, and Myth* (1997) Cohen focuses on a religious uprising in northern China one hundred years ago. He makes no explicit reference to Korea or May 18. However, the framework he adopts for analyzing the historiography of the Boxer uprising is, I believe, applicable to May 18.

Cohen suggests that we distinguish three different ways of viewing and discussing important historical events. First, we need to distinguish the contemporaneous reports of those who were actual eyewitnesses or participants from the accounts historians weave from those reports later. He points out that later reconstructions of an event by historians are quite different from what those who actually participated in or witnessed that event saw and heard. For one thing, historians have the benefit of multiple accounts, which allows them to integrate what happened at the same time in different places into a single narrative. They also have the benefit of hindsight telling them which particular incidents in an event are more important (i.e., have more significant consequences) than others and therefore merit more attention. In other words, historians are able to make sense of an event in a way those present when the event occurred are unable to because participants and contemporary observers, first, witness only a part of what is going on and, second, do not know yet what impact the events they witnessed will have in the long term.[1]

Cohen suggests that we should not only distinguish the historian's retelling of an event from the accounts of individual participants and observers but should also notice that beyond the retelling and reconstruction of an important event is a third perspective generated by the significance ascribed to that event. When later generations draw lessons from a significant historical event in order to guide them in coping with problems they face in their own time, they change the way that event is viewed and discussed. Cohen calls this third perspective, refashioning the past to meet the needs of the present, the construction of a "myth."

He uses the term "myth" not to imply that historical lessons are drawn from misleading premises, but to emphasize that the mythical retelling of an event is designed not so much to relate what actually occurred as it is to encourage certain sentiments, arouse certain emotions, serve certain political functions, or fulfill certain psychological needs.[2] As Cohen uses the term, "myths" are not necessarily false. By their nature, however, they are normally one-sided because they tend to focus on or isolate particular elements of an event, taking them out of their original historical context in order to make them more applicable to more recent concerns. A prime example of such myth making is general-turned-president Park Chung Hee's 1970s exaltation of military heroes such as Admiral Yi Sun-sin far beyond the regard they were held in by their peers. Another example would be the twentieth-century interpretation of the fifteenth-century invention of the Korean alphabet, which is often anachronistically portrayed as an attempt to create a graphic representation of the distinctiveness of Korean civilization.

Cohen's dissection of history into three categories—eyewitness reports, historian's narratives, and hortatory reiteration—proved useful to me as I grappled with what the events of May 18 mean to me, and how I should talk to my students about Kwangju in the broader context of modern Korean history. His analysis of the historiography of the Boxer Rebellion has reminded me that, in order to better appreciate the significance of May 18 for modern Korean history, I need to go beyond my own isolated individual memories and those of others who were there. He has also reminded me that I need to dig beneath the surface of historical reconstructions of the events that transpired between May 18 and May 27 to see how those events have been "mythologized," given a significance for Korea today. In other words, I need to investigate how the raw data of experienced history (eyewitness accounts) and the narratives of reconstructed history (attempts by historians to weave various threads of experienced history into coherent narratives) have provided the foundations on which a usable past (Cohen's "myth") has been erected.

One route to identifying the significance imparted to May 18 over the last two decades is to examine how May 18 is portrayed in popular culture: literature, music, drama, and movies. This can tell us what May 18 means, or at least what writers, musicians, and movie producers want it to mean.

A preliminary and admittedly incomplete examination of those four avenues to recreating May 18 has led me to the tentative conclusion that there are now two intertwined but nonetheless distinguishable approaches to May

18, two "myths" in Cohen's terminology. In the first, the people of Kwangju are portrayed as innocent victims who were mostly apolitical until they were attacked by Chun Doo Hwan's paratroopers. In the second "myth," the people of Kwangju are depicted as heroes, idealistic political activists who risked their lives in a noble attempt to build a democratic and just society on the Korean peninsula.

Yin and Yang, Victims and Heroes

It might be useful to distinguish these contrasting interpretations of May 18 in terms of yin and yang. The focus on the people of Kwangju as victims, a focus more on what happened to them than on their resistance to brutality and injustice, would be the "yin" perspective, borrowing a term from traditional Sino-Korean philosophy for the things, events, and processes in the universe that are more passive than active, more like water than metal. The emphasis on how the people of Kwangju responded to the brutality of the martial law forces would, in contrast, be the "yang" perspective, using the traditional term for things strong and forceful. The labels yin and yang indicate more than the contrast of passive suffering with active resistance. Yin and yang in traditional Korean thought, and on the flag of the Republic of Korea today, are intertwined, reminding us that active and passive define and create each other. Any attempt to understand yin without reference to yang would produce incomplete, and therefore distorted, knowledge of both yin and yang. In this respect, the relationship between yin and yang is like the relationship between heat and cold. Cold is always defined relative to heat and vice versa. Nevertheless, in most situations either yin or yang, heat or cold, is more salient.

The same holds true with interpretations of May 18. Though we can find both victims and heroes in most accounts of what happened over those ten days, some interpretations are more colored by a yin focus on innocent victims and others by a yang focus on heroic resisters.

Early narratives of May 18 generally focused on the victimization rather than the heroism of the people of Kwangju. The men and women of Kwangju were primarily remembered during the Chun Doo Hwan years as innocent victims who rose up in spontaneous outbursts of righteous anger at the brutality of Chun's martial law forces. Back then, the events of May 1980 were usually referred to as a *haksal* (massacre) or, in milder terms, a *sakŏn* (incident). Only near the end of the 1980s did the characterization of May 18 as a *minjuhwa undong* (democratization movement) began to gain favor.

Later, as the memories of pain and fear faded, the image of the people of Kwangju as victims began to be complemented by an image of the people

of Kwangju as heroes, fighting for the abstract ideal of democracy or for social justice. This change in the image of Kwangjuites is graphically represented by the difference between the old, unofficial Mangwŏl-dong cemetery, with nothing but graves and mementos of the dead, and the new,
official Mangwŏl-dong cemetery, with its somber rows of tombs protected
by statues of heroic resisters behind a democracy gate and a people's resistance memorial tower.[3]

In the 1990s, as monuments were erected at Mangwŏl-dong and elsewhere
to honor those who died during those terrible ten days in May, narratives of
the events that led to their deaths grew more diverse, complex, and nuanced.
On the one hand, those who preferred to talk about the people of Kwangju as
heroes highlighted the roles played by Yun Sang-wŏn and other Kwangjuites
who had an ideological agenda and earned for Kwangju the proud titles "city
of justice" and "Mecca of democracy." On the other hand, those who emphasized consequences more than motives expanded the label of victim to cover
not only those who were killed and wounded by martial law forces but also
those who served in those martial law forces.

Almost every narrative of Kwangju recognizes that there were both heroes
and victims in Kwangju in May 1980, and that many times the same person
was both a victim and a hero. However, narratives differ on where they prefer
to place emphasis: on the heroic aspects of the struggle against brutality or on
the tragic impact of that brutality on the men, women, and children who were
in Kwangju between May 18 and May 27, 1980.

Literature

Literature is a good place to start searching for indications of how the general
population understands an important historical event. In this sense, the dominant image of the people of Kwangju is that they were the innocent victims
of an unjustified attack on May 18.

Probably the best known piece of literature directly related to Kwangju is
the poem by Kim Chun-t'ae entitled "Kwangju, the Cross of Our Nation"
(Kwangju, ah Kwangju, uri nara ŭi shipchaga). Kim was a high school teacher
of Korean literature in Kwangju and wrote this poem in the midst of tragedy.
The following stanza gives some indication of how Kim saw his fellow
Kwangjuites at that time.

> Our father: Where has he gone?
> Mother: Where has she fallen?
> Our sons: Where were they killed and buried?
> And our lovely daughters

Where are they lying, mouths agape?
Where were our spirits
torn apart, ripped to shreds?[4]

There are no heroes in this poem, no Citizens' Army recruits raising their guns high or fighting valiantly against paratroopers. Instead, there are only the innocent dead, mourned by their parents, children, or siblings. Kwangju as the cross of Korea is not the cross held high as a triumphant symbol of resurrection in Roman Catholic religious processions. Instead, it is the crucifix on which Christ, the lamb of God, died. It is a symbol of suffering.

Fiction writers have tended to focus on the innocent victims who suffered from the brutal military assault on Kwangju rather than the leaders who called out for democracy and fought against the martial law forces. For example, in the short story "Spring Day" (Pom nal), by Im Cheol-woo (Im Ch'ŏr-u), originally published in 1984, the main character is a young man named Sang-ju who becomes suicidal and insane out of guilt at the death of his friend Myŏng-bu. He believes that Myŏng-bu pounded on his family's gate to ask that it be opened so that he could escape the paratroopers. When Sang-ju and the rest of his family failed to open that gate, Myŏng-bu was caught by the paratroopers and killed.

That Myŏng-bu was killed during May 18 is clear. He is said to be buried in the Mangwŏl-dong cemetery, and there are references to the tragic events of May years earlier. However, there is no explicit description of the events in Kwangju, and whether Myŏng-bu was an active member of the resistance or was chased down just because he was a young man is not clear; the narrator notes only that Myŏng-bu believed in fighting against injustice. In this story, it is not what Myŏng-bu did or did not do that May that is important. Rather, the impact of his death on Sang-ju, who was not an active resister, is the focus of the narrator's concern.[5]

Another Im Cheol-woo story published about the same time, "Shared Journey" (Tonghaeng), does take as one of the main characters a leader of the Kwangju resistance. However, the focus is not on his role in the resistance but on how he has been on the run ever since, and how both his life and the lives of his friends have been changed for the worse by the events of May 18.

In "Shared Journey," a friend of the narrator suddenly appears after a year and a half absence, disguised as a Hyundai employee. The narrator expresses concern about meeting someone who is wanted by the police but meets him anyway. Neither the narrator nor his friend is presented as a particularly heroic individual. In fact, they are described as lonely, exhausted, and more than a little depressed. The hunted man, for example, is described as always on the move, unable to maintain regular contact with friends and family.

Kwangju itself is portrayed as traumatized by May 18, turning into a city full of isolated individuals who are emotionally dead.[6]

Another popular story set in Kwangju is Kong Sŏn-ok's "Parched Season" (Mok marŭn kyejŏl, 1993). This story takes place twelve years after the Kwangju tragedy, yet the people of Kwangju apparently are still suffering in its aftermath.

The characters in Kong's story are impoverished women who live in public housing in Kwangju. The only mention of someone who actually was involved in May 18 is a brief reference to the death of the boyfriend of a bar waitress named Cho. Her boyfriend, we are told, had never recovered physically or mentally from fighting in the Citizens' Army in 1980. The major characters in this story include a woman who runs a bar and gets thrown in jail when she hires two underage waitresses. Other key characters include the bar owner's mute and deaf daughter as well as the waitress Cho, whose handicap is an artificial leg, and the narrator herself, who is a divorced, unemployed mother. The characters are not particularly heroic. Nor are they particularly political, though they appear depressed over Kim Dae Jung's defeat in the 1992 presidential election, an obvious allusion to the fact that Kwangju had lost again. Kong's short story, though not about May 18 per se, reinforces an image of the people of Kwangju as victims, people who have not been dealt with fairly by life.[7]

Even though Kwangju was heartened when Kim Dae Jung finally won the presidency in 1997, more recent fictional treatments of May 18 and its aftermath still tend to portray May 18 more as a tragedy than a heroic epic. One surprising example of this victimization theme is a recent novel by the highly political writer Hwang Sŏg-yŏng. *An Old Garden* (Orae toen chŏngwŏn) is a love story and not just a fictional recreation of the events of May 18.[8] In fact, May 18 takes up only a small part of this two-volume work. Most of this novel is set years later, when the primary narrator, O Hyŏn-u, is released from prison in 1998, after eighteen years behind walls for antigovernment activity, and reads the diary left for him by his common-law wife, who died before he was released.

That diary relates events in the lives of fictional characters both before and after May 1980. For example, the wife, Han Yun-hŭi, participates in the compiling of eyewitness accounts of May 18, which were then distributed underground. Hwang clearly relishes the irony of having his fictional character play a role in the publication of a book that very closely resembles an actual publication, *Beyond Death, Beyond the Darkness of the Age* (Chugŭmŭl nŏmŏ shidae ŭi ŏdŭmŭl nŏmŏ). It first appeared under his name, though he was not the actual author.[9] Hwang also takes advantage of this fictional episode to describe the savagery of the martial law forces and the heroism of those who resisted. In the picture he draws of May 18, the people of Kwangju appear heroic. For example, he describes young Kwangjuites risking death by grabbing any sort of weapon they could find, even a kitchen knife, and marching toward the Provincial Office building to confront the paratroopers.

The major character, O Hyŏn-u, sat in a prison cell for what should have been the most productive years of his life. But when he finally regained his freedom, he learned that his wife had died and that he had a daughter who did not know him. In the final analysis, his life is more tragic than heroic, and he is more to be pitied than admired. Nor is Han Yun-hŭi especially heroic. She is free to participate in the fight for democracy and a more just society, while her jailed husband is not. In fact, the reader is given the distinct impression that she is drawn into the post-1980 antigovernment movement reluctantly and almost accidentally. As portrayed by Hwang, she is a "passive activist" (if I may coin an oxymoron), someone who drifts through life rather than someone who makes a conscious decision to dedicate her life to struggling against injustice and oppression.

An Old Garden is more likely to sadden its readers than inspire them and suggests that the people caught up in the events of May 18 were victims, or at least caught up in events beyond their control. The same cannot be said for Song Ki-suk's *A Faint Smile in May* (Owŏl ŭi miso).[10] Song, like Hwang, was in Kwangju in May 1980. Unlike Hwang, he was arrested and spent almost a year in prison for his role on the Citizens Settlement Committee. That may explain why Song's novel exudes much more anger than does Hwang's. Song admits that he wrote *A Faint Smile in May* after he was inspired by the 1996 shooting of An Tuhŭi, who had assassinated Kim Ku almost fifty years earlier, as a warning against any pardon or amnesty for Chun Doo Hwan and Roh Tae Woo, the architects of May 18.

In an early signal that he would adopt a more radical approach to May 18, Song gives the leading role in his novel to a man who had joined the Citizens' Army in 1980 and taken up arms against the martial law forces. The story is set in 1997, but about fifty pages are devoted to relating what happened in Kwangju between May 18 and May 27 as recalled by the narrator seventeen years later. Though there are plenty of victims in this story, such as a young woman who is driven insane by her memories of May 18, the overall tone is one of militancy (the narrator carries a gun) reinforced by a refusal to forget what happened or forgive those who ordered troops to attack the people of Kwangju.

Despite the militant tone, Song's characters do not espouse any particular political agenda other than exposing the truth about May 18 and demanding that those who were at the top of the chain of command pay for their crimes. Unlike the characters in *An Old Garden,* Song's characters are not involved in

any broader movements for democratization or social justice. Nor are they
angry at everyone who was on the wrong side in 1980. Among the narrator's
friends are two men who served in the martial law forces in Kwangju in 1980.
One of the principal story lines is about the drowning of one of the men and
the false accusation leveled against the other that he had deliberately caused
the death of that man, who had been his commander in the Special Forces in
1980.

A third novel that is shaping memories today about what happened twenty
years ago is Im Cheol-woo's *Spring Day* (Pom nal). Im, who was also in
Kwangju during May 18, has become known as a May 18 writer, drawing on
that experience to create disturbing fictional portraits of guilt-ridden survivors. By the time he wrote this novel, a decade and a half had passed since
he published his short stories "Shared Journey" and "Spring Day," which describe the impact of May 18 on a few individuals. In the novel *Spring Day,* a
work not only longer but also with different characters from his short story of
the same name, Im supplements his personal memories with the recollections
of others, creating a narrative more historical than autobiographical. As a result, *Spring Day* is not only much longer (five volumes) than either of his short
stories, it is also quite different, though the undertones of guilt and fear are the
same.

In *Spring Day,* Im uses his formidable writing skills to relate actual events
over those ten days as experienced or witnessed by several fictional characters,
drawing on over five hundred eyewitness accounts collected by the Center for
Research on Contemporary Korean History in 1990 and published under the
title *A Comprehensive Collection of Historical Documents on the May People's
Uprising* (Kwangju owŏl minjung hangjaeng saryo chŏnjip). Im begins his account at dawn, May 16, 1980, before martial law was declared nationwide. His
narrative ends with the assault on the Provincial Capitol building on the
morning of May 27. We watch the events from the vantage points provided by
a number of different characters, ranging from a student activist to a paratrooper. The result is a novel in which there are more frightened, confused,
and self-reproaching characters than epic heroes.[11]

Im downplays the politics that motivated some of the resisters in Kwangu
in favor of an emphasis on the brutality that forced normally apolitical citizens into resistance and drew the people of Kwangju together into a community united by fear and anger. Even Yun Sang-wŏn, who appears as Yun Sang-
hyŏn, is portrayed as less ideological than many of those who were with him
in the final days at the Provincial Capitol building now remember him being.
For Im, May 18 was not an organized resistance movement. The political activists who could have served as leaders had either fled town or been arrested
by the morning of May 18. As a result, there was no specific ideology behind

the resistance, nor any conscious strategy. Instead, the Kwangju uprising occurred when the people themselves spontaneously organized to resist violence
against their family, their friends, and their community. This to him is what
makes the Kwangju resistance extraordinary, and why he felt compelled to
write a five-volume glimpse of what happened there.[12]

Drama

In spring 2000, many events were staged to remind Koreans of what happened to their compatriots in Kwangju twenty years earlier. Im's novel *Spring
Day* was transformed into a play and performed at the National Theater in
Seoul and in Kwangju. (The stage production was also aired on MBC television on May 18.) On stage, the characters in *Spring Day* appeared a lot more
politically charged, and a lot more heroic, than they did on the printed page.
The stage version of *Spring Day* was filled with characters shouting slogans
and raising their fists high into the air in defiance of Chun Doo Hwan and his
martial law forces. For example, one character shouts, "Let's all go to Main
Street and fight for democracy!" before leading a crowd of young people
downtown to confront the martial law forces.

At the same time, however, another drama about May 18, closer to the picture of Kwangju presented in the printed version of *Spring Day,* could be seen
at the outdoor theater behind the Seoul Arts Center south of the Han River.
Like the novel *Spring Day, May Bride* (Owŏl sinbu) stayed true to the Kwangu
I heard about in the immediate aftermath of May 18. Instead of brave individuals seizing weapons to bring democracy and social justice to Korea, the
characters in *May Bride* are drawn into battle with martial law forces in self-
defense or in anger at the violence inflicted on their friends, relatives, and
neighbors.

As playwright Hwang Chi-u explained in the program notes, he made a conscious decision to focus on the most dramatic part of 5-18—the clash between
the martial law troops and the citizen militia—rather than devote much attention to Chun Doo Hwan, Roh Tae Woo, or other political actors responsible for
May 18. He was concerned that too much attention paid to leaders in Seoul
would detract from the image of May 18 he wanted to convey, one in which
both the fear and the bravery of the protagonists is more salient than the evil
of their opponents. It is with the same intent that Hwang delineates even individual paratroopers in the martial law forces as ordinary people caught up by
fate in an unfortunate situation. He refused to fall into the trap of making a political point by creating characters who are symbols of good and evil rather
than real human beings with mixed motives and mixed emotions.[13]

These characters for the most part represent real people in Kwangju who were victims of paratrooper violence. The play opens in a psychiatric hospital, with a former member of the citizen militia, driven crazy by survivor guilt, whirling naked around the stage and crying out "I am so happy!" It ends with the marriage of the character who most closely represents Yun Sang-wŏn and the character who most closely represents the young woman who drove through the streets of Kwangju on the morning of May 27 in a sound truck, calling on citizens to rush to the Provincial Capitol building to save the lives of those under attack there. (She is the May bride of the title.) Both characters are killed shortly after the wedding.

If the characters in this play are victims caught in a situation beyond their control, they are also heroes because they refuse to accept their misfortune quietly. Their resistance to brutality, despite the overwhelming odds against them, gives them the aura of heroism. They are not political activists fighting for abstract ideals such as democracy or a more just society. Rather, as Hwang depicts them, they are ordinary human beings who were mostly apolitical until the savagery of the martial law forces frightened them, angered them, and finally forced them to fight back. Combining victimization with heroism, they are ennobled by the suffering they endure and their brave response to it.

Movies

Movies have been more one-sided, tending to focus less on the heroism exercised by Kwangjuites in spring 1980 and more on the suffering they endured then and for a long time afterward. Movies also expand the reach of victimization to encompass not only those who were attacked by martial law forces but their attackers as well.[14]

The first mainstream movie to comment on May 18 was Pak Kwang-su's *Black Republic* (Kŭdŭldo uri ch'ŏrŭm), which appeared in 1990. The film makes no explicit reference to Kwangju but focuses on a young political activist who is hiding from Chun Doo Hwan's police several years after May 18. A couple of times in that film that young man has flashbacks to street battles with police and riot troops. When I questioned Pak Kwang-su after a screening of the film at the Vancouver International Film Festival, he told me that he wanted to use actual footage from the military suppression of the Kwangju democracy movement for those flashbacks, but the Roh government would not let him do so.

The fugitive in this film is portrayed as a caring human being who is now trying to avoid political activity so that he will not come to the attention of the authorities. However, he maintains his sense of justice and his sympathy for the underdog, so he steps between a local big shot and the prostitute he is beating up in a tearoom. His involvement in that tearoom brawl destroys his plan to stay inconspicuous. As the movie ends, he is leaving town again, once more on the run, more victim than hero.

In 1996, after Roh had left office and was replaced by the civilian Kim Young Sam, a movie appeared that was allowed to show scenes of the carnage of May 18—Jang Seon-woo's (Chang Sŏn-u) *A Petal* (Kkonnip). It was based on a novella by Ch'oe Yun, *There a Petal Silently Falls* (Chŏgi sori ŏpsi hamjŏm kkonnip-i chigo), which was first published in 1988.[15] Though it was not a particularly well-written movie, the portrayal of a young girl victimized by the events of May 18 was so strong that some of my students cried when I took them to see it.

The central character in *A Petal* is a young girl driven crazy by the shock of seeing her mother shot when the martial law forces fired on demonstrators in Kwangju (a scene shown in all its gory detail on the big screen). With no family left, she has no one to take care of her and begins wandering aimlessly through the small towns of the Chŏnnam region, where she is raped by a number of different men. There is absolutely nothing heroic or political about her. If she is supposed to represent the people of Kwangju, then they are clearly portrayed as innocent victims.

In 1995, a TV miniseries took a different approach to the participants and victims of May 18. *Hourglass* (Morae sigye), aired on SBS in 1995, is primarily a melodramatic love story that was immensely popular in Korea and among young Korean Americans who watched it on rented videos. The main characters in *Hourglass* are adversely affected by their participation in the events of May 1980, one as a resistance fighter and the other as a member of the martial law forces.

In a twist from previous fictional accounts of May 18, the most admirable main character in the TV drama, Kang U-sŏk, is a paratrooper dispatched to Kwangju in May 1980. He is a man of high principles who later became a prosecutor in order to fight corruption and injustice. As a man of conscience, he feels guilty over his participation in the suppression of the uprising.

The character who was once a resistance fighter in Kwangju, Pak T'ae-su, is less admirable. Pak is a good-hearted gangster. We learn that his father had been a partisan—a communist guerrilla—reinforcing the stereotype held by some that the Kwangju demonstrations were instigated and led by radical leftists.

This twist on the previous portrayal of the people of Kwangju as the primary victims of May suggests a legacy of ambiguity in the general population about what really happened those ten days in May. This minidrama clearly shows that the martial law forces used excessive force but it also hints that those who fought back against them were not from the better classes of society.

In February 2000, another movie appeared in Korean theaters that featured May 18 as a formative influence in the life of a main character. Just as in *Hourglass*, the main character is one of those responsible for the shooting and killing, not one of those killed or injured. Yi Ch'ang-dong's *Peppermint Candy* (Pak'a sat'ang) is an unusual movie in that we meet a drunk and suicidal man at the beginning of the movie and then go back in time through a series of episodes from his life to show how he became the thoroughly despicable person we see in the first scene.

In the last scene in the movie, set in 1979, he is a flower-sniffing, poetry-loving night school student. The scene before that, set in 1980, shows him as a conscripted soldier sent to Kwangju, where he accidentally kills a high school girl who is trying to return to her home. That marks the beginning of his deterioration. In earlier scenes, from the years after Kwangju, we see him as an unfaithful husband and a policeman who tortures political prisoners. The movie implies that his guilt over what he did on May 18 changed him irrevocably for the worse.

Documentaries

In literature and films designed for entertainment, the victim narrative dominates the depiction of the events and impact of May 18. Documentary films offer a different kind of narrative, one in which the people of Kwangju are presented as heroes of Korea's fight for democracy, or even as heirs to the righteous tradition of the Tonghak rebels of 1894 and anti-Japanese activists during the colonial period.

The first documentaries adopted the victim-centered perspective, since they were produced after seven years of government-imposed silence concerning what had happened during May 1980. Few Koreans outside of Kwangju knew what Kwangjuites had endured. The first such documentary, produced in 1987 by the Kwangju Catholic Priests Committee for Peace and Justice, was *May Such a Tragedy as May 18 Never Occur Again* (Owŏl, kŭ nari tasi omyŏn). A video shown in church halls, it was screened to let the rest of Korea know about the misfortune that had befallen the people of Kwangju seven years earlier. Within two years, those shocking scenes had gone beyond church halls to the TV screen. In 1989, the MBC network aired *A Mother's Song* (Ŏmŏni ŭi norae), which told the story of May 18 from the perspective of the mother of a nineteen-year-old man who was shot and killed. Not to be outdone, KBS aired its own exposé of paratrooper violence and government cover-up, *Kwangju Speaks* (Kwangjunŭn malhanda).

The emphasis remained on the people of Kwangju as victims until 1996, when MBC in Kwangju produced a ninety-minute special called *Yun Sang-wŏn: A Soldier in the Citizens' Army* (Simin'gun Yun Sang-wŏn). A year earlier, in 1995, the Kwangju chapter of the Korean Artists Alliance (Han'guk minjok yesurin ch'ongyŏnhap) had already signaled a shift in the perception of May 18 by producing a video emphasizing the heroic role of the citizens of Kwangju, especially the citizen militia. That documentary, entitled *The Kwangju Popular Uprising of May 18: May Such a Day Never Come Again* (5.18 Kwangju minjung hangjaeng: Owŏl kŭ nari tasi omyŏn), doesn't ignore the suffering of the people of Kwangju. In fact, one of the two photos on the back of the case containing the video is of a mother crying before the coffin of her son in the Sangmu Judo Studio. The other photo is of young men riding a commandeered jeep, waving their guns in the air.

This video opens with depictions of the Tonghak rebellion, the 1907 right-eous armies, the 1929 anti-Japanese student demonstrations (which began in Kwangju), and the demonstrations of April 16, 1960, which led to the over-throw of Syngman Rhee. Clearly the intent is to portray May 18 as the latest example of the righteous people of the southwest rising up against injustice and oppression.[16] This video puts May 18 into historical perspective, tracing the rise of Chun Doo Hwan back to Park Chung Hee's declaration of the Yusin system in 1972 and Kim Chae-gyu's assassination of Park in 1979. What hap-pened on May 18 is shown to be a part of a much longer and larger struggle by the Korean masses to achieve democracy, not just a spontaneous protest against paratrooper brutality.

After showing, without narration, several scenes of paratrooper savagery as well as citizen resistance, this video ends with the poetic presentation of Kwangju as victim, Kim Chun-t'ae's "Kwangju, Ah Kwangju," scrolling down the screen.

This video, produced after Kim Young Sam's government announced in July 1995 that it lacked the authority to indict Chun and Roh, appears to be part of a campaign to arouse popular sentiment against Chun and Roh and put pressure on the government to try them for their crimes.

A documentary video prepared in 1998 by the city of Kwangju, as Kim Dae Jung was finally elected president, returns to the Kwangju as victim theme, but with a twist. Although the citizens of Kwangju were victimized by Chun and Roh in 1980, they eventually gained victory over them. This video, *The Kwangju Uprising, May 18, 1980,* opens with the famous photo of a small child holding the funeral portrait of his father. It quickly shifts to the March 1996 trial of former presidents Chun and Roh. It then shows how Chun rose to power illegitimately, arguing explicitly that the uprising in Kwangju was justi-fied (it was a "fight for democracy").

Some scenes in this video were designed to evoke sadness and sympathy for the victims of May 18. For example, we are told that the first fatality was a young deaf man, beaten to death by paratroopers. We are also shown a picture of Pak Kwan-hyŏn, the chairman of the Chŏnnam University student council, speaking to demonstrators, and we are told that was the last speech of his life.[17] There are many more scenes of bloodied corpses than there are of healthy, armed young men fighting back against paratrooper brutality.

The unspoken theme of this video is that May 18 was a response to the military brutality wielded to enforce the military seizure of power. There is no mention of the broader issues of economic or social injustice that are commonly believed to have motivated the Tonghak rebels, for example. The role of the citizen militia, though not ignored, is downplayed. It is mentioned only briefly, and then only as armed rebels who not only resisted the martial law forces but also "maintained social order." Nothing is said of the progressive political agenda of activists such as Yun Sang-wŏn. In the final frames of this video, we see the people of Kwangju victorious over their oppressors, with the election of Kim Dae-jung to the presidency. The video concludes by referring to Kwangju as the "Mecca of democracy" and displaying the words "for those who gave their lives for democracy." No distinction is made between those who died because they were inadvertently caught in the line of fire and those who died because they fired back at the martial law troops forcing their way into the Provincial Capitol building on the morning of May 27.

Music

The difference in focus among video documentaries on the people of Kwangju—as innocent victims, as heroic victims forced in self-defense to fight for democracy, or as heroic heirs to a centuries-old tradition of active resistance to injustice—can also be heard in two attempts to narrate the events of May 18 with music. Both musical narrations are in *p'ansori* format, for a couple of reasons.[18] First, *p'ansori* has a particularly close connection with the culture of the Honam region in which Kwangju is situated. Second, *p'ansori* is an appropriate musical form for expressing the *han* (the pain of having been treated unjustly) of the people of Kwangju.[19] As the music critic Chin Hŭi-suk noted in her liner notes to Im Chin-t'aek's *Kwangju That May: An Original P'ansori Composition* (Ch'angjak p'ansori owŏl Kwangju), *p'ansori* has the power to convey both the rage that memories of May 18 evoke, as well as the tears those same memories bring to our eyes.

The first *p'ansori* retelling of the events of May 18 appeared in 1993. Synnara produced a CD entitled *May That Day Never Be Forgotten: Songs of the May*

18th Kwangju Democratic Uprising (Kŭ nariyŏ yŏngwŏn hara: 5.18 Kwangju minju hangjaeng ŭi norae). Both the cover picture, of a child standing amid a pile of bones, and the line on the cover that reads "this recording is dedicated to all those who were sacrificed in the Kwangju Democratic Uprising," indicate the interpretation of May 18 that shapes the ten *p'ansori* songs it contains. The focus is almost exclusively on the people of Kwangju as victims.

There are brief references to the people of Kwangju showing the same admirable spirit the Tonghak rebels displayed almost a century earlier, but otherwise little is sung about the citizen militia or other forms of active resistance. Nor is much said about political ideas motivating the people of Kwangju, not even the desire for free elections. Instead, the songs are about a son, an older brother, and an older sister who died. This CD also includes "Kwangju, the Cross of Our Nation," Kim Chun-t'ae's poem enumerating the various dead, intoned *p'ansori* style.

One year later, Im Chin-t'aek, already known for his *p'ansori* rendering of Kim Chi-ha's poems, recorded a different *p'ansori* interpretation of May 18. His *Kwangju That May: An Original P'ansori Composition,* from Seoul Ŭmban, celebrates the resisters more than it mourns the dead. Im writes in the liner notes that he was a friend of Yun Sang-wŏn and, in fact, one of the songs praises Yun for his hard-line stance against disarming before the army reentered the city.

Im sings an epic tale of the people of Kwangju, people with a revolutionary past forcing oppressive martial law forces to vacate their city. He provides a detailed narrative of the events from Park Chung Hee's assassination to the army attack on the Provincial Office building on the morning of May 27. One of the more poignant songs is entitled "A Certain Female University Student" and is about the young woman in the sound truck who rode through the streets of Kwangju on the morning of May 27 calling for the people of Kwangju to come downtown and fight the martial law forces that had just launched their final assault on their city. Despite frequent references Im makes to those who died in the Kwangju uprising, his focus is on the heroic qualities of the Kwangju resistance fighters, on what they sacrificed their lives for rather than their sacrifice per se.

Conclusion

Whether literature, movie, play, or *p'ansori,* these dramatic forms not only evoke painful memories of May 18 but reshape them. When we are shown scenes of coffins filling the Sangmu Judo Studio and battered bodies filling the beds of pickup trucks, we forget about the dedicated political activists among them. On the other hand, if we are exposed to literature, movies, plays, or music that portray the citizens of Kwangju as heroes fighting against not only dictatorship but all forms of oppression and injustice, then our memories are reshaped in another direction. We look at pictures of young men waving their weapons high, scenes we can see at the new Mangwŏl-dong cemetery as well as in documentary videos, and forget how frightened and confused most of the people in Kwangju were during those terrible ten days.

We thus have competing "myths" of May 18. Whichever interpretation of May 18 we adopt, we run the risk of simplifying, and therefore distorting, the full complexity of the events in Kwangju two decades ago. That is why Cohen calls such interpretations of the past "myths." To the extent that such interpretative reconstructions ascribe motives to actors that the actors themselves may not have been conscious of, and to the extent that such renditions of past events ascribe a significance to the events that were not clear to participants at that time, they take one step beyond the chronological narrative of events reconstructed by historians and thus are two steps beyond the past as experienced by eyewitnesses and participants.

Nevertheless, such "myths," such constructions of usable pasts, are not to be condemned, for a past with no significance for the present dishonors those who preceded us. Whether or not the people of Kwangju knew at the time that they were laying a foundation from which a democratic government would rise more than a decade later, and whether their resistance to martial law forces was inspired by political idealism or by anger and self-defense, Korea is a much better place today for the sacrifices they made and the examples they set twenty years ago. Whether they were victims or heroes, their contributions to the birth of democratic Korea must be recognized, but not at the cost of historical fidelity.

As a historian I share my interpretations of the past, my "myths," with younger generations, and I face a dilemma. If I focus on the people of Kwangju as victims and talk to my students about the majority of the population, those who had not planned to resist the martial law forces until paratrooper brutality left them no choice, I err on the side of caution. I may excuse my reluctance to ascribe a life-or-death commitment to democracy to the average man or woman in Kwangju in 1980 by pointing out that such a generalization would anachronistically add hindsight to the experience of those who were there at the time. However, such a prosaic account of what transpired that May might blind my students to the fact that it was the blood of the people of Kwangju that fertilized the ground out of which democracy later sprouted.

I lean too far in the other direction if I impart self-consciously political motivations to Kwangjuites who at the time were concerned with self-defense or were acting out of anger more than ideology. Focusing too heavily on Yun Sang-wŏn and other ideologically driven resisters would blind us to the fact that the majority of those who demonstrated against, and fought against, martial law forces were fighting in self-defense or to protest attacks on their friends and family members. An ideological interpretation risks turning Kwangju into a more politically aware community than it actually was in May 1980. I would dishonor the dead if I denied them the complexity of motives that is the mark of a real human being.

To make matters more difficult, I have to remember, when talking to my students about what I saw and heard in Kwangju in May 1980, that even eyewitnesses to a particular historical event such as May 18 cannot rely on their own memories. First, as Cohen pointed out in his discussion of eyewitness accounts of the Boxer Rebellion, an important historical event is normally far too multifaceted and takes place over far too much space and time for any individual to have a clear and comprehensive view of what happened. Second, memories change as time passes. As we describe to others what we saw and heard and they tell us what they saw, heard, or read, we unconsciously try to reconcile differences among those various accounts, modifying our own memories in the process.

In other words, the stories we hear from others affect the stories we tell. That includes stories we hear in movies, dramas, literature, and music. That is one of the reasons it is so difficult, twenty years after the fact, for even eyewitnesses to provide an accurate account of what really happened on May 18. We want to make sense out of events that appeared senseless at the time they occurred. In so doing, we join with others in highlighting some aspects of those events and downplaying others. We need such "myths" in order to impart comprehensible coherence to the chaos that is everyday experience, but we should also keep in mind that such interpretations by their very nature contain elements of selectivity and subjectivity and thus should not be confused with objective reality. Only then can we approach important events such as May 18 with an appropriate humility, humility I lacked fourteen years ago when I promised to describe what really happened on May 18.

We will never have a totally objective and comprehensive understanding of the events that took place in Kwangju from May 18 to May 27, 1980. But if we include both victims and heroes in our account of what happened, our interpretation will be less subjective and more objective than it otherwise would have been. Just as yin is best understood in terms of its relationship to yang, and yang is best understood in terms of its relationship to yin, so there can be no truly usable past of May 18 without both the yin of its many victims and the yang of its many heroes. We should not forget that the people of Kwangju on May 18 were not one-dimensional caricatures but multifaceted human beings, with all the complexity and mixed emotions that entails; many of them were victimized heroes as well as heroic victims. The best myth of May 18 would include the political ideals of the heroes, those who fought for democracy and social justice. It would also include the deaths of those who were simply in the wrong place at the wrong time. Though the young schoolgirl in *Peppermint Candy* and the mother in *A Petal* are fictional, there were many real people like them in Kwangju in May 1980. Remembering both the heroes and the victims of May 18, and remembering that they were a diverse group with a variety of reasons for the roles they played, is the best way to honor the memory of all those who died there twenty years ago, to render their deaths meaningful, and to uphold the commitment to democracy they have come to represent.

Notes

1. Paul Cohen, *History in Three Keys: The Boxers as Event, Experience, and Myth* (New York: Columbia University Press, 1997), 4–11.
2. Cohen, *History*, 213.
3. For more on the two Mangwŏl-dong cemeteries, see Sallie Yea, *"Rewriting Rebellion and Mapping Memory in South Korea: The (Re)presentation of the 1980 Kwangju Uprising through Mangwol-dong Cemetery,"* Asian Studies Institute Working Paper, no. 13 (Wellington, New Zealand: Victoria University of Wellington, 1999). Pictures showing the differences between the old and the new cemeteries can be found on pages 20-23.
4. Kim Ch'un-t'ae, "Kwangju: The Cross of Our Nation," *Korea Communiqué*, October 5, 1980, 25. Translated by David McCann.
5. Im Ch'eol-woo (Im Ch'ŏr-u), "Spring Day," *Manoa* 11, no. 2, "The Wounded Season," 48–63. Translated by Susie Jie Young Kim.
6. Im Ch'eol-woo, "Shared Journey," in *Land of Exile: Contemporary Korean Fiction* (New York: Sharpe, 1993), 264–84. Translated by Bruce and Ju-chan Fulton.
7. Kong Sŏn-ok, "Parched Season," *Manoa* 11, no. 2, "The Wounded Season," 160-78. Translated by Susie Jie Young Kim.
8. Hwang Sŏg-yŏng, *Orae toen chŏngwŏn* (Seoul: Ch'angjak kwa pip'yŏngsa, 2000).
9. The primary author of that book, Lee Jae-eui, explains in his preface to the English edition that Hwang Sŏg-yŏng allowed his name to appear on the title page both to enhance the book's credibility and to protect the actual authors who, not being as famous as Hwang, would have been more vulnerable to government persecution when the book first appeared in 1985. Lee Jae-eui, *Kwangju Diary: Beyond Death, Beyond the Darkness of the Age*, trans. Kap Su Seol and Nick Mamatas (Los Angeles: UCLA Asian Pacific Monograph Series, 1999). The original edition appeared as Hwang Sŏg-yŏng, *Chugŭmŭl nŏmŏ sidae ŭi ŏdumŭl nŏmŏ* (Seoul: P'ulpit, 1985).
10. Song Ki-suk, *Owŏl ŭi miso* (Seoul: Ch'angjak kwa pip'yŏngsa, 2000).

11. Im Ch'ŏr-u, *Pom nal* (Seoul: Munhak kwa chisŏngsa, 1997–1998).

12. Im Ch'ŏr-u, "Kwangju and My Literary Tribulations [Na ŭi munhakjŏk konoe wa Kwangju]," *Yŏksa pip'yŏng* 51 (Summer 2000): 292–303.

13. Hwang Chi-u, *Owŏl ŭi sinbu* (Seoul: Munhak kwa chisŏngsa, 2000).

14. Chŏng Kŭn-sik and Min Hyŏng-bae, "Yŏngsang kirok ŭro pon waegok kwa chinsil [Facts and falsifications in documentary accounts of May 18]," *Yŏksa pip'yŏng* 51 (Summer 2000): 267–91.

15. Ch'oe Yun, "There a Petal Silently Falls," trans. Bruce and Ju-chan Fulton, *Korea Journal* (Winter 1997): 221–38; (Spring 1998): 356–92.

16. A similar linking of May 18 to these popular resistance movements from the past is on display at the new Mangwŏl-dong cemetery. A portion of that cemetery called "History Square" includes bas-relief sculptures of scenes from those same historical events, with one change: the 1907 resistance to the Japanese is replaced in History Square with the popular resistance to the Japanese invasion three centuries earlier, in the 1590s.

17. Pak died in prison in 1983 after going on a hunger strike to protest prison conditions.

18. *P'ansori* is a traditional form of drama in which a single performer alternately speaks and sings an entertaining and morally uplifting story. That performer is accompanied by one musician, a drummer.

19. *Han* is a Korean term so rich in emotional connotations that it is difficult to provide a concise English translation for it. In recent decades, it has been used as shorthand for the mental suffering and righteous anger of those who have been oppressed for a long time but have been unable to escape the unjust situation they find themselves in and, to make matters worse, have had to repress their resentment at the way they have been treated. Women, peasants, workers, and the people of Kwangju are the groups in Korea usually considered to possess the strongest *han*. For more on *han*, see Jae Hoon Lee, *The Exploration of the Inner Wounds: Han* (Atlanta: Scholars, 1994).

8

Reinventing the Region: The Cultural Politics of Place in Kwangju City and South Chŏlla Province

Sallie Yea

THROUGHOUT KOREA'S PREMODERN AND MORE RECENT HISTORY, the Chŏlla region (comprising North and South Chŏlla provinces) has been subject to persistent discrimination and political-economic marginalization within the Korean nation-state.[1] Since the onset of rapid economic development during the past four decades in particular, the region has suffered especially severe discrimination in virtually all areas of social, economic, and political life. Indeed, while the Kwangju uprising was part of a nationwide movement for the restoration of democracy in South Korea, many believe it was most pronounced and severe in Kwangju for reasons that can be traced back to this legacy of marginalization.

Since the election of Kim Dae Jung (a native of South Chŏlla province) as president in late 1997, this history of marginalization has been both subverted and reinvented (indeed embellished). There are a variety of expressions of this, including the emerging touristic promotion of the region for its largely unspoiled environment and cultural heritage, the promotion of the region as a center for civil society and sustainable development, and the political promotion of the region, and Kwangju city in particular, as an emerging center (or Mecca) for democracy, social justice, and human rights. These place-based promotions rely on a consciously articulated image of the region that neatly fuses civil society, culture and environment, and politics. While the former two expressions of this place promotion embrace the whole province, the latter relates specifically to Kwangju city.

The Kwangju uprising is central to this emerging narrative of Kwangju as a democratic center (even though the uprising also drew support from a number of surrounding counties in South Chŏlla province). Connected to this supposed legacy of radicalism symbolized by the Kwangju uprising is the promotion of Kwangju as a city where civil society and organizations dedicated to social justice are deeply entrenched. The retelling/historicization of the uprising has become an important part of the current effort to rework the city's political legacy (of radicalism, dissent, etc.) into a narrative of radical-progressive politics. This narrative draws heavily on the tropes of democracy, social justice, human rights, and equality. This chapter focuses particularly on the political expression of Chŏlla's new regionalist vision and explores efforts to promote Kwangju city as a major center for human rights and democracy. The Kwangju uprising, as a particularly salient reference point in sustaining such a vision, will be given particular attention. With the twentieth anniversary of the uprising in May 2000, the discourse on Kwangju as a democratic city intensified even further. This chapter draws on recent work in cultural geography and postcolonial studies that views regions/places as sociocultural and historical constructs which continually undergo transformation and reinvention. This peculiar historical juncture in Korea has presented an opportunity for reinvention in Kwangju city and South Chŏlla province that both breaks with and draws from the past.

First, I introduce the theoretical and conceptual discussions in cultural geography on which this research draws. Second, I provide a brief background on the dimensions of Chŏlla's historical and contemporary marginalization, which helps situate and explain current efforts at reinventing the region in Korea's wider regional geography. Third, I discuss recent reconfigurations of regional identity in Chŏlla, beginning with an overview of the three elements of this vision and the ways in which the current domestic (and Asian) context is precipitating its emergence. Fourth, I discuss the ways in which the Kwangju uprising enters a broader discourse of democracy that lies at the core of the region's efforts to reinvent itself in the twenty-first century.

Rethinking Regions

Recently the influence of postcolonial studies in cultural geography has led to new ways of understanding regions, cities, and entire nations. Regions and cities are no longer viewed simply as material-spatial constructs, but also as discursive-historical and cultural constructs produced by multiple interests and containing discrepant voices. Summarizing much of these recent efforts to "rethink the region" is the suggestion by Allen, Massey, and Cochrane that

> spaces/places are constructed both materially and discursively, and each modality of this construction affects the other. Moreover, every place or region "arrives" at the present moment trailing long histories: histories of economics and

politics, of gender, class and ethnicity; and histories, too, of the many different stories which have been told about all of these. The complex ways in which the region is constructed at any time is a result of these histories and of what is made of them.[2]

This focus on the constructed (and contested) nature of cities and regions allows us to explore the processes and agencies of their production through time and space. Such an understanding draws on Edward Said's concept of imaginary geographies, or "symbolic territories"[3] in which the discursive production of places is as significant as the material political-economic reality, and indeed is intertwined with such a reality.

Regions are thus constantly made and remade, building on, denying, reworking, and reinventing legacies of the past to sustain a vision of the present and future. This process of ongoing construction involves negotiation, cooperation, and contestation among groups and actors within and beyond the region itself and according to the needs of the present. Local, national, and global actors can combine to produce the dominant understanding of a region at any point in time, conferring on such a construction material and symbolic support.

Regions are also relational constructs, drawing their identity as much from what they are not as what they are. Thus in any nation we can identify peripheral and central regions, growth regions and marginal/stagnant regions, and so on. In understanding the production of the southeast as the dominant growth region in the United Kingdom, Allen, Massey, and Cochrane argue that

> the regional identities are relational, marking out the differences and contrasts between regions, and, whilst they are open to reinterpretation, they carry a legacy of meaning. It would jar, for example, to refer to central Scotland or East Anglia as core or lead regions, because the resonances of the past, the regional identities over the past century or so, render such labels implausible. It is not that the identities of the two regions are fixed; they can and do shift, but only as part of an historical play of differences between regions.[4]

"Terrain of resistance" is often used to describe specifically dissident or radical places.[5] According to Routledge, a terrain of resistance is "the specific geographical, historical, political, economic, ecological and cultural context of movement agency."[6] This term draws attention to the specific geographical context in which a social movement arises, providing a framework within which to understand why movements occur where they do and the sociospatial specificity of movement practice. In the case of the Kwangju uprising, the history of struggle, resistance, dissent, and marginality within the Chŏlla region powerfully explain why Kwangju became the focal point of popular protest in May 1980. These factors, including the struggle for democracy and cherishing of ideals of justice and equality, also help explain the characteristics of the movement itself, including cooperation, the formation of an "absolute community," solidarity, and so on.[7] Importantly, a terrain of resistance is not just a physical place but also a physical expression that "endow[s] space with meanings—be they symbolic, spiritual, ideological, cultural or political. A terrain of resistance is thus both metaphorical and literal. It constitutes the geographical ground upon which conflict takes place, and is a representational space."[8] This symbolic or representational aspect means that a space of resistance is constituted through a symbolic landscape—the subject of ongoing construction after the movement/uprising has taken place—and draws on its legacy.

In sum, to understand the construction of a region or city one must look beyond the material, physical elements of its geography to its discursive production over time-space. This production may involve a variety of agencies operating (competitively or cooperatively) at a variety of scales (including the local, national, and global). The construction of a region or city usually also involves some elements of oppositional imagery: places are often understood as much by what they are not, as what they are. These constructions normally draw on historical, cultural, and sociopolitical legacies, including important events and personages, but these are reworked and reinvented according to the needs of the present. The reproduction of a particular place over time is thus contingent in large part on the system of representation that accompanies it. In the case of both Kwangju and South Chŏlla province the characteristics that constitute the representations, images, and symbols of the region have been remarkably durable over time. The Kwangju uprising, as a major event that is complicit with these broader tropes that define the region, has been drawn into this system of representations where it has continued to inform the imaginary geography of the region. However, in the 1990s and beyond these same tropes are taking on a new meaning, in accordance with the shifting domestic and international political context.

Chŏlla's History of Marginality and Radicalism

Chŏlla's imaginary geography is perhaps more powerful and provocative than that of the other regions in South Korea. Clues as to why this may be the case can be found in the region's long history of economic and social marginalization, as well as the wholesale repression of the region in national political life and the region's history of popular protest and resistance, which is itself an expression of these multiple and protracted processes of exclusion and marginalization. From the Tonghak uprising in the late nineteenth century to the Kwangju uprising in May 1980 and post-1980 protests, the history of the region can be narrated through episodes of dissent and radicalism. Even before this in the much earlier premodern history of Korea, much of the territory that today comprises the Honam region was at one time or another subject to severe discrimination and repression as the Korean nation-state came into existence. Nonetheless, it is certainly true that, historically, other provinces had equally as pronounced episodes of popular protest and suffered similar levels of political discrimination to Chŏlla.[9] Chŏlla's particular claims to this legacy need to perhaps be understood not only as a fact of history but, equally, as a consequence of present efforts at rebuilding that history by the architects of this area's new regionalist vision. It is nonetheless worth exploring the historical fabric by which this current narrative has been carefully woven.

The struggle between the regions, especially the southeast and southwest, for territorial hegemony on the Korean peninsula provides an important mechanism for understanding how and why regional divisions first appeared in Korea. The formation of distinct territorially based groups, particularly in what today roughly coincides with the regions of Kyŏngsang (the southeast), Chŏlla/Ch'ungch'ŏng (the southwest),[10] and what is now North Korea (the north), began early in Korean history when these three regions existed as the separate states of Silla, Paekche, and Koguryŏ respectively. Toward the end of this Three Kingdoms period (seventh century) the three states were forcibly integrated by the state of Silla into one unified nation, a move that incited particularly bitter and protracted resistance from the Paekche people in the southwest.

Regional group cohesiveness was exacerbated in the newly unified and centralized state of Koryŏ (918–1392) and its successor, Chosŏn (1392–1910), as interregional divisions became implicated in the emerging political culture, social order, and economic relations. During this time laws and institutional edicts based on the *p'ungsu chirisŏl* (geomancy, or literally theory of wind and water) came to be written with the deliberate purpose of excluding former Paekche people from politics, thus rendering the region isolated and disadvantaged in a permanently united Korea (from 918 on). This attitude toward Paekche people was undoubtedly grounded in the previous bitter experiences of interstate conflict and Paekche resistance to unification. One edict, the *Hunyo sipjo* (ten principles of rule), was particularly important in legitimizing the political and social emasculation of the former state of Paekche. With the installment of the new Koryŏ dynasty in 918, this ten-article constitution was drawn up by the first king, T'aejo. As was the normal procedure for a new dynasty, such principles of rule were strictly adhered to throughout the remainder of the dynasty, which in this case was

475 years. Given the particularly bitter experiences with Paekche radicalism and the former state's persistent assertions of independence, King T'aejo feared that Paekche people would again attempt to regain power and territory and divide the country. Fearing loss of control over the peninsula, he decided to invoke *p'ungsu chirisŏl* to legitimize his exclusion of Paekche people from important government positions and military posts. The eighth article of the constitution thus states:

> The topographical features of the territory south of Kongju [behind the Chaeryŏng Mountains] and beyond the Kongju River are all treacherous and disharmonious, and its inhabitants are also treacherous and disharmonious. For that reason, if they are allowed to participate in the affairs of state, to intermarry with the royal family, aristocracy, and royal relatives and to take the power of the state, they might imperil the state or injure the royal safety—grudging the loss of their own state (Paekche) and being resentful of the unification.

T'aejo declared that the Chaeryŏng Mountains and Kongju River would be the dividing line that would determine where rebellious people *(paeyŏgin)* lived. T'aejo knew that, while Silla people integrated easily into the new Koryŏ state, Paekche people would continue to be resistant and rebellious. The *p'ungsu chirisŏl* was thus intentionally manipulated by the new state to legitimize the exclusion of Paekche people from access to any political power and social privilege for 475 years.

A new element in the discrimination of Chŏlla people involving Confucian scholarship emerged following the establishment of the Chosŏn dynasty in 1392. Particularly during the late Chosŏn period, literature and scholarship flourished under the conditions of state endorsement and patronage of Confucian learning. Benefiting from the new environment created by the promotion of scholarship, many scholars devoted themselves to publishing works on Korean society, culture, and geography. While these treatises are interesting in themselves, most important for our purposes were the comments these scholars and bureaucrats made about the populations of the various regions, their characters, intelligence, aptitudes, ritual life and cultural activities, and achievements. The "Augmented Survey of the Geography of Korea" is one of the most comprehensive works building on an original description, rendered in English simply as *Geographical Description of the Eight Province*s (1432). In addition to the practical information it provided, the document also described the people from each province, thus giving an insight into how Chŏlla, as well as the other regions, was viewed in the Chosŏn dynasty. Chŏlla people were characterized as kindhearted and gentle, but also highly intelligent, manipulative, and calculating. In addition they were described as ardent followers of shamanism (or "ghost worship"), ritual, and ancestor worship. Shamanism had become marginalized in both the Koryŏ and Chosŏn dynasties as Buddhism and Confucianism respectively became more fully institutionalized as providing the nation's moral, ethical, and religious needs. The scholars and bureaucrats of the Chosŏn dynasty viewed shamanism as a historic vestige, inappropriate for progressive Korean society.[11] According to the *Geographical Description*, then, Chŏlla people lacked application and the ability to diligently study Confucianism. They were consequently seen to be immoral, impolite, and needing special attention if they were to be appropriately educated.

These types of geographical treatises on Chŏlla and various legal mechanisms to exclude Chŏlla from state institutions, such as the *Hunyo sipjo*, constituted important mechanisms by which Chŏlla was mapped in the premodern period. But these laws and treatises also acted in concert with Chŏlla's evolving regional economy and social relations, and with the protest and rebellion that these relations produced. Especially during the Chosŏn dynasty, the history of radicalism, as well as the broader cultural and political terrain that constitutes the region as dissident, became closely wedded to its agrarian landscape. Historically, Chŏlla, like Ch'ungch'ŏng, possessed an agrarian culture and economy based on a highly polarized rural class structure in which a small number of powerful landlords ubiquitously exploited a large number of classless farm laborers and tenant farmers. Working in concert with this economic exploitation was the exclusion and isolation of Chŏlla from national politics, which helped ensure high levels of material exploitation of the region. This, in turn, had the important effect of perpetuating rebellion and protest there.

During the nineteenth century Chŏlla's peasants extended their protests to criticism of the state and its (Confucian) ideological underpinnings. In particular, the Tonghak rebellion of 1894 galvanized the image of Chŏlla touted by the state and the factional groups that dominated it as indeed rebellious and radical (a subject that received much attention in many of the regional geographies that were written during the late Chosŏn period). This agrarian structure has conferred two intertwining legacies in modern South Korea. The first is a tradition of egalitarian and communitarian political practices and ideology, as well as a populist folk culture in which politics is expressed through performative elements and oral traditions such as *p'ansori* (narrative operatic performance), *t'alch'um* (masked dance), and *minjung munhak* (populist literature). In both political ideology and cultural practice the overriding themes of usurping authority, reasserting the popular, reclaiming culture, and achieving social justice evince these origins in agrarian class struggles. Today the Tonghak rebellion has become a central narrative in *minjung* discourses of resistance and popular struggle, thus necessarily locating both Chŏlla and Ch'ungch'ŏng in such populist politics.

Many of these themes were extended during the period of Japanese colonial rule (1910–1945). A primary objective of the Japanese colonial administration in Korea was to exploit the agricultural surplus, particularly in rice, thus freeing up Japanese resources to concentrate on industrial expansion and war preparation. The exploitation of Korea's agrarian sector was precipitated by the reorganization of land holdings through a cadastral survey conducted between 1911 and 1918. This survey resulted in a dramatically high concentration of ownership of land generally. Given that topographical conditions in the Ch'ungch'ŏng and Chŏlla provinces were most suitable to extensive holdings, the regionalist implications of this emerging pattern of agrarian restructuring were marked, with land expropriation by the Japanese being most intense in the southwest (although this pattern was also evident in both South Ch'ungch'ŏng and South Kyŏngsang provinces). In 1918, immediately after the cadastral survey, 42.6 percent of all land under private Japanese ownership was concentrated in the two Chŏlla provinces. Increasing Japanese landlordism and rising tenancy became more entrenched as the colonial period continued. By 1942, 68.4 percent and 52.3 percent of the paddy fields in North Chŏlla and South Chŏlla respectively belonged to large landlords. These figures were by far the highest of any region in the country. In North Chŏlla a remarkable 85 percent of total farm households were classified as either landless tenants or semitenants. In addition, the southwest had the largest proportion of "servile" workers anywhere in the country. By 1943, 54.2 percent of servile workers were employed by landlords in the two Chŏlla provinces. Consequently, the greatest number of farm households suffering in the spring famine was concentrated in the two Chŏlla provinces and South Ch'ungch'ŏng province. The incidence of peasant protest and tenancy disputes in the southwest thus remained the highest in the country throughout the colonial period.[12]

In the postcolonial period Chŏlla's position within the South Korean nation-state has been established through the enduring legacy of economic exclusion and social and political marginalization that evolved during earlier times. While regionalism *(chiyŏkjuŭi),* regional "sentimentalism" *(chiyŏk kamjŏng),* and regional economic differentiation remain highly sensitive subjects in South Korea, a few studies have emerged that document the economic marginalization,[13] social subordination,[14] and political repression[15] by which Chŏlla is situated in the "modern" South Korean nation-state.

In the modern period Chŏlla's marginalization is most starkly revealed in political-economic trends. Attention to the social bases of the developmental (post-1960) Korean state, for example, reveals the highly exclusive regional origins of senior bureaucratic personnel. Similarly, political leaders during this period tended to be predominantly from North and, later, South

Kyŏngsang provinces. The trend became most entrenched during the Chun regime (1980–1987) but first became apparent during the Park regime (1961–1979). More recently, despite the formal transition to democracy in South Korea, critics maintain that regional identification of politicians persists as one of the major influences on political processes and in the composition of the bureaucracy, thus thwarting efforts to establish a "true" democracy in the country. Indeed, despite President Kim Dae Jung's plea to end the regionalization of politics, his own administration was prominently staffed with advisors from his native Chŏlla region, and his accession to the presidency was carefully orchestrated through a Chŏlla-Ch'ungch'ŏng alliance that directly worked against Kyŏngsang.

Park Chung Hee, from North Kyŏngsang province, provides the classic case of this type of regionalization of politics. Park established a political power base through the development of tactical alliances with leading political figures and senior military personnel (mainly generals) from his home province. In fact, Presidents Park, Chun, and Roh all drew their major base of support from North and South Kyŏngsang provinces. For Park and Chun the geographical bases of support were even more localized, as both presidents formed their allegiances more particularly around their hometown of Taegu (the so-called TK, or Taegu-Kyŏngbuk, faction). Selection of senior ranking state officials was determined largely by the internal political pretensions of the core power elites of the government. After his accession to power, Park deliberately set about removing politicians from regions other than his own from the government, as well as forging strong relationships with those from North Kyŏngsang province. By the strategic allocation of key government positions, including minister, vice minister, and director generals, Park ensured that there would be minimal opposition and maximum support from within the government structure for his regime, and that these key figures would actively contribute toward the continuation of Park's rule and the perpetuation of his personal image of authority and power.

The regionalization of bureaucratic authority and political power may be easily seen through an analysis of the provincial origin of both bureaucrats and politicians. The number of southeasterners (from both North and South Kyŏngsang provinces) who occupied high government positions in successive governments since liberation from Japanese occupation is exceptionally high. Southeasterners occupied an average of 30.1 percent of high government positions throughout this period. Taking into account the regional populations at the time, southeasterners were overrepresented by 2.5 times in central governmental positions. This regionalization of government appears even starker when it is considered that Chŏlla people were 0.7 times underrepresented.[16]

The other major dimension of regionalization of the state was the persistent monopolization of key positions in the Korean Central Intelligence Agency (KCIA), Economic Planning Board (EPB), and Ministry of Home Affairs (MHA) by persons from Kyŏngsang. These core bureaucratic institutions maintained centralized control of Korea's economic and security environment, and thus possessed enormous power in the developmental and repressive spheres. From 1961 to 1980, the total number of government ministers whose home province was Kyŏngsang was seventy-nine, or 27.5 percent, compared with forty-two (14.6 percent) from Ch'ungch'ŏng provinces, and thirty-six (12.5 percent) from Chŏlla. In particular, among the thirteen successive EPB ministers from 1963 to 1984, 40 percent were from Kyŏngsang, and none were from Chŏlla. This also meant that direct bureaucratic support for the development of the southeast far outweighed that given to other regions. Southeasterners accounted for an average of 38.4 percent of all positions of director general and above in the economic ministries of the central bureaucracy. Positions in the EPB, Ministry of Construction (MOC), Ministry of Finance (MOF), and Ministry of Commerce and Industry (MOCI) had particularly important implications for the spatial pattern of economic development. This disparity was particularly marked in the MOC, which acted as the state's central vehicle for national spatial development. Hence many cite the Honam region's relative lack of rapid economic development at levels in line with the nation's overall successful experience of rapid development as directly linked to this monopolization of bureaucratic and political power.[17] It is also common belief among Koreans, and a view held by the vast majority of people in Chŏlla, that the dominance of the Kyŏngsang provinces in postcolonial national politics has disadvantaged Chŏlla more than any other region, in line with the long-standing enmity that exists between the two regions.

The political tropes of radicalism and dissent and the sociocultural tropes of egalitarianism and communitarianism that define Chŏlla as a distinctive place in Korea's geographical imaginary can be traced to these historical and contemporary fortunes. These historical and contemporary vicissitudes have also provided an enduring thematic in much of the populist literature that has emerged from within Chŏlla. This literature has made a considerable contribution toward helping to galvanize the circumstances of Chŏlla into a popularly accessible literary project that bespeaks the region as a politically radical and resistant place. Thus the imagined map of Chŏlla arises from a configuration of the culture, history, and political realities of the region and the various ways these have been expressed and reworked through populist literature.

These regional characteristics and their (re)production through populist literature and other cultural, political, and physical (landscape) forms help explain why Kwangju was an especially likely center of resistance to authoritarianism, as well as a particularly strong advocate for democracy and justice/equality. They help answer the question of why dissent and containment were most vehemently expressed in Kwangju, thus constituting a formidable terrain of resistance.

Contextualizing the Reinvention of Kwangju City and South Chŏlla Province

As South Korea enters the new millennium, the status of Kwangju city and South Chŏlla province is undergoing a dramatic transformation, with expressions in all aspects of political, cultural, and social life. Before exploring the substance of these changes, I will briefly review the context in which they have occurred.

The most marked change in Chŏlla's relative status involves the region's position in national politics. In February 1998 Kim Dae Jung, a long-time dissident political figure in South Korean politics, was sworn in as president. Kim, a native of South Chŏlla province, had been the key political figure for the region for several decades. Kim's election was particularly significant because of the regionalized nature of politics in the country. Political regionalism is one of the key characteristics defining the politics in South Korea—both in terms of voting patterns and party/factional formations. Thus, understood in terms of South Korea's political regionalism, Kim's election heralded the ascendancy of his home region in national politics (this despite Kim Dae Jung's pre- and postelection promises to end political regionalism).

At a more general level the entire political environment in Korea is also undergoing a major departure from the past. The election of Kim Young Sam in early 1993 represented the realization of formal democracy in Korea. With the election of Kim Dae Jung, the consolidation of democratic processes was further extended at a formal level, since Kim's election represented the transfer of power from government to opposition, a commonly accepted indicator of democratic consolidation. Civil society and social movement groups have also benefited from this new political environment and have expanded enormously, both in numbers and public support, over the last few years. With democracy being expressed at a national level, and civil society playing a greater role in shaping politics and social futures in the country, a regionalist vision that also contains these ideals is bound to be more readily accepted than it was under the authoritarian governments of the past. Indeed, in this new context Kwangju/Chŏlla's long history of egalitarianism and human rights has been received quite differently than it was in the past.

The Kwangju uprising was central to attempts by Kim Young Sam's inaugural democratic government to legitimize itself. The Kim government attempted, through various means discussed below, to insert itself into the uprising narrative, principally by aligning itself to the spirit and objectives of the movement. In addition to supporting memorialization and commemoration, the government took measures to investigate the "truth" about the uprising, addressing the level of violence and repression by the Korean military, receiving testimonies from citizens involved in the uprising, and documenting human rights abuses that emerged during and after the uprising. The arrests of former Presidents Chun and Roh are also at least partly explained by their respective roles in both the uprising and broader human rights abuses in Korea.[18]

If the structural circumstances associated with Korea's political economy have helped facilitate the realization of a new regionalist vision in Chŏlla, then its realization has been due to the conscious effort of people within the region. Implicit in all efforts to reinvent South Chŏlla province and Kwangju city is the desire to overcome their marginal position within Korea. Nowhere is this more clearly articulated than in one of the promotional brochures for the memorialization of the Kwangju uprising. Near the beginning of this brochure is the pronouncement that "Kwangju citizens are making every effort to throw off the shadow of isolation, underdevelopment, and depression in order to make a future full of prosperity and hope under the motto, 'Vanguard of Democracy, Vibrant New City.'"[19] Recognition of this marginal status has been the subject of extensive discourse on regional development within Chŏlla/Kwangju throughout the rapid development period since the early 1960s. The question of how to develop Chŏlla/Kwangju and shrug off an image of radicalism and marginality has been a perplexing one that has informed a large number of public discussions in the region over recent years. In 1995, for example, the Ministry of Construction undertook the task of formulating a new regional development plan for South Chŏlla province. Prominent personages in the region, including academics, civil servants, and politicians, took part in a series of public meetings to discuss issues related to education, industry, agriculture, environment, and so on. The course of the discussions revealed in no uncertain terms that regional deprivation, underdevelopment, and backwardness in large part defined people's self-understanding in the region. This was further confirmed by the results of two questionnaire surveys of citizens in the region conducted around the time of the meetings. When asked about the status of the region in comparison with other regions, the vast majority of respondents clearly identified Chŏlla as underdeveloped and backward.[20]

The ability of provincial peoples to exert a greater voice in determining the future of their region or city also received a boost with the decentralization of Korean politics. In May 1995 the first local elections were held, thus breaking down the previous system of appointment of local representatives by the central government. Local elections and the decentralization of politics *(chibang chach'ije)* have helped ensure that local representatives have a more direct and sustained interest in their region. Indeed, South Chŏlla and Kwangju city are not the only places in Korea to embark on ambitious self-promotion strategies. Pusan, for example, has begun hosting an annual film festival. Within South Chŏlla province itself, other counties are also embarking on strategies to promote popular folk culture specific to the county. Chindo, for example, has begun promoting itself as "a village of arts such as poems, calligraphy and folk song as well as a treasury of traditional folklore."[21] In much the same way as Kwangju, Chindo's county officials and folklore troupe have linked to "exilic culture" created by "the literary exiles and peculiar folk customs."[22]

In sum, the election of Kim Dae Jung as president helped provide both a degree of legitimacy and financial support for efforts to reinvent Chŏlla/Kwangju. The emergence of a broadly democratic polity and an active, assertive civil society in South Korea since the early 1990s have also lent legitimacy to any vision for the future that is dependent on the tropes of human rights, democracy, and social justice. Increasing local autonomy through local elections has also helped insert local people into debates and planning processes for regional development. Finally, overcoming a legacy of marginalization and repression that has historically informed people's self-understanding within Chŏlla/Kwangju acts as a powerful impetus for endogenously directed efforts to reinvent the region.

The Discourse of Democracy in Chŏlla/Kwangju

The three dominant elements in Chŏlla's new place promotion are democratic politics, civil society/community, and culture/environment. Expressions of culture/environment are well developed and include the touristic promotion of culture *(munhwa sanŏp)* and an annual *Biennale* in which progressive/alternative artists and performers gather in Kwangju for an artistic festival. The region has established international links with artists and undertaken an extensive review of cultural ties and "hearths," or origins. This last project has been realized in a number of historical/archaeological studies claiming to locate the origins of Japanese culture in the southwest's Paekche period. In the *Guide to May 18 Historical Sites* (n.d.), these efforts are summarized with the self-proclamation that "in particular Kwangju is renowned as 'a Cradle of Korean Arts' *[yehyang]*. Our citizens' love of nature and the arts has nurtured some unique southern cultural art forms, such as *p'ansori* and traditional Korean paintings."[23]

The strength of civil society and social movement groups in South Chŏlla province has also been drawn into the new regionalist vision; indeed, these organizations themselves are often conscious articulators of such a vision. The Kwangju Futures Society (Pit koŭl mirae sahoe yŏn'guwŏn) and the related Kwangju Citizens Solidarity (Simin yŏndae moim) are the central organizations involved in the promotion of Chŏlla/Kwangju under the guise of sustainable and just futures. The rationale for the establishment of Kwangju Citizens Solidarity (KCS) is worth quoting in this regard:

> KCS is working toward the development of the community, society and the reunification of the Korean peninsula. KCS would like to build a better community with a clear vision for the up-coming 21st century.... KCS would like to link with any individual or organization that is struggling for freedom, democracy, justice and peace anywhere in the world as a member of the international human rights network.[24]

The Kwangju Futures Society, which was formed in 1993 involving thirteen local citizens groups, put forward four objectives: promoting democracy in Korea, protecting human rights and environment, promoting regional development, and establishing solidarity among international and domestic NGOs. A consortium of NGOs in Kwangju has been responsible for the organization of conferences (including the annual 5-18 conference and the series of seminars on regional development held in 1995), international symposiums, and recently the signing of the Asian Human Rights Charter in Kwangju.

The trope of democratic politics is the most well developed of the three elements of this new regionalist vision and draws on several associated political images/elements including human rights, social justice, and equality. This democratic image has been projected through the motto chosen for Kwangju: "Vanguard of Democracy, Vibrant New City" (Minjujuŭi sŏngin si, kŏn'gang-han sae Kwangju). In the *Guide to May 18 Historical Sites* this impulse to ensure justice is summarized as one of the major elements that defines Kwangju as a place:

> ... Kwangju has long been known as a city of patriotism and justice. Whenever the nation has been in peril, Kwangju's people have courageously risen and taken the lead in defending our national sovereignty. Due to our people's commitment to end injustice, the tradition of patriotism and justice has continued to the present.[25]

The recent publication of a book entitled *Kwangju as an International Place for Democracy* locates Kwangju as one of the major sites for democracy in the world alongside places such as Beijing (due to the Tiananmen Square uprising).

The Kwangju Uprising in Chŏlla's New Regionalist Vision

Central to the reinvention of the Chŏlla region through the trope of democracy is the Kwangju uprising. The uprising is invoked within the discourse of Chŏlla's democratic politics as the central event in heralding democratic reform in the country, and within the discourse of human rights as the symbolic center and exemplar of human rights struggles.

Situated within this new regionalist vision, the Kwangju uprising is the subject of an elaborate commodification process centering on its memorialization through statues, monuments, and buildings in and around Kwangju city, and its elaboration through texts and conferences. So extensive has this process become that people in the region have labeled it "the memorial industry" *(kinyŏm sanŏp)*. Facilitated by growing financial resources available to the Kwangju city government since the mid-1990s, the memorialization of the uprising has proceeded apace.[26]

The Kim Young Sam government was the first to devote financial resources to the memorialization of the uprising. Kim instituted three symbolic gestures that together constituted the Korean government's official apology for the uprising, and began the rectification of the uprising's meaning and significance as a national movement heralding the realization of democracy in the country. The three gestures included National Commemoration Day on May 18 (including a memorial ceremony) beginning in 1997, the establishment of a Kwangju Uprising Special Law (which specifically allowed for the exoneration of some Kwangju Uprising leaders), and the (re)construction of a number of important sites that figured in the uprising as memorials. In addition, the 5-18 Foundation was formed in 1994, and many of the May movement organizations that had been struggling to realize compensation claims and/or official recognition and apology for the uprising merged to join the foundation.[27]

Through the memorialization of the Kwangju uprising democratic and human rights struggles become embedded in the symbolic landscape of Kwangju. The three sites selected for memorialization are Mangwŏl-dong cemetery, which was designated as a national cemetery in 1994, the Toch'ŏng (the Provincial Hall, or South Chŏlla Provincial Capitol Building), which was the site of the last stand of the Kwangju Citizens' Army before the city was forcibly retaken by the Korean army, and Sangmudae, the Martial Law Branch Headquarters for North and South Chŏlla provinces. Sangmudae was an important uprising site because it was used for the detention, beating, and torture of the citizens arrested during the course of the uprising. In the *Guide to May 18 Historical Sites* the Toch'ŏng is described as "the central symbolic location during the May 18 uprising," while Provincial Hall Square, which acted as a center for larger rallies, has been renamed "May 18 Democracy Square." The section of the *Guide to May 18 Historical Sites* entitled "Progress of the Memorial Project" clearly inserts Kwangju within the trope of democracy, as the following pronouncement reveals: "When this Memorial Project, centering around the Mangwŏl-dong cemetery, the Provincial Capitol Building and Sangmudae, is completed, Kwangju will take its proud place as a Mecca of Democracy in the hearts of all those in the world who long for freedom, democracy and justice."[28]

The memorialization of Mangwŏl-dong cemetery is particularly important from the standpoint of locating Kwangju within the trope of democratic struggle. In 1994 a memorial project to build a new Mangwŏl-dong cemetery commenced. The new Mangwŏl-dong cemetery contains several memorials/statues that deliberately foreground democratic struggle. These markers include Democracy Gate (Minjujuŭi mun), Democracy Square (Minjujuŭi kwangjang), the May 18 Democratization Movement Memorial Tower (Oilp'al minjung hangjaeng ch'umot'ap), and the Garden for Democracy (Minju tongsan). In addition, the *Guide to May 18 Historical Sites* accords an actively symbolic role to the cemetery:

> The May 18 Cemetery is located in a cozy knoll with a commanding view of Mt. Mudung [Mudŭng]. This place will stand as a stern historical reminder that we must never allow injustice and tyranny to flourish in this land again. . . . The revered spirits of the victims of May are resting in peace in the May 18 Cemetery, standing as enduring symbols of democracy in the hearts of people all over the world who struggle for freedom, democracy and justice.[29]

The old Mangwŏl-dong cemetery has been neglected in memorialization efforts. Many in Kwangju/South Chŏlla who oppose the memorialization and commodification of the Kwangju uprising make a conscious effort to visit the old cemetery as a form of passive protest.[30]

Even before the conscious re-visioning of the Kwangju uprising through these commodification processes, the specificity of Kwangju in democratic struggles has been captured in popular writings about the uprising. In Lee Jaeeui's *Kwangju Diary*, for example, this has been clearly articulated:

> A general respite or lull was reached throughout the country, but Kwangju alone was an exception. Instead, some thirty thousand people, even more than on the previous days, gathered in front of the provincial administration building with a vast display of blazing torches. After October 26, the strong hope for democratization reached far greater levels in Kwangju than in other regions; and one can point to several reasons for this. First, from the Tonghak farmers' rebellions through the Righteous Armies [of the turn of the twentieth century] through the

Kwangju Student Rebellion [of 1929] and other events, there had come into existence a family-like tradition of outstanding pride and self-awareness regarding the democratization movement.[31]

Narratives such as Lee's act to situate Kwangju at the center of democratic struggle through a historical legacy of dissent, so that it became the historical right (indeed responsibility) of Kwangju citizens to lead in taking a stand against the repressive authoritarianism and injustice. Poems too have become a popular cultural medium through which to develop a narrative connection between Kwangju and its citizens' struggles. In *minjung* poet Ha-lim Choi's poem "Today, We Too" (Onŭlŭn uri do), Choi celebrates the role of Kwangju/Chŏlla citizens in populist struggles through their agency in the Kwangju uprising:[32]

> We were the hope and we were the scream
> We were the warriors and we were apostles
> We were blood and we were corpses
> We were a light province and a light province's Mongol-dong and
> We were a plane tree and the bricks of Kŭmnam-no where the leaves
> of the plane tree flourish . . .
>
> The dream of the people who couldn't help dying revives
> We were a large ground and a chorus . . . Kwangju.

The repetition of "we" in the poem consciously locates Chŏlla/Kwangju people at the center of Korea's democratic movement and locates the center of the movement in Kwangju, drawing on significant places that became meaningful in the context of the Kwangju uprising.

Citizens' testimonies of their involvement in the uprising give the general impression that South Chŏlla citizens viewed themselves as the defenders of democracy:

> The Kwangju incident is not a communist riot but a righteous movement against oppression of democracy and freedom. Thus, the main force behind this noble movement is neither mobs nor communists. It was we, the democracy-loving Chŏnnam people, who rose to protect our rights in the name of democracy.[33]

Or consider the following excerpt of testimony given by a religious leader in Kwangju: "Every citizen was sharing everything. Our heroic and proud warriors fight for democracy. How can they be mobs or communists? Aren't they the true patriots?"[34]

Other testimonies further develop the idea of Kwangju citizens as patriots—defenders or warriors of democracy. These testimonies stand in direct contrast to, and openly contradict, the official Chun government interpretation of the uprising as "a communist-backed plot" or "a rebellion backed by some seditious power" by locating historical agency with the insurgents in Kwangju.[35]

Conferring historical agency on Kwangju citizens through their role in past movements has been consciously drawn into the Kwangju uprising commodification process. The 5-18 Institute at Chŏnnam National University, for example, relates its establishment in the following way:

> The Institute was established to build up the academic ground for the historical value of May 18 of 1980 and to revitalize its role over democracy and human rights. Kwangju/South Chŏlla area has a historical tradition to value justice through the historical background of Citizens Troops, Tonghak [Eastern Learning], Kwangju Students Independence Movement and May 18 in 1980. Particularly May 18 demolished bureaucracy and created modern democratization building up the electoral government, which led to the tradition of democratization.[36]

One may liken the self-understanding of Kwangju and Chŏnnam citizens involved in the uprising to the construction of a heroic analysis. Elaborating this idea through an analysis of the glorification of Irish history through public statuary, Nuala Johnson notes that such a "process was predicated on the assumption that heroic histories would articulate and legitimize present day circumstances or future aspirations."[37] Thus in Kwangju it is important that previous official histories are displaced, and the construction of the uprising through a narrative of heroic struggle by sanctioned Kwangju citizens is legitimized in its place. In the process Kwangju citizens become the righteous defenders of Korea's democracy and human rights.[38]

Invoking the Kwangju uprising in Chŏlla's emerging narrative of democracy is not just a process that centers on historical analysis. The emerging discourse of Kwangju as a democratic center is also future oriented and universalized. The future orientation of the uprising is perhaps most neatly captured by Lee Jae-eui in his author's preface to the English edition of *Kwangju Diary*.[39] According to Lee,

> I hope that the history of resistance in Kwangju will bring hope to those who still suffer from inhuman institutions and violence. I believe that Kwangju in 1980 was typical of the efforts of humanity in keeping with its universal value, a value that is inherent in both East and West. In that respect, the struggle of Kwangju still continues. It is because our efforts to defend our dignity will continue, as long as the inhumanity of what happened in Kwangju exists anywhere in the world. Now, we will share the bitter experience we had to go through in Kwangju with the world, and with the new generations.

In some recent official materials produced in the context of the reinterpretation of the uprising, the continuity and universality of the uprising are also evident. *The May 18 Kwangju Democratic Uprising* (n.d.) is a book intended to "re-estimate the uprising and its achievements and to assign it its proper place in the history of Korea and in the larger history of world-wide struggles for democracy" (p. 5). Authored by the May 18 History Compilation Committee of Kwangju City, it states that "the Kwangju Democratic uprising should not be considered the painful, frustrated chapter of an age, but should be placed in the modern history of this country as the starting point of democratization. The Kwangju Democratic uprising should go down in national history and national consciousness as an inspiring stand for human freedom and dignity."[40]

The twentieth anniversary of the uprising provides an important opportunity for the globalization of its meaning. The Global Symposium on the Twentieth Anniversary of the Kwangju Uprising, organized by the 5-18 Institute and held in Kwangju in May 2000, expressed the following objective:

> Both the Korean government and the citizens of Kwangju . . . agree to make up a new program of May 18 globalization which will promote the futuristic global vision of May 18 research, rather than focus on national political struggles or the movement for political reforms of the past. To blend the significant spirit of May 18 with the fundamental values of all the human race, the Global Symposium on Democracy and Human Rights will be held in Chŏnnam University from May 15 to May 17 this year. We expect the eyes of the world to watch this historic event in terms of emphasizing the unstoppable trend toward democracy in developing countries.[41]

Kwangju thus becomes not just a place to reevaluate and historicize the uprising but also a place that can articulate a universal democratic vision for the future, which has the uprising as its reference point. "Through various academic and social activities . . . it [5-18 Institute] has progressively attained the status of research Mecca for the study of democracy and human rights in the Third World."[42]

Conclusion

In this chapter, I have examined the way the Kwangju uprising figures in the broader project of reinventing Chŏlla as a unique region and Kwangju as a unique city in the twenty-first century. I have attempted to locate much of the current discourse about the Kwangju uprising—academic, popular, statuary, organizational—within the context of Chŏlla's regionalist vision for the future. This task has been informed by recent work in cultural geography that draws on the postcolonial understanding of places and regions as constructed and contested entities scripted by various agencies according to the needs of the time. Thus regions and cities are constructs of space-time and the social and political relations and histories that inform them.

The Kwangju uprising has been the object of interpretation, historicization, and invocation by different groups and individuals for different purposes. Most recently, with the realization of (formal) democracy in South Korea, a certain degree of legitimacy has been conferred on the uprising, which in turn has opened the way for new interpretations of the event, many of which draw on previously unsanctioned sources and contraband materials. Consequently, the uprising has been inserted into a broader popular national discourse of democratic reform, human rights, and social justice.

In this new context (of democracy) South Chŏlla province and Kwangju city figure as prominent places. This context has presented people in the region an opportunity to consciously sculpt South Chŏlla/Kwangju as democratic sites. Such place promotion draws heavily on the Kwangju uprising as the central event heralding democracy in South Korea. These efforts are imparted through conferences, seminars, statuary and memorials, and organizations (NGOs such as Kwangju Citizens Solidarity and those devoted specifically to the Kwangju uprising, such as the 5-18 Foundation).

In this chapter, I aimed to recognize and document the ways in which the Kwangju uprising has continued to be reworked as a central part of efforts to establish Kwangju as a major center/Mecca of world/Korean democracy. My intent was to raise questions about what such a project means for the future of Kwangju and South Chŏlla province and the way the region and city are coming to view themselves in the twenty-first century. In beginning to answer this question, I point to several emerging trends. First, even though both Chŏlla provinces (North and South) and Kwangju city have advanced materially since formal democratization in the 1990s, the tropes on which the region's self-understanding are drawn remain tied to the legacies of political radicalism and dissent of the past. In this new context these legacies have been the subject of elaboration through statuary, writing, conferences, tourist promotions, and so on. Second, this rather pronounced continuity in the substance of regional identity in Chŏlla may be explained in large part by another enduring feature of Korea's regional geography: despite the rising material status and political ascendancy of the Chŏlla provinces in recent years, a social and cultural bias against the region persists in Korean society. This has prompted efforts within the region to appeal to a wider, global audience to achieve a degree of legitimacy long denied in the national context. Contrary to the predictions of many social theorists, globalization has, in the case of Kwangju and Chŏlla, resulted in the elaboration of a unique and particular identity rather than an erosion of place-based distinctiveness. The global, as well the national, has helped reconstitute the local in ways that both break with and draw from the past(s) of both South Chŏlla province and Kwangju city.

Notes

1. Hereafter Korea unless contrasted with North Korea.

2. John Allen, Doreen Massey, and Allan Cochrane, *Rethinking the Region* (London: Routledge, 1998), 9.

3. Edward Said, *Orientalism* (London: Penguin, 1979).

4. Allen, Massey, and Cochrane, *Rethinking,* 10.

5. Paul Routledge, "Backstreets, Barricades, and Blackouts: Urban Terrains of Resistance in Nepal," *Environment and Planning D: Society and Space* 12 (1994): 559–78.

6. Routledge, "Backstreets," 559.

7. See Jung-Woon Choi, "The Kwangju People's Uprising: Formation of the Absolute Community," *Korea Journal* 39, no. 2 (1999): 238–82; and Sang-Jin Han, "Popular Sovereignty and a Struggle for Recognition from a Perspective of Human Rights," *Korea Journal* 39, no. 2 (1999): 184–204.

8. Routledge, "Backstreets," 561.

9. In the nineteenth century, for example, popular revolts took place in other provinces in Korea, including P'yŏngan, Kyŏngsang, and Cheju Island.

10. We should be careful, nonetheless, to place North and South Chŏlla provinces together and this regional entity together with the Ch'ungch'ŏng provinces. Geographically, we might well group North Chŏlla province more closely with South Ch'ungch'ŏng province, since North and South Chŏlla provinces are separated by the rugged Noryŏng Mountains. Historically, a regionalist strategy that places the Tonghak rebellion together with the Kwangju uprising as part of a history of dissent is a conscious invocation by the architects of South Chŏlla's current regional image. In fact, the Tonghak rebellion took place largely in northern Chŏlla and southern Ch'ungch'ŏng provinces (although many insurgents traveled from southern Chŏlla to join the rebellion).

11. During this period shamans could be found nationwide, and Yŏngdŭngp'o, south of Seoul just across the river, was traditionally one of the most famous centers of shaman residence. The richest source of shamanism is probably the eastern coastal regions around North and South Kyŏngsang provinces. Therefore we can interpret the association of Chŏlla with shamanism and, further, the negative scholarly perceptions of shamanism at this time as a further effort of Confucian scholars to legitimize the exclusion of Chŏlla people from official/governmental capacity.

12. See Gi-Wook Shin, *Peasant Protest and Social Change in Colonial Korea* (Seattle: University of Washington Press, 1996).

13. See Myung-Rae Cho, *Political Economy of Regional Differentiation: The State, Accumulation, and the Regional Question* (Seoul: Hanul Academy Publishing, 1991); and Soo-Hyun Chon, "Political Economy of Regional Development in Korea," in

Richard P. Appelbaum and Jeffery Henderson, eds., *States and Development in the Asia Pacific Rim* (Newbury Park: Sage, 1992), 150–75.

14. Mun Sŏng-nam, Chŏng Kŭn-sik, and Chi Pyŏng-mun, *Chiyŏk sahoe wa sahoe ŭisik: Kwangju-Chŏnnam chiyŏk yŏn'gu* [Regional society and social consciousness: Kwangju-Chŏnnam regional research] (Seoul: Munhak kwa chisŏng-sa, 1994).

15. Sallie Yea, "Regionalism and Political-Economic Differentiation in Korean Development: Power Maintenance and the State as Hegemonic Bloc," *Korea Journal* 34, no. 2 (1994): 5–29.

16. Kim Man-hŭm, *Han'guk ŭi chŏngch'i kyunyŏl e kwanhan yŏn'gu: chiyŏk kyunyŏl ŭi chŏngch'i kwajŏng e taehan kujojŏk chŏpkŭn* [A study on political cleavage in Korea: a structural approach to the political process of regional cleavage"] (Ph.D. diss., Seoul National University, 1991).

17. See Sallie Yea, "Regionalism," for further details of the economic imbalance between Chŏlla and other regions of South Korea during the period of rapid economic development between 1960 and 1980. There were, however, strategic and geographic rationales for disproportionately favoring the two Kyŏngsang provinces as locations for investment. Often cited are the natural deep water harbors off the coast of South Kyŏngsang province, which would provide easy access for Korean exports to Japan, and the strategic consideration of locating industry as far as possible from the lines of a possible North Korean invasion.

18. The arrest of Chun and Roh was motivated explicitly by the demand for a full investigation into the Kwangju uprising and for the punishment of those responsible for the brutal suppression of Kwangju by the military, including the order to fire on civilians. The arrest was the result of popular demands for punishment and accompanying protests that began to intensify during 1995. The prosecutor's office under Kim Young Sam decided in July 1995 that because the statute of limitations had run out, those responsible for the Kwangju uprising could not be tried on charges of "high treason." As the protests intensified following this pronouncement, Kim ordered the arrest of Chun and Roh and instituted a Special Law to allow for the punishment of those implicated in the Kwangju uprising. Nonetheless, the arrests of the two former presidents came about as a result of an inquiry into graft and corruption, rather than the Kwangju uprising itself. The arrests did, nonetheless, manage to quell the growing popular demand for punishing those responsible for the uprising.

19. Kwangju City Government, *A Guide to May 18 Historical Sites* (Kwangju: Kwangju City Government, n.d.), 2.

20. Sallie Yea, *Maps of the Imaginary, Geographies of Dissent: The Marginalisation of South Chŏlla Province, South Korea* (Ph.D. diss., Monash University, 1999).

21. Available at www.visitkorea.go.kr/html/event/cult.

22. Available at www.visitkorea.go.kr/html/event/cult.

23. Kwangju City Government, *Guide to May 18 Historical Sites*.

24. Kwangju Citizens Solidarity (KCS), *Introductory Booklet* (Kwangju: Kwangju Citizens Solidarity, n.d.).

25. Kwangju City Government, *Guide to May 18 Historical Sites*.

26. There is a growing cleavage among Kwangju uprising memorialization groups, with some claiming that current "mainstream" and officially sanctioned efforts are di-

luting the true meaning and spirit of the uprising. Prominent among these groups are radical student organizations based mainly in Kwangju at Chŏnnam National University and Chosun University. At the twentieth anniversary commemoration of the Kwangju uprising, held in Kŭmnam Avenue, these student groups organized an "alternative" concert that was held about half a kilometer from the official concert.

27. A good treatment of the struggle for compensation by the Kwangju uprising victims can be found in Ju-na Byun and Linda S. Lewis, eds., *The Kwangju Uprising after Twenty Years: The Unhealed Wounds of the Victims* (Seoul: Taehae, 2000).

28. Kwangju City Government, *Guide to May 18 Historical Sites.*

29. Kwangju City Government, *Guide to May 18 Historical Sites.*

30. For further discussion of the difference between the new and old cemeteries and the infrapolitics that construction of the new cemetery has generated, see Sallie Yea, "Rewriting Rebellion and Mapping Memory in South Korea: The (Re)presentation of the 1980 Kwangju Uprising through Mangwol-dong Cemetery," ASI Working Paper no. 13, Victoria University of Wellington, New Zealand, 1999.

31. Jae-eui Lee, *Kwangju Diary: Beyond Death, Beyond the Darkness of the Age* (Los Angeles: UCLA Asian Pacific Monograph Series, 1999).

32. Ha Lim Choi, *Into an Open Abyss* (Seoul, 1991).

33. Emphasis added. Kwangju 5-18 Historical Materials Compilation Committee, *Oilp'al Kwangju minjuhwa undong charyo ch'ongsŏ* [Collected materials of the Kwangju democratization movement of May 18] (Kwangju: Kwangju 5-18 Historical Materials Compilation Committee, 1997), 10:218.

34. Testimony of Kim Song-yong, in Han'guk hyŏndaesa saryo yŏn'guso, ed., *Kwangju owŏl minjung hangjaeng saryo chŏnjip* [The complete collection of the historical record of the Kwangju May people's uprising] (Seoul: P'ulpit, 1990), 176.

35. May 18 History Compilation Committee of Kwangju City, *The May 18 Kwangju Democratic Uprising* (Kwangju, n.d.), 62.

36. Emphasis added. 5-18 Institute, *Information Booklet on Global Symposium on the 20th Anniversary of the Kwangju Uprising* (Kwangju: 5-18 Institute, 2000), 3.

37. Nuala C. Johnson, "Sculpting Heroic Histories: Celebrating the Centenary of the 1789 Rebellion in Ireland," *Transactions of the Institute of British Geographers* 19 (1994): 78.

38. There is some tension between Kwangju citizens' self-perceived roles in the Kwangju uprising and the roles of Chŏnnam citizens from surrounding counties. The location of historical agency *only* in Kwangju citizens' remembrance of the uprising has met with considerable opposition from groups from the surrounding counties who traveled to Kwangju to participate in the uprising. Many of these groups feel they have been unfairly excluded in commemoration and memorialization efforts. Oh Soosung, personal communication with author, Chŏnnam National University, November 1999.

39. Jae-Eui Lee, *Kwangju Diary*, 15.

40. May 18 History Compilation Committee of Kwangju City, *Oilp'al Kwangju minjuhwa undong charyo ch'ongsŏ*, 67.

41. 5-18 Institute, *Information Booklet*, 2.

42. 5-18 Institute, *Information Booklet*, 3.

Afterword

Kwangju: The Historical Watershed

Kyung Moon Hwang

T IME HAS VINDICATED KWANGJU. Over the past two decades the victims and resistors of May 1980, along with their supporters among students, laborers, and political activists, have seen their cause ceremonially embraced by the intellectual, cultural, and (belatedly) political leaders of South Korea. Much of this support stems from the now solidly orthodox view of Kwangju as an indispensable source of Korean democratization—a process that, to many, ultimately achieved a resolution approaching heavenly justice with the election of President Kim Dae Jung in 1997. Indeed, the organized retrospectives over the past few years, including the one in Los Angeles that spawned the chapters in this book, have progressed beyond debating the array of forces good and bad. While such gatherings continue to illuminate the events of May 1980, they tend to focus on extracting a larger meaning, and in full consideration of what has happened in the aftermath. The period of citizen autonomy in Kwangju (what Jung-woon Choi in this volume calls an "absolute community" and others have called the days of the "Kwangju Republic"), for example, has been vested with standing as a consummate realization of democracy, harmony, and cooperation that can inspire the ongoing quest for social and political reform. As several of the contributors (Jung, Baker, Yea, Lewis, and Byun) demonstrate, the memory of Kwangju has taken on a life of its own, contested, shaped, preened, and appropriated for purposes sometimes far removed from what the participants in 1980 could have imagined. In sum, the Kwangju uprising has grown into a rich source of historical inquiry, on several levels.

The contributions to this volume attest to the appeal and significance of approaching a retrospective on Kwangju in this manner. In this afterword I seek to broaden the historical scope and examine the Kwangju uprising as not only the source of important events but also the culmination of longer-term developments in the context of Korean history. May 1980 crystallized many of the fissures, conflicts, and changes within Korean society that had accumulated over the previous century as Koreans struggled to forge their modern existence. In this sense, Kwangju became a product of most of the major historical factors that marked the nation's turbulent twentieth century: the left-right ideological split, communism (or anticommunism), volatile economic growth trajectories, regional imbalances and resentments, dictatorship and resistance, mobilization and regimentation of the populace, the foreign presence—there are strong traces of all of these phenomena converging on Kwangju. The uprising, then, marked a historical moment in which these forces, and the divisions that these forces generated, exploded onto the landscape to substantially shape the subsequent path of Korean history.

The Modern Heritage of Resistance

May 18 represents a watershed in the long history of modern resistance movements that together constitute a proud heritage of opposition to oppressive and unjust political authority. Beginning with the Tonghak rebellion of 1894, which originated in the southwestern region of Korea in which Kwangju lies, and continuing on to the anti-Japanese "righteous army" *(ŭibyŏng)* bands at the turn of the twentieth century, this resistance tradition sprang from the birth pangs of Korea's modernity. The twin targets for insurgency—government abuse and foreign exploitation—continued to provoke mass uprisings: the March First independence movement of 1919 against Japanese colonial rule; the postliberation rebellions in Taegu, Yŏsu-Sunch'ŏn, and Cheju Island in the late 1940s against the nascent southern system; and the constant resistance—often clamorous, sometimes covert—against authoritarian regimes in South Korea in the decades following the Korean War. All Koreans in 1980 could recall this heritage, just as Koreans now can readily locate Kwangju in their annals of popular resistance.

Particularly significant were the connections to the modern history of student activism. As in Kwangju, students sparked mass protests against oppressive rule throughout the twentieth century. The declaration of independence that set off the March First demonstrations of 1919 drew much of its intellectual inspiration from nationalist students studying in Japan, some of whom had drafted a preliminary independence manifesto in February. In 1929 students in Kwangju itself led a fierce revolt against local authorities, which soon spurred a nationwide anticolonial student movement unprecedented in scale since March First.[1] Following liberation in 1945, students constituted the staunchest, most consistent agitators against the South Korean dictatorships, mobilizing to overthrow the corrupt Syngman Rhee regime in 1960, rallying against the normalization treaty with Japan in 1965, joining forces with religious leaders, laborers, and others to apply relentless pressure on the excessive Yusin dictatorship of the 1970s, and taking to the streets en masse in early 1980, when Park Chung Hee's death engendered not liberalization but rather a reincarnation of Yusin in the hands of another military dictator. Student demonstrations sparked the chain of events leading to the soldier–student confrontation in front of Chŏnnam University on May 18, which soon descended into the bloodbath of Kwangju.

As with popular uprisings as a whole, Kwangju represented a historical fulcrum in student activism. The suppression of the city may have temporarily stifled outward resistance, but things would never be the same. The persecutions of the Chun Doo Hwan regime in the 1980s served only to intensify the seething antigovernment resentment among the students who, armed with their memories of Kwangju, gradually ratcheted up the pressure until it burst forth irrepressibly in 1987.[2] By then, the place of Kwangju in the heritage of student activism was unmistakable.

Democratization

We cannot measure concretely the causal connection to the enormous demonstrations of 1987 that brought forth democratization, but clearly the motivation and inspiration for the vanguard of agitators in 1987 drew from the indelible remembrance of Kwangju, churned through underground channels by way of clandestine organizational activities and through the circulation of banned testimonials and video footage. But the grounds for warranting Kwangju a hallowed place in the story of South Korean democratization rest also on the fact that May 1980 capped off a long series of struggles waged by a growing civic movement in the early 1970s, when Park promulgated the Yusin constitution and took absolute control.[3] By the late 1970s, the cycle of defiance and dictatorship had reached a boiling point, as workers staged fierce strikes and tens of thousands took to the streets in Pusan and Masan. No one could have expected that Park himself would become the most memorable casualty of this turmoil, but most could have anticipated that, following his assassination, the era of military dictatorship would come to an end. It did not, and with a brutal vengeance. From December 1979 to May 1980, Chun's path toward power was strewn with many victims, with those in Kwangju numbering and suffering the most.

Was the brave resistance to Chun's tyranny, though, enough to warrant calling the uprising itself a striving for "democracy"? The South Korean government's recognition of Kwangju not as an "incident" *(sat'ae)* but rather as a "democratization movement" *(minjuhwa undong)*[4] has sanctioned and standardized this widely accepted perception of Kwangju, but I propose that we consider this issue more carefully.

As Keun-sik Jung suggests in this volume, the context of political developments in late 1979 and early 1980 points clearly toward a longing for democratic reform throughout the country, and Kwangju itself occurred as Koreans realized that yet another major opportunity at lasting political reform was dissipating. One cannot divorce Kwangju, in other words, from the mass demonstrations throughout the country in the days preceding May 18 that inspired the Chŏnnam University students to confront the soldiers. One also finds a kind of elemental, mass democracy at work during the period of the "absolute community" as described by Jung-woon Choi, and during the halcyon days following the expulsion of government troops on May 21, when the Kwangju citizens sustained an autonomous, controlled, cooperative community.

Considering, however, the extraordinary circumstances of the uprising within an isolated environment and in an institutional vacuum, we must be careful before readily linking the kind of group behavior seen in Kwangju— even if we consider this a more direct, pure form of democracy—with the formal democratic reforms that Koreans sought both before and after the uprising. It could be argued, in fact, that insisting on the term "democratization movement" for the uprising itself excessively privileges Kwangju over the dozens of other struggles against dictatorship in South Korea.[5] More importantly, as several of this volume's chapters and testimonials indicate, the Kwangju citizens' actions were driven first and foremost by rage in the face of the unspeakable brutality of the government troops. Notwithstanding the cries for political reform and the pervasive atmosphere of participatory communal behavior among the citizens during the uprising, ultimately the severity of state violence and the scale of antistate resistance, more than an idealistic striving for democracy, appear most compellingly to distinguish Kwangju in South Korean history.

Illegitimacy of the System

The savagery unleashed against civilians in May 1980 shattered the sheen of legitimacy of the Chun regime (even before it formally began), and in fact heightened suspicions about the entirety of government rule over the previous three decades. It was a ruling system that had justified itself as the people's protectors against communism but had constructed a military and security apparatus that consistently battled not North Korean troops but rather its own citizens. In Kwangju the forces meant to wage war against North Korea were brought down on the very citizenry it purported to defend, and with shocking proficiency. The state-directed anticommunist indoctrination, piped through the education system and the press from the founding of the South Korean republic, now appeared exposed for what it really was: a means of sustaining autocratic rule. Kwangju demonstrated that the constant red scare—which, once again, the authorities cooked up to legitimate the martial law decree of May 17, 1980—not only produced a military easily manipulated by a willful dictator but might also have aroused the soldiers to step beyond their humanity. The simple pronouncement from their superiors that a leftist insurrection had broken out in Kwangju appears to have given license to barbarity.[6]

The deep distrust of the South Korean government that followed Kwangju had a pronounced effect on the subsequent development of some segments of society. To intellectuals, students, and others, Kwangu uncovered the multiple support mechanisms that had sustained the system: the regimentation and militarization of society for both economic and political goals, the tight-fisted censorship of the press, the domination of the economy by a few select family-owned monopolies, the suppression of labor, the harassment of student and civic groups, dependence on American military protection, and, some argued, the perpetuation of national division itself. All of these factors played a role in the onset and eventual conclusion of the Kwangju uprising, and rumination on and analysis of this web during the past two decades have only strengthened a semipermanent opposition movement composed of students, laborers, and intellectuals. This movement, so clearly on display in mocking the official twentieth anniversary commemoration of Kwangju in May 2000,[7] could not be placated even with the ascension of Kim Dae Jung, who, at his inaugural, publicly embraced Chun Doo Hwan in a gesture of reconciliation. From the perspective of this opposition, the essential character of the South Korean ruling order that abused the citizens of Kwangju through authoritarianism, anticommunism, and collusion with American military power remains in place.

Sobering View of America

Reliance on U.S. military protection has fueled a raging anti-Americanism among these opposition activists. Suspicion concerning American influence in various sectors of life has spread throughout the Korean population on a scale unimaginable before 1980, when the overwhelming majority of citizens viewed the United States as not only a protector but also the embodiment of progress and the champion of democracy. These illusions have dissipated, thanks largely to Kwangju. To be sure, anti-Americanism is a complex phenomenon that arose in the 1980s from the convergence of a variety of factors. But undoubtedly Kwangju was the spark.[8] Agitated debate continues over when and how the American command learned about what was taking place in Kwangju, and about how much control the Americans had over the troops sent to Kwangju. But recent memoirs by Ambassador William Gleysteen and General John Wickham do not dispel what the events originally suggested: American priorities lay primarily in procuring security and stability on the peninsula, and only secondarily in ensuring human rights or democratic rule.[9] Although the government of the United States may issue sweeping idealistic pronouncements about humanity, in the end it invariably acts according to its own interests. The deflation felt by many Koreans during and after Kwangju ironically mirrored the solemn disappointment of the 1919 independence movement leaders, who, having been deluded by postwar Wilsonian idealism, quickly saw their hopes punctured.[10]

The parallels to March First do not end there. Just as the 1919 mass uprising overcame its immediate defeat by spawning multiple independence movements as well as productive reflection on Korean nationhood within the sphere of Japanese domination, the Kwangju uprising instilled an energetic reconsideration of Korea's place in the larger world of the Cold War, particularly under American hegemony. The picture that emerged was not pretty. Stimulated in part, ironically, by American scholarship,[11] this reexamination of the Korean–American relationship unveiled significant American involvement in many of the sadder details of South Korean history, including vital support for dictators Syngman Rhee, Park Chung Hee, and Chun Doo Hwan and heavy responsibility for national division in the first place. The palpable anti-Americanism that I felt acutely among Koreans, especially students, in the late 1980s and 1990s has moderated, but the questioning of American influence in South Korea continues. If this healthy skepticism can be considered a legacy of May 1980, then Kwangju, too—perhaps like March First—has ultimately overcome its initial defeat by creating something far more productive and lasting than bitterness.

Regionalism

A final product of Kwangju, regionalism, is the embodiment of bitterness itself. All agree on the harm caused by regionalism's pervasive influence today—

seen most glaringly in electoral behavior, but also, as Sallie Yea points out, in common perceptions about a particular region's people and culture. There is, however, no resolution in sight. This suggests perhaps an ingrained trait. Did regional particularism constitute a powerful force in Korean life before Kwangju? One can certainly point to the economic and bureaucratic favoritism toward Kyŏngsang province under the rule of Kyŏngsang generals[12]—from the 1960s to 1980s—which carved out a corridor of rapid economic development that stretched from Seoul to Pusan and excluded only one area of population concentration: the Chŏlla provinces. But this kind of political chauvinism presents only half the equation. Did the people of Chŏlla, where Kwangju is situated, in turn harbor strong feelings of exclusion and resentment? Here the answer is mixed. A sense of persecution might have sustained the élan of Kwangju citizens during the siege, but voting patterns before the uprising did not display such a pronounced tilt,[13] and furthermore antiregime fervor was widespread throughout the country (except perhaps in the Taegu area, the home region of Park and Chun).

After the uprising, however, regionalism flared into a suffocating menace, as people outside Chŏlla subscribed to the government-drawn portrayal of that region's populace as rebellious and backward. The people of Chŏlla, in turn, grew increasingly maligned and desperate, with their sense of betrayal expressing itself in electoral behavior. Once again, the ruling authority appears to have played a major role in fanning the flames, with the Chun regime dismissing Kwangju (when it allowed mention of it at all) as a local insurrection. Despite the liberalization of information access and the expanded understanding of the uprising in the 1990s, this initial perception remains tough to overcome. Surveys continue to demonstrate a regional slant in popular perceptions about Kwangju and about the proper approach to its memory.[14] Understandably, the designated gatekeepers of the May 18 memory have grown sensitive to the regionalist coloring, emphasizing (as the Lewis and Byun chapter demonstrates) the national character of this event—as they should—and extending the lessons from Kwangju to universal human rights implications, as reflected in Keun-sik Jung's chapter. This most recent transformation of the memory of Kwangju testifies to the lasting and continuing power of this momentous event in shaping both Korean history and perceptions about Korean history.

Notes

1. The Kwangju student movement, in the closing months of 1929, began as scuffles between Korean and Japanese secondary students that quickly escalated into

demonstrations against colonial education policies. When the local authorities arrested several of the Korean student leaders, the response was to expand the resistance effort into one against colonial rule as a whole. Kwangju was particularly ripe for such an explosion, having developed into a hotbed of nationalist sentiment and organizations in the late 1920s, and these various forces soon came together into a concerted movement throughout the region. Their demands included the immediate release of jailed student leaders, greater autonomy for Korean schools, and freedom of assembly and publication. By December, Korean sympathizers throughout the country joined in these protests through attendance strikes and school closings, and by the end of the movement nearly two hundred schools and fifty thousand students had participated, constituting the largest mass demonstrations since the March First movement of 1919. Several thousand students were jailed or expelled as a result.

2. See Jung-kwan Cho's chapter in this volume.

3. See Sunhyuk Kim, *The Politics of Democratization in Korea: The Role of Civil Society* (Pittsburgh, Pa.: University of Pittsburgh Press, 2000), 67.

4. As others have noted in this volume, there are various monikers in Korean for this event, but *Kwangju sat'ae (Kwangju incident)* has become almost taboo, as this term is associated with the 1980s government distortion of the event.

5. Tim Lee, one of the discussants for the Kwangju conference of April 2000, convincingly issued this reminder in his comments.

6. Kim Ch'i-nyŏn, one of the paratroopers unleashed against the uprising, recalled getting instructions from his commander beforehand that "procommunist elements" were instigating the rebellion toward an extremist bent. The power of this testimony is heightened when considering that Kim was making the larger argument that the blame for the uprising's brutality lay on both sides. See Kim's memoir in "Chŏnt'unŭn issŏtchiman haksarŭn ŏpsŏtta [Combat yes, but massacre no]," *Wŏlgan Chosŏn* (April 1996), in *5-18 Kwangju minjuhwa undong charyo ch'ŏngsŏ* [Complete documents of the May 18th Kwangju democratization movement], v. 11 [(Kwangju: Kwangju kwangyŏksi 5-18 saryo p'yŏnch'an wiwŏnhoe)], 726. There remains strong suspicion (and strong evidence to support it) that labeling the uprising as communist/leftist was a concerted effort, from Chun on down to his field commanders, to destroy Kim Dae Jung, long-time nemesis of the military dictatorships, once and for all.

7. Witnessing this scene myself, I was awestruck by the enormous scale of this countercommemoration, as well as by its brazenness—held on the same hallowed Kŭmnam Avenue (scene of the 1980 mass confrontation with government soldiers) as the "official" celebrations of the twentieth anniversary. This relatively small but nonetheless substantial and dedicated group of activists, composed mostly of laborers and their sympathizers among students and intellectuals, has never accepted the fundamental top-down power structure of the country, centered on the state and big business. Their competing commemoration of the twentieth anniversary of Kwangju clearly indicated that they viewed even the Kim Dae Jung government as having been coopted into this power structure, which it was now enforcing. Their slogans, as expressed in the leaflets, placards, and speeches of that night, indicated a hostility especially toward the continuing presence of and reliance on the American military stationed in Korea.

8. See Gi-Wook Shin, "South Korean Anti-Americanism: A Comparative Perspective," *Asian Survey*, August 1996, 787–803, 793–94; John Ki-chiang Oh, "Anti-Americanism and Anti-Authoritarian Politics in Korea," in Ilpyong J. Kim, ed., *Two Koreas in Transition: Implications for U.S. Policy* (Rockville, Md.: In-Depth Books), 245–62.

9. John A. Wickham, *Korea on the Brink* (Washington, D.C.: National Defense University Press, 1999); William H. Gleysteen, *Massive Entanglement, Marginal Influence: Carter and Korea in Crisis* (Washington, D.C.: Brookings Institution, 1999).

10. Linda Lewis, one of this book's contributors and an eyewitness to the events, recalled in an earlier article that many Kwangju citizens actually expected the United States to intervene to halt the brutality. See Lewis, "The Kwangju Incident Observed: An Anthropological Perspective on Civil Uprisings," in Donald N. Clark, ed., *The Kwangju Uprising: Shadows over the Regime in South Korea* (Boulder: Westview, 1988), 15, 23–24.

11. The 1981 publication of Bruce Cumings's *Origins of the Korean War* had a particularly jarring effect, circulating underground among students and intellectuals and helping inspire a full-scale academic assault on the accepted wisdom about American intervention in the postliberation period.

12. See the chapter by Sallie Yea in this volume.

13. Regionalism in electoral behavior has been most conspicuous in the presidential elections. Among the three presidential elections prior to 1980—in 1963, 1967, and 1971—only the 1971 election, with Kim Dae Jung the main opposition candidate to Park Chung Hee, revealed a regionalist bent in Chŏlla province voting patterns. But even then, Park pulled in around 35 percent while approximately 62 percent went for Kim. This pro-Kim favoritism pales in comparison to the support he received in the Honam region in the presidential elections of 1987, 1992, and 1997—receiving 85 percent of the vote. See Bae Sun-kwang and James Cotton, "Regionalism in Electoral Politics," in James Cotton, ed., *Korea under Roh Tae-woo: Democratisation, Northern Policy, and Inter-Korean Relations* (St. Leonards, Australia: Allen & Unwin, 1993), 170–83.

14. The compilation of various citizen surveys about Kwangju, taken in the second half of the 1990s, presents an unmistakable—and somber—reminder that regional background still colors Korean perspectives about the uprising and its aftermath. To cite one example, the answer to the question of whether the significance of the Kwangju uprising was regional or national in scope differs considerably between Chŏlla citizens and those outside Chŏlla. See Kim Tong-wŏn et al., eds., *Kungmini ponŭn 5-18* [Citizens' perspective on Kwangju] (Kwangju sahoe chosa yŏn'guso, 1998).

Appendix

A Research Report by Ju-na Byun:
A Study on the Violation of the Kwangju Civil Uprising Victims' Right to Life Satisfaction and Happiness

Subjects and Methods

ONE HUNDRED FIFTY-SIX MEMBERS OF THE 5-18 INJURED VICTIMS ASSOCIATION were surveyed for six months, from July through December 1997, at monthly meetings. For objectivity and validity of the quantitative research, two kinds of internationally standardized social psychology measurement apparatuses were employed. These apparatuses and methods are explained below.

For measuring degree of life dissatisfaction perceived in everyday life, the life satisfaction ladder (ranging 1 to 10)[1] was used as the internationally standardized self-report measurement apparatus. Each month, subjects were asked to mark scores of life satisfaction that they felt at each of six relevant points of time—before May 1980, right after May 1980, after the 1990 compensation, after the 1995 Special Law enactment, at the present time (1997), and in the future in 2002, five years away. For measuring scores of unhappiness, the Memorial University of Newfoundland Scale of Happiness (MUNSH: Cronbach's Alpha = 0.90: ranging from −24 <unhappy> to 24 <happy>) was used.[2] MUNSH had been used before to study Korean immigrants in Chicago[3] and is recognized as an adequate apparatus for measuring self-reports of Koreans.[4] The subjects were given twenty-four questionnaires. In cases where the question is in the form of a negative sentence, the subject gets −1 point when he/she answers "no"; 0 points when the answer is "inapplicable"; and 1 point when the answer is "no." If the question is stated as a positive sentence, the points given are reversed. The total points range from −24 to +24. The score toward −24 is interpreted as unhappy, and the score toward +24 as happy.

Results

1. Demographic Characteristics

Ninety percent of the subjects are male. As for the age distribution, 30.2 percent of them are 40–49 (21–29 in 1980), 16.3 percent are 30–39 (10–19 in 1980), and 2.3 percent 20–29 (1–9 in 1980). The present employment status is: unemployed 56.8 percent, merchant 12.3 percent, driver 11.7 percent, farmer 4.5 percent, handyman 2.6 percent, and company employee 2.3 percent. The cause of unemployment is: aftermath of injuries 42.5 percent, old age 17.4 percent, and business failure 9.0 percent. Educational background is: elementary school graduate 31.3 percent, middle school graduate 19.3 percent, high school graduate 28.9 percent, college graduate 12 percent, and not educated 8.4 percent. As for housing conditions, 53.1 percent do not have their own house. As for welfare benefits, 6.4 percent of them receive residential care, 5.6 percent self-support care, and 88.0 percent have no welfare benefits.

2. Characteristics of Physical Injuries

Forty-two percent of the subjects are currently under treatment for physical illness, 18.0 percent for mental illness, and 40.0 percent for both physical and mental illness. As for degrees of disability (determined according to Workmen's Accident Compensation), 36.1 percent of the subjects are classed as degree 13–14 (with the loss of 10.5 percent of working capability), and 31.7 percent as degree 2–8 (with the loss of more than 50 percent of working capability). 1.5 percent of them have lost their total working capability. 95.9 percent of the subjects receive medical care in relation to the 5-18 uprising. As for kinds of injuries, 75.3 percent were contusion, 12.4 percent gunshot wound, 8.6 percent complicated injury, 3.0 percent stabbing, and 0.7 percent burn. As for regions of injury, 24.0 percent of the injuries were in the head, 23.9 percent over the whole body, 21.9 percent in the chest, 18.4 percent in the abdomen, 6.0 percent in the neck and spine, and 5.8 percent in the four limbs. As for treatment need, 44.7 percent of all the victims need further treatment. However, in the group with first- through third-degree disability, 80 percent of them need further treatment; in the group with fourth- through sixth-degree disability, 73.2 percent; and in the group with seventh- through ninth-degree disability, 65.4 percent. As for availability of clinics, 0.9 percent of the victims have no clinic where they can be treated, 50 percent of them have one clinic, 27.8 percent of them two clinics, 11.1 percent of them three clinics, 6.5 percent of them four clinics, and 1.9 percent of them five clinics or more.

3. Characteristics of Life Dissatisfaction

To the questions regarding life satisfaction in everyday life, 97 percent of the subjects answered "not satisfied." Among these negative answers, 45.1 percent were "very unsatisfied." No subject answered "very satisfied." The mean ladder score of the life satisfaction measurement was 2.94, which is at the level of one-third toward the lowest.

The life satisfaction scores at each point of time change as follows: right before the 5-18 uprising, the score is 5.66, but after the uprising it goes 4 ladders down to the lowest point. Right after the 1990 compensation, it goes 1 ladder up to 2.94. Right after the enactment of the 5-18 Special Law, it goes up 1 more ladder to 3.58, but at the present time of 1997, it goes down 1 ladder again to 2.94. As for the future, in 2002, the score is expected to be 4.45, 1.5 times more satisfied than now, but this score is still lower than that before the uprising.

4. Characteristics of Unhappiness

The mean score of happiness of the victims is -13.06, which is at the level of medium unhappiness. As for the distribution of major unhappy feelings, 95.0 percent of them complain of perplexity; 90.0 percent a sense of being sick; 87.5 percent painfulness; 72.5 percent misery; 62.5 percent exhaustion; 59.0 percent a sense of aggravation; and 50.0 percent depression. Illness also has a significant impact on the score of unhappiness. The group with physical illness (the score of -18.7) suffers from 11.6 times greater unhappiness than the group with no physical illness (the score of -1.61). The group with mental illness (the score of -14.2) is 4.6 times unhappier than those with no mental illness (the score of -3.09). The group with both physical and mental illness (-23.5) is 21.9 times unhappier than those without illness (the score of -1.07). Also, it is found that the group with both physical and mental illness (the score of -23.5) shows significantly greater unhappiness compared to the group with mental illness only (score of -14.2). Scores of unhappiness are significantly varied according to degrees of disability. The group with the first- through fourth-degree disability (score of -17.0), whose injuries were the most serious, shows 1.6 times greater unhappiness than that with tenth- through fourteenth-degree disability (score of -10.8). Employment status also has significant influence on unhappiness scores. The unemployed victims (score of −17.0) are 1.8 times unhappier than victims who work as company workers (score of −9.3). The result of the multiple regression analysis of the variables of their unhappiness proves that the illness variable explains 47.4 percent of their unhappiness and the employment variable 31.3 percent.

Discussion

This research shows that the victims of the 5-18 Kwangju uprising have experienced serious life dissatisfaction and unhappiness since 1980. The factors of their loss of happiness are injuries at the time of 1980, lack of available clinics, and financial pressure due to unemployment.

The victims are at the lowest level of the life satisfaction ladder. Their life satisfaction score is 2.3 times lower than the 6.7 score for ordinary Korean American in Chicago and 2.0 times lower than the 5.8 score for Korean Chinese laborers in Korea.[5] The highest score of the victims, 5.66, occurred before 1980. This score, however, has never been regained, even after compensation and the enactment of the Special Law. The victims do not expect this much happiness even in the year 2002. This implies that the victims' right to happiness, violated during the bloody incident, will not be completely recovered.

The mean score of unhappiness of the victims is −13.06, showing that they feel medium unhappiness. According to the happiness measurement research of Hur and Kim on Korean Americans in Chicago, the men's score is 10.3 and the women's is 9.7, both leaning toward happiness. According to the happiness measurement research of Ju-na Byun on Korean American victims of the 1992 Los Angeles riots, the mean happiness score of the Korean victims of the riots is −6.32 in the direction of unhappiness.[6] However, the unhappiness score of the 5-18 victims is so high that it is almost beyond comparison with those of the above two groups. According to Hur and Kim, Korean Americans in Chicago reach the lowest point of happiness (a men's score of −0.55 and a women's score of −0.50) and come to face the critical stage or exigency one to two years after arrival. They are at risk for mental problems at this point in time. In light of the above, it can be affirmed that most of the 5-18 victims are already suffering from mental illness, since they show twenty-four times greater unhappiness than Korean Americans in the critical stage.

Notes

1. H. Cantril, *The Patterns of Human Concerns* (New Brunswick, N.J.: Rutgers University Press, 1965).

2. A. Kozma and M. J. Stone, "The Measurement of Happiness: Development of Memorial University of Newfoundland Scale of Happiness," *Journal of Gerontology* 35 (1980): 906–12.

3. Won-moo Hur and Kang-cheong Kim, *Uprooting and Adjustment: A Sociological Study of Korean Immigrants' Mental Health,* final report submitted to the National Institute of Mental Health (U.S. Department of Health and Human Services, 1988).

4. M. S. Han, "Social Interaction and Life Satisfaction among the Elderly" (Ph.D. diss., St. Louis University, 1980).

5. So-jung Kim, "The Changes of Life Satisfaction of the Korean Chinese Laborers in Korea," *Overseas Korean Research* 6, no. 1 (1998): 142–58.

6. Ju-na Byun, "The Impact of Racial Conflict on Life Happiness and Health Status of Korean American Victims from the 1992 Los Angeles Riots," *Korean Stress Research* 6, no. 1 (1998): 39–53.

Index

About the Contributors

Jong-chul Ahn currently serves as the Director-General of the Discrimination Investigation Bureau of the National Human Rights Commission of Korea. He received his Ph.D. in political science from Chŏnnam National University and has produced numerous studies on the Kwangju uprising. He has worked also in the prime minister's office as a specialist in the Compensation Committee for Korean Democratization.

Don Baker is a professor in the Department of Asian Studies and the director of the Centre for Korean Research at the University of British Columbia. He was first introduced to Korea as a Peace Corps volunteer in Kwangju from 1971 through 1974. He was also in Korea from 1978 through 1980 to conduct research for his doctoral dissertation in Korean history from the University of Washington. Most of his research and publications focus on the history of religion, philosophy, and science in the Chosŏn dynasty and the twentieth century. He was a coeditor of *Sourcebook of Korean Civilization, Volume II* (1996).

Ju-na Byun received her Ph.D. in medical anthropology from the University of Florida, with a dissertation that examined the psychophysical impact of the 1992 Los Angeles riots on Korean Americans. Thereafter she has published extensively on the impact of the Kwangju uprising. Her latest books are *Torture and Torture Survivors* (2002) and *The Unhealed Wounds of the Kwangju Civil Uprising After 20 Years* (2000).

Jung-kwan Cho is assistant professor at the College of Social Sciences, Hanshin University, Korea. He received his Ph.D. from Yale University in 2000 with a dissertation titled, "From Authoritarianism to Consolidated Democracy in South Korea." He has research interests in various aspects of modern Korean politics. His recent publications include "Taming the Military to Consolidate Democracy: The South Korean Experience," *Pacific Focus*, Vol. 16, No. 1.

Jung-woon Choi is professor at Seoul National University. He received a Ph.D. in political science from the University of Chicago in 1989 and has published two books, *Chisik kukkaron* [Theory of the knowledge state] (1992), and *Owŏl ŭi sahoe kwahak* [May in the social sciences] (1999), the latter of which dealt with the Kwangju uprising. His current research is on modern and contemporary Korean political thought. He is preparing a book in Korean with a working title of *The Birth of the Minjung* (masses): *The Origin of Korean Anti-Intellectualism.*

Keun-sik Jung is professor of sociology and director of the Honam Cultural Institute at Chŏnnam National University, Kwangju. He also serves as secretary for the Korean Committee of East Asian Peace and Human Rights. He received his Ph.D. from Seoul National University and has published widely on Korean historical sociology. Currently he is conducting research into the relationship between the modern subject and colonial power in Korea.

Kyung Moon Hwang is assistant professor in the Department of History at the University of Southern California. He received his Ph.D from Harvard University in 1997, and his research has focused on the modern transformation of state and society in Korea from the late Chosŏn dynasty to the twentieth century.

Linda S. Lewis is professor of anthropology and director of the East Asian Studies Program at Wittenberg University (OH). She first went to Korea in 1970 as a Peace Corps Volunteer and later did her doctoral dissertation research in the district court in Kwangju in 1979–1980. As an eyewitness to the events of May 18, she has had a long-standing personal and scholarly interest in the Kwangju uprising; her recent publications include *Laying Claim to the Memory of May: A Look Back at the 1980 Kwangju Uprising* (2002).

Gi-Wook Shin is associate professor of sociology and senior fellow at the Institute for International Studies at Stanford University. He is also acting director of Stanford's Asia/Pacific Research Center and in charge of building Stanford's Korean studies program. He has published numerous articles and books, including *Peasant Protest and Social Change in Colonial Korea* (1997) and *Colonial Modernity in Korea* (1999, co-editor), and is currently writing a book on ethnic nationalism in Korea. Shin taught at the University of Iowa and UCLA, has written op-eds in Korean and American newspapers, and sits on many councils and advisory boards in the United States and Korea. Shin received his Ph.D from the University of Washington.

Jean W. Underwood was appointed a missionary by the United Presbyterian Church and arrived in Korea in 1954. She and her husband, John T. Underwood, a third-generation missionary in Korea, served in the city of Ch'ungju for twelve years before being assigned to Kwangju in 1967. In addition to teaching at the Honam Theological Seminary, she wrote three articles published by the Christian Literature Society: "A Short History of Church Music," "Dictionary of Hymnology," and "Programmed Instruction for Sunday School Teachers."

Sallie Yea is senior research fellow in international development, School of Social Science and Planning, RMIT University in Melbourne, Australia. She completed her Ph.D. in 1999 on the topic of regionalism and the marginalization of the Chŏlla region in South Korea, from Monash University, Melbourne. She has published extensively on this subject, including articles in *Urban Studies* (2002) and *Futures* (1999). Currently she is researching migrant communities and identity in South Korea, with a focus on trafficked women.